BARRON'S
STUDENTS' #1 CHOICE

PASS KEY
TO THE
PSAT/NMSQT*

W9-AWB-859

Second Edition

Sharon Weiner Green
Former Instructor in English
Merritt College, Oakland, California

Ira K. Wolf, Ph.D.
President, PowerPrep, Inc.
Former High School Teacher, College Professor,
and University Director of Teacher Preparation

BARRON'S EDUCATIONAL SERIES, INC.

Adapted from *How to Prepare for the PSAT/NMSQT,* 11th Edition © 2002 by
Barron's Educational Series, Inc. Math section also adapted from *Pass Key
to the SAT I,* 4th Edition © 2001 by Barron's Educational Series, Inc.

All inquiries should be addressed to:
Barron's Educational Series, Inc.
250 Wireless Boulevard
Hauppauge, New York 11788
http://www.barronseduc.com

Library of Congress Catalog Card No. 2002038539

International Standard Book No. 0-7641-2017-4

Library of Congress Cataloging-in-Publication Data
Green, Sharon.
    Pass key to the PSAT/NMSQT / Sharon Weiner Green, Ira K. Wolf.—2nd ed.
        p. cm.
    Rev. ed. of: Barron's pass key to the PSAT/NMSQT / Samuel C. Brownstein,
Mitchel Weiner, Sharon Weiner Green. c1995.
    ISBN 0-7641-2017-4 (alk. paper)
        1. Preliminary Scholastic Aptitude Test—Study guides. 2. National Merit Scholarship
    Qualifying Test—Study guides. I. Wolf, Ira K. II. Brownstein, Samuel C., 1909–
    Barron's pass key to the PSAT/NMSQT. III. Title.

    LB2353.56 .B765 2003
    378.1'662—dc21   2002038539

PRINTED IN THE UNITED STATES OF AMERICA
9 8 7 6 5 4 3 2 1

Contents

Preface

Welcome to the Second Edition of *Barron's Pass Key to the PSAT/NMSQT*. If you are preparing for the PSAT, this is the book you need.

It features two full-length model tests identical to the PSAT in length and difficulty, two crucial "dress rehearsals" for the day you walk into the examination room.

It prepares you for the writing skills section, teaching you how to spot errors and polish rough drafts so that you can shine on that section.

It briefs you on vocabulary-in-context and critical reading questions, giving you key tips on how to tackle these important verbal question types.

It takes you step by step through double reading passages, showing you how to work your way through a pair of reading passages without wasting effort or time.

It introduces you to quantitative comparison questions as well as the non-multiple-choice questions in the mathematics section, teaching you shortcuts to solving problems and entering your own answers on a sample grid.

It offers you advice on how (and when) to use a calculator in dealing with quantitative comparison, multiple-choice, and "grid-in" questions.

It gives you the *newly revised and enlarged* 300-word PSAT High Frequency Word List, 300 vital words that have been shown by computer analysis to occur and re-occur on actual published PSATs.

The PSAT is your chance to get yourself set for two important tests—the SAT I and SAT II: Writing. It's also your chance to qualify for some of the nation's most prestigious college scholarships. Go for your personal best; take the time to learn how to prepare for the PSAT.

Acknowledgments

The authors gratefully acknowledge all those sources who granted permission to use materials from their publications:

Pages 9–10: From *Summer of '49* by David Halberstam © 1989 by David Halberstam. Reprinted by permission of HarperCollins Publishers Inc.

Page 10: From *Take Time for Paradise* by permission of the estate of A. Bartlett Giamatti, published by Summit, © 1989, pp. 40–42.

Pages 189–191: From "Huge Conservation Effort Aims to Save Vanishing Architect of the Savannah" by William K. Stevens, © 2001 by the New York Times Co. Reprinted by permission.

Pages 200–201: From "Let's Say You Wrote Badly This Morning" by David Huddle in *The Writing Habit,* University Press of New England, Hanover, 1994.

Pages 201–202: From "My Two One-Eyed Coaches" by George Garrett. Virginia Quarterly Review, V. 63 N. 2.

Pages 245–246: From *Black Americans in the Roosevelt Era* by John B. Kirby, University of Tennessee Press, copyright © 1980.

Pages 257–258: From "The Feeling of Flying" by Samuel Hynes. First published in *The Sewanee Review,* vol. 95, no. 1, Winter, 1987. Copyright 1987 by Samuel Hynes. Reprinted with permission of the editor.

Pages 258–259: From "The Stunt Pilot" by Annie Dillard, © 1989, in *The Best American Essays,* Ticknor & Fields.

PSAT/NMSQT Actual Test Time 2 Hours and 10 Minutes

Section 1:	**Verbal Reasoning**	Sentence Completions
		Analogies
		Critical Reading
Time—25 minutes		*25 questions*
Section 2:	**Mathematical Reasoning**	Multiple-Choice
Time—25 minutes		*20 questions*
	5-Minute Break	
Section 3:	**Verbal Reasoning**	Sentence Completions
		Verbal Analogies
		Critical Reading
Time—25 minutes		*27 questions*
Section 4:	**Mathematical Reasoning**	Quantitative Comparison
		Student-Produced Response (Grid-In)
Time—25 minutes		*20 questions*
	1-Minute Break	
Section 5:	**Writing Skills**	Identifying Sentence Errors
		Improving Sentences
		Improving Paragraphs
Time—30 minutes		*39 questions*

1 The PSAT/National Merit Scholarship Qualifying Test

Your plan to take the PSAT/NMSQT is perhaps your first concrete step toward planning a college career. The PSAT/NMSQT, the SAT I—what do they mean to you? When do you take them? Where? What sort of hurdle do you face? How do these tests differ from the tests you ordinarily face in school? In this chapter we answer these basic questions so that you will be able to move on to the following chapters and concentrate on preparing yourself for this test.

SOME BASIC QUESTIONS ANSWERED

What Is the PSAT/NMSQT?

The PSAT/NMSQT is a standardized test designed to measure your ability to do college work. It is given once a year, in mid-October. Most schools administer the exam on a Saturday; some, however, give it on a Tuesday.

While some high schools recommend that their students take the test "for practice" as sophomores, most students take it only once, in the beginning of their junior year.

The test consists of five sections, two testing verbal reasoning skills, two testing mathematical skills, and one testing writing skills. Fifty minutes is allowed for answering the verbal questions, fifty for the mathematical questions, and thirty minutes for the writing questions.

Why Is the Test Called the PSAT/NMSQT?

This Preliminary SAT is also the qualifying test for the scholarship competitions conducted by the National Merit Scholarship Corporation (NMSC). NMSC has been cosponsoring this test since 1971.

What Are Merit Scholarships?

Merit Scholarships are prestigious national awards that carry with them a chance for solid financial aid. Conducted by NMSC, an independent, nonprofit organization with offices at 1560 Sherman Avenue, Suite 200, Evanston, Illinois 60201-4897, the Merit Program today is supported by grants from over 600 corporations, private foundations, colleges and universities, and other organizations. The top-scoring PSAT/NMSQT participants in every state are named Semifinalists. Those who advance to Finalist standing by meeting additional requirements compete for one-time National Merit $2000 Scholarships and renewable, four-year Merit Scholarships, which may be worth as much as $10,000 a year for four years.

What Is the National Achievement Scholarship Program for Outstanding Black Students?

This is a program aimed at honoring and assisting promising African-American high school students throughout the country. It is also administered by NMSC. Students who enter the Merit Program by taking the PSAT/NMSQT and who are also eligible to participate in the Achievement program mark a space on their test answer sheets asking to enter this competition as well. Top-scoring African-American students in each of the regions established for the competition compete for non-renewable National Achievement $2000 Scholarships and for four-year Achievement Scholarships supported by many colleges and corporate organizations.

Note: To be considered for this program, you *must* mark the appropriate space on your answer sheet.

How Can the PSAT/NMSQT Help Me?

If you are a high school junior, it will help you gauge your potential score on the SAT I and the Writing SAT II that you will take in the spring. It will give you some idea of which colleges you should apply to in your senior year. It will give you access to scholarship competitions. It will definitely give you practice in answering multiple-choice questions where timing is an important factor.

In addition, you may choose to take advantage of the College Board's Student Search Service. This service is free for students who fill out the biographical section of the PSAT/NMSQT. If you fill out this section, you will receive mail from colleges and search programs.

How Do I Apply for This Test?

You apply through your school. Fees, when required, are collected by your school. Fee waivers are available for students whose families cannot afford the test fee; if this applies to you, talk to your counselor.

The test is given in October. In December the results are sent to your school and to the scholarship program that you indicated on your answer sheet in the examination room.

What Makes the PSAT Different from Other Tests?

The PSAT is trying to measure your ability to reason using facts that are part of your general knowledge or facts that are included in your test booklet. You are not required to recall any history or literature or science. You are not even required to recall most math formulas—they are printed right in the test booklet.

Your score depends upon how many correct answers you get within a definite period of time. You can't go too slowly; however, accuracy is even more important than speed. You have to pace yourself so that you don't sacrifice speed to gain accuracy (or sacrifice accuracy to gain speed).

The biggest mistake most students make is to answer too many questions. It is better to answer fewer questions correctly, even if you have to leave some out at the end of a section.

How Is the PSAT Different from the SAT I?

The PSAT is a mini-version of the SAT I. For most students, it serves as a practice test. The PSAT takes two hours and ten minutes. The SAT I takes three hours. You have to answer fewer verbal and math questions on the PSAT than you do on the SAT I; however, the questions are on the same level of difficulty.

The PSAT also serves as a preview of the SAT II: Subject Test in Writing. The writing skills section of the PSAT has the same kinds of multiple-choice questions as the SAT II: Subject Test in Writing. There are just fewer of them.

How Are the Results of Your PSAT/NMSQT Reported?

About six to eight weeks after the test, you will receive, through your school, the following:

1. a Report of Student Answers with your scores
2. a copy of the answers you gave
3. a copy of the correct answers
4. a Selection Index, which identifies those eligible for NMSC programs
5. a copy of the original test booklet that you used in the examination room

Can I Do Anything If I Miss the Test but Still Want to Participate in Scholarship Competitions?

If you fail to take the PSAT/NMSQT because you were ill or involved in an emergency, you still may be able to qualify for a National Merit or National Achievement Scholarship. You need to contact the NMSC to find out about alternate testing arrangements that would enable you to take part in the National Merit competitions.

Likewise, if you are of Hispanic descent, you need to contact the National Hispanic Scholar Recognition Program run by the College Board. You can arrange to be considered for this program by communicating with The College Board, Suite 600, 1233 20th Street NW, Washington, DC 20036.

SAMPLE PSAT QUESTIONS

The purpose of this section is to familiarize you with the kinds of questions that appear on the PSAT by presenting questions like those on recent PSATs. Knowing what to expect when you take the examination is an important step in preparing for the test and succeeding in it.

The directions that precede the various types of questions are similar to those on the PSAT. For all except the student-produced response questions, you are to choose the best answer and fill in the corresponding blank on the answer sheet.

VERBAL REASONING

The verbal reasoning sections consist of fifty-two questions to be answered in fifty minutes. A typical test is made up of thirteen sentence completion questions, thirteen analogy questions, and twenty-six questions testing critical reading and vocabulary in context.

Sentence Completions

The sentence completion question tests your ability to use words in context and is in part a test of reading comprehension. Select the best answer to the following questions, then fill in the appropriate space on your Answer Sheet.

Each of the following sentences contains one or two blanks; these blanks indicate that a word or set of words has been left out. Below the sentence are five words or phrases, lettered A through E. Select the word or set of words that best completes the sentence.

EXAMPLE:

Fame is ----; today's rising star is all too soon tomorrow's washed-up has-been.

(A) rewarding   (B) gradual   (C) essential
    (D) spontaneous   (E) transitory

ⒶⒷⒸⒹ●

---

1. Folk dancing is ---- senior citizens, and it is also economical; they need neither great physical agility nor special accoutrements to enjoy participating in the dance.

   (A) bewildering to (B) costly for (C) foreign to (D) appropriate for
   (E) impracticable for

2. Holding her infant son, the new mother felt an ---- greater than any other joy she had known.

   (A) affluence (B) incentive (C) assurance (D) incredulity (E) elation

3. The author contended that his insights were not ----, but had been made independently of others.

   (A) derivative (B) esoteric (C) fallacious (D) hypothetical (E) concise

4. Suspicious of the ---- actions of others, the critic Edmund Wilson was in many ways a ---- man, unused to trusting anyone.

   (A) altruistic . . cynical
   (B) questionable . . contrite
   (C) generous . . candid
   (D) hypocritical . . cordial
   (E) benevolent . . dauntless

5. Although Roman original contributions to government, jurisprudence, and engineering are commonly acknowledged, the artistic legacy of the Roman world continues to be judged widely as ---- the magnificent Greek traditions that preceded it.

   (A) an improvement on (B) an echo of
   (C) a resolution of (D) a precursor of
   (E) a consummation of

6. ---- though she appeared, her journals reveal that her outward maidenly reserve concealed a passionate nature unsuspected by her family and friends.

   (A) Effusive (B) Suspicious (C) Tempestuous (D) Domineering
   (E) Reticent

7. Crabeater seal, the common name of *Lobodon carcinophagus*, is ----, since the animal's staple diet is not crabs, but krill.

   (A) a pseudonym (B) a misnomer (C) an allusion (D) a digression
   (E) a compromise

Answer Explanations

Sentence Completion Questions

1. **(D)** *Because* senior citizens don't need great physical agility to enjoy folk dancing, it is an *appropriate* activity for them.

2. **(E)** If the missing word is an emotion greater than *any other joy*, then it too must be a form of joy. *Elation* is a feeling of great joy.

3. **(A)** If the author got his insights independently, then he did not get or derive them from the insights of other people. In other words, his insights were not *derivative*.

4. **(A)** Someone given to distrusting the motives and actions of others is by definition *cynical*. Such a person would question even the *altruistic*, unselfish deeds of others, suspecting there to be ulterior motives for these charitable acts.

5. **(B)** The view of Rome's contributions to government, law, and engineering is wholly positive: these original additions to human knowledge are generally acknowledged or recognized. *In contrast*, Rome's original contributions to art are *not* recognized; they are seen as just an *echo* or imitation of the art of ancient Greece.

   Note that *Although* sets up the contrast here.

6. **(E)** Her outward appearance was one of "maidenly reserve" (self-restraint; avoidance of intimacy). Thus, she seemed to be *reticent* (reserved; disinclined to speak or act freely), even though she actually felt things passionately.

7. **(B)** Because these seals eat far more krill than crabs, it *misnames* them to call them crabeater seals. The term is thus a *misnomer*, a name that's wrongly applied to someone or something.

   Beware of eye-catchers. Choice A is incorrect. A *pseudonym* isn't a mistaken name; it's a false name that an author adopts.

Analogies (Word Relationships)

The analogy question tests your ability to see relationships between words. These relationships may be degree of intensity, part to whole, class and member, synonyms, antonyms, or others, which are discussed fully in Chapter 4.

Each of the following questions introduces a pair of words or phrases in capital letters, linked by a colon(:); this colon indicates that these words are related in some way. Following the capitalized pair are five pairs of words or phrases lettered A through E. Select the pair whose relationship is most similar to the relationship illustrated by the capitalized pair.

EXAMPLE:

CLOCK:TIME::   (A) watch:wrist
(B) pedometer:speed
(C) thermometer:temperature
(D) hourglass:sand   (E) radio:sound

8. WOLF:PACK::   (A) horse:saddle   (B) goose:flock   (C) fox:lair   (D) pig:sow
   (E) lion:cub

9. BRANCH:TREE::   (A) lid:eye   (B) strap:sandal   (C) sand:beach
   (D) frame:picture   (E) wing:building

10. FOIL:SCHEME::   (A) alter:decision   (B) conceal:weapon
    (C) sketch:blueprint   (D) block:passage   (E) lose:competition

11. FLIMSY:PRETEXT::   (A) frail:illness   (B) shaky:alibi
    (C) apprehensive:risk   (D) sorrowful:confession   (E) final:judgment

12. EMBRACE:POSITION::   (A) disentangle:knot   (B) espouse:cause
    (C) propose:ceremony   (D) reverse:decision   (E) enforce:law

13. EAGER:OVERZEALOUS::   (A) alluring:repulsive   (B) finicky:fussy
    (C) temperate:abstemious   (D) guileless:ingenuous
    (E) thrifty:parsimonious

14. QUACK:CHARLATANRY::   (A) miser:extravagance   (B) braggart:flattery
    (C) insurgent:revelry   (D) ascetic:misanthropy   (E) blackguard:knavery

Answer Explanations

Analogy Questions

8. (B) A *wolf* belongs to a *pack*. A *goose* belongs to a *flock*.

(Group and Member)

9. (E) A *branch* is an offshoot from the main part of a *tree*. A *wing* is an extension from the main part of a *building*.

(Part to Whole)

10. (D) To *foil* a *scheme* is to hinder or obstruct it. To *block* a *passage* is to close or obstruct it.

(Function)

11. (B) A *flimsy pretext* (pretended reason) is by definition too weak to stand up to close examination. A *shaky alibi* (excuse to avoid blame) is likewise too weak to stand up to close examination.

Beware of eye-catchers. Choice A is incorrect. While illness may make someone frail, an illness can't be described as being frail.

(Defining Characteristic)

12. (B) To *embrace* a *position* is to choose a particular point of view; to *espouse* a *cause* is to support a particular movement.

(Function)

13. (E) Someone *overzealous* is excessively *eager*; someone *parsimonious* (stingy) is excessively *thrifty*.

(Degree of Intensity)

14. (E) A *quack* (impostor; fraud) is noted for *charlatanry* (making fraudulent claims). A *blackguard* (scoundrel; rogue) is noted for *knavery* (behaving villainously).

(Defining Characteristic)

Critical Reading

Your ability to read and understand the kind of material found in college texts and the more serious magazines is tested in the critical reading section of the PSAT/NMSQT. Passages generally range from 400–850 words in length. You may be asked to find the central thought of a passage, interpret just what the author means by a specific phrase or idea, determine the meaning of individual words from their use in the text, evaluate the special techniques the author uses to achieve his or her effects, or analyze the author's mood and motivation. You will also be asked to answer two or three questions that compare the viewpoints of two passages on the same subject. You can expect to spend about three-quarters of your verbal testing time reading the passages and answering the twenty-six critical reading questions.

> The questions that follow the two passages in this section relate to the content of both, and to their relationship. The correct response may be stated outright or merely suggested in the passages and in any introductory or footnoted material included.

Questions 15–21 are based on the following passages.
The following passages are excerpted from books on America's national pastime, baseball.

Passage 1

DiMaggio had size, power, and speed. McCarthy, his longtime manager, liked to say that DiMaggio might have stolen 60 bases a season if
he had given him the green light. Stengel, his new manager, was equally
Line impressed, and when DiMaggio was on base he would point to him as
(5)   an example of the perfect base runner. "Look at him," Stengel would say
as DiMaggio ran out a base hit, "he's always watching the ball. He isn't
watching second base. He isn't watching third base. He knows they
haven't been moved. He isn't watching the ground, because he knows
they haven't built a canal or a swimming pool since he was last there.
(10) He's watching the ball and the outfielder, which is the one thing that is
different on every play."

DiMaggio complemented his natural athletic ability with astonishing
physical grace. He played the outfield, he ran the bases, and he batted
not just effectively but with rare style. He would glide rather than run, it
(15) seemed, always smooth, always ending up where he wanted to be just
when he wanted to be there. If he appeared to play effortlessly, his team-
mates knew otherwise. In his first season as a Yankee, Gene Woodling,
who played left field, was struck by the sound of DiMaggio chasing a fly
ball. He sounded like a giant truck horse on the loose, Woodling thought,
(20) his feet thudding down hard on the grass. The great, clear noises in the
open space enabled Woodling to measure the distances between them
without looking.

He was the perfect Hemingway hero, for Hemingway in his novels
romanticized the man who exhibited grace under pressure, who withheld
(25) any emotion lest it soil the purer statement of his deeds. DiMaggio was
that kind of hero; his grace and skill were always on display, his emotions
always concealed. This stoic grace was not achieved without a

terrible price: DiMaggio was a man wound tight. He suffered from insom-
nia and ulcers. When he sat and watched the game he chain-smoked and
(30) drank endless cups of coffee. He was ever conscious of his obligation to
play well. Late in his career, when his legs were bothering him and the
Yankees had a comfortable lead in a pennant race, columnist Jimmy
Cannon asked him why he played so hard—the games, after all, no
longer meant so much. "Because there might be somebody out there
(35) who's never seen me play before," he answered.

Passage 2
Athletes and actors—let actors stand for the set of performing artists—
share much. They share the need to make gestures as fluid and economical as possible, to make out of a welter of choices the single, precisely
right one. They share the need for thousands of hours of practice in
(40) order to train the body to become the perfect, instinctive instrument to
express. Both athlete and actor, out of that abundance of emotion,
choice, strategy, knowledge of the terrain, mood of spectators, condition
of others in the ensemble, secret awareness of injury or weakness, and
as nearly an absolute *concentration* as possible so that all externalities
(45) are integrated, all distraction absorbed to the self, must be able to
change the self so successfully that it changes us.

When either athlete or actor can bring all these skills to bear and
focus them, then he or she will achieve that state of complete intensity
and complete relaxation—complete coherence or integrity between what
(50) the performer wants to do and what the performer has to do. Then, the
performer is free; for then, all that has been learned, by thousands of
hours of practice and discipline and by repetition of pattern, becomes
natural. Then, intellect is upgraded to the level of an instinct. The body
follows commands that precede thinking.
(55)   When athlete and artist achieve such self-knowledge that they transform the self so that we are re-created, it is finally an exercise in power.
The individual's power to dominate, on stage or field, invests the whole
arena around the locus of performance with his or her power. We draw
from the performer's energy, just as we scrutinize the performer's
(60) vulnerabilities, and we criticize as if we were equals (we are not) what is
displayed. This is why all performers dislike or resent the audience as
much as they need and enjoy it. Power flows in a mysterious circuit
from performer to spectator (I assume a "live" performance) and back,
and while cheers or applause are the hoped-for outcome of performing,
(65) silence or gasps are the most desired, for then the moment has
occurred—then domination is complete, and as the performer triumphs,
a unity rare and inspiring results.

15. In Passage 1, Stengel is most impressed by DiMaggio's

(A) indifference to potential dangers
(B) tendency to overlook the bases in his haste
(C) ability to focus on the variables
(D) proficiency at fielding fly balls
(E) overall swiftness and stamina

16. It can be inferred from the content and tone of Stengel's comment (lines 5–11) that he would regard a base runner who kept his eye on second base with

(A) trepidation   (B) approbation
(C) resignation   (D) exasperation
(E) tolerance

17. The phrase "a man wound tight" (line 28) means a man

(A) wrapped in confining bandages
(B) living in constricted quarters
(C) under intense emotional pressure
(D) who drank alcohol to excess
(E) who could throw with great force

18. Which best describes what the author is doing in the parenthetical comment "let actors stand for the set of performing artists" [line 36]?

(A) Indicating that actors should rise out of respect for the arts
(B) Defining the way in which he is using a particular term
(C) Encouraging actors to show tolerance for their fellow artists
(D) Emphasizing that actors are superior to other performing artists
(E) Correcting a misinterpretation of the role of actors

19. To the author of Passage 2, freedom for performers depends on

(A) their subjection of the audience
(B) their willingness to depart from tradition
(C) the internalization of all they have learned
(D) their ability to interpret material independently
(E) the absence of injuries or other weaknesses

20. The author's attitude toward the concept of the equality of spectators and performers (lines 57–61) is one of

(A) relative indifference
(B) mild skepticism
(C) explicit rejection
(D) strong embarrassment
(E) marked perplexity

21. The author of Passage 2 would most likely react to the characterization of DiMaggio presented in lines 30–35 by pointing out that DiMaggio probably

(A) felt some resentment of the spectator whose good opinion he supposedly sought
(B) never achieved the degree of self-knowledge that would have transformed him
(C) was unaware that his audience was surveying his weak points
(D) was a purely instinctive natural athlete
(E) was seldom criticized by his peers

Answer Explanations

Critical Reading Questions

15. (C)   Stengel's concluding sentence indicates that DiMaggio watches "the one thing that is different on every play." In other words, DiMaggio *focuses on the variables*, the factors that change from play to play.

16. (D)   The sarcastic tone of Stengel's comment suggests that he would be *exasperated* or irritated by a base runner who had his eye on second base when he should have been watching the ball and the outfielder.

17. (C)   Look at the sentences following this phrase. They indicate that DiMaggio was a man *under intense emotional pressure*, one who felt so much stress that he developed ulcers and had problems getting to sleep.

18. (B)   The author is taking a moment away from his argument to make sure the reader knows exactly who the subjects of his comparison are. He is not simply comparing athletes and actors. He is comparing athletes and *all* performing artists, "the set of performing artists," to use his words. Thus, in his side comment, he is *defining* how he intends to use the word *actors* throughout the discussion.

19. (C)   Performers are free when all they have learned becomes so natural, so internalized, that it seems instinctive. In other words, freedom depends on *the internalization* of what they have learned.

20. (C)   The author bluntly states that we spectators are not the performers' equals. Thus, his attitude toward the concept is one of *explicit rejection*.

21. (A)   Passage 1 indicates DiMaggio always played hard to live up to his reputation and to perform well for anyone in the stands who had never seem him play before. Clearly, he wanted the spectators to have a good opinion of him. Passage 2, however, presents a more complex picture of the relationship between the performer and his audience. On the one hand, the performer needs the audience, needs its good opinion and its applause. On the other hand, the performer also resents the audience, resents the way spectators freely point out his weaknesses and criticize his art. Thus, the author of Passage 2 might well point out that DiMaggio *felt some resentment* of the audience whom he hoped to impress with his skill.

MATHEMATICAL REASONING

There are three types of questions on the mathematics portion of the PSAT:

1. multiple-choice questions
2. quantitative comparison questions
3. grid-in questions

Examples of each type will be given in this chapter. In Chapter 7, you will learn some important strategies for handling each one. The math questions are in Sections 2 and 4 of the PSAT. In each of those sections there are twenty questions; you are allotted twenty-five minutes to complete each section.

- Section 2 has twenty multiple-choice questions (Questions 1–20)
- Section 4 has twelve quantitative comparison questions (Questions 21–32) followed by eight grid-in questions (Questions 33–40).

Within each group, the questions are presented approximately in order of increasing difficulty. In fact, on the score report, which you will receive about seven weeks after taking the PSAT, each question will be rated E (Easy), M (Medium), or H (Hard), depending on how many students answered that question correctly. On a recent PSAT, for example, the ranking of the math questions was as follows:

	Easy	Medium	Hard
Multiple-choice	1–7	8–13	14–20
Quantitative Comparison	21–25	26, 27, 29, 30	28, 31, 32
Grid-in	33	34–36	37–40

As a result, the amount of time you spend on any one question will vary greatly. We will discuss this in detail in Chapter 2 when you learn the best way to pace yourself and how to make educated guesses.

Multiple-Choice Questions

Half of the forty mathematics questions on the PSAT are multiple-choice questions. Although you have certainly taken multiple-choice tests before, the PSAT uses a few different types of questions in these sections, and you must become familiar with all of them. By far, the most common type of question is one in which you are asked to solve a problem. The straightforward way to answer such a question is to do the necessary work, get the solution, then look at the five choices and choose the one that corresponds to your answer. In Chapter 7 we will discuss other techniques for answering these questions, but for now let's look at a couple of examples.

EXAMPLE 1

What is the average (arithmetic mean) of −2, −1, 0, 1, 2, 3, and 4?

(A) 0   (B) $\dfrac{3}{7}$ (C) 1   (D) $\dfrac{7}{6}$ (E) $\dfrac{7}{2}$

To solve this problem requires only that you know how to find the average of a set of numbers. Ignore the fact that this is a multiple-choice question. *Don't even look at the choices.*

- Calculate the average by adding the 7 numbers and dividing by 7.

- $\dfrac{-2+-1+0+1+2+3+4}{7} = \dfrac{7}{7} = 1$

- Now look at the five choices. Find 1 listed as Choice C, and blacken in C on your answer sheet.

EXAMPLE 2

Emily was born on Wednesday, April 15, 1987. Her sister Erin was born exactly 1200 days later. On what day of the week was Erin born?

(A) Tuesday   (B) Thursday   (C) Friday   (D) Saturday   (E) Sunday

Again, you are not helped by the fact that this question is a multiple-choice question. You need to determine the day of the week on which Erin was born, and then select the choice that matches your answer.

- The 7 days keep repeating in exactly the same order: 1 day after Emily was born was a Thursday, 2 days after Emily was born was a Friday, and so on. Make a table.

	Thurs.	Fri.	Sat.	Sun.	Mon.	Tues.	Wed.
Days after Emily	1	2	3	4	5	6	7
was born	8	9	10	11	12	13	14
	and so on.						

- Note that whenever the number of days is a multiple of 7 (7, 14, 21, . . . , 70, . . .) a whole number of weeks has gone by, and it is again a Wednesday.
- If 1200 were a multiple of 7, the 1200th day would be a Wednesday.
- Is it? No. When 1200 is divided by 7, the quotient is 171 and the remainder is 3.
- Since $171 \times 7 = 1197$, the 1197th day completes the 171st week, and hence is a Wednesday.
- The 1198th day starts the next week. It is a Thursday; the 1199th day is a Friday; and the 1200th day is a Saturday.
- The answer is D.

NOTE: Did you notice that the solution didn't use the fact that Emily was born on April 15, 1987? This is unusual. Occasionally, but not often, a PSAT problem contains extraneous information.

In contrast to Examples 1 and 2, some questions *require* you to look at all five choices in order to find the answers. Consider Example 3.

EXAMPLE 3

For any numbers a and b: $a \odot b = a^2 + b^2$? Which of the following is *not* equal to $6 \odot 8$?
(A) $-10 \odot 0$ (B) $-8 \odot -6$ (C) $9 \odot \sqrt{19}$ (D) $(6 \odot 9) - (4 \odot 1)$
(E) $2(3 \odot 4)$

The words *which of the following* alert you to the fact that you are going to have to examine each of the five choices and determine which of them satisfies the stated condition—in this case, that it is *not* equal to $6 \odot 8$.

Do not be concerned that you have never seen the symbol "$\odot$" used this way before. No one has. On the PSAT there is always at least one question that uses a symbol that the test makers have made up. All you have to do is read the question very carefully and follow the directions exactly. In this case we have: $6 \odot 8 = 6^2 + 8^2 = 36 + 64 = 100$.

Now check each of the five choices, and find the one that is *not* equal to 100.

(A) $-10 \odot 0 = (-10)^2 + 0^2 = 100 + 0 = 100$
(B) $-8 \odot -6 = (-8)^2 + (-6)^2 = 64 + 36 = 100$

(C) $9 \odot \sqrt{19} = 9^2 + (\sqrt{19})^2 = 81 + 19 = 100$

(D) $(6 \odot 9) - (4 \odot 1) = (6^2 + 9^2) - (4^2 + 1^2) = (36 + 81) - (16 + 1) =$
$117 - 17 = 100$

(E) $2(3 \odot 4) = 2(3^2 \ 1 \ 4^2) = 2(9 + 16) = 2(25) = 50$, which is *not* equal
to 100.

So, the correct answer is E.

Another kind of multiple-choice question that appears on the PSAT is the Roman numeral-type question. These questions actually consist of three statements labeled I, II, and III. The five answer choices give various possibilities for which statement or statements are true. Here is a typical example.

EXAMPLE 4

In $\triangle ABC$, $AB = 3$ and $BC = 4$. Which of the following could be the perimeter of $\triangle ABC$?

I.   8
II. 12
III. 16

(A) I only   (B) II only   (C) I and II only   (D) II and III only
(E) I, II, and III

- To solve this problem, examine each statement independently.
  I.   Could the perimeter be 8? If it were, then the third side would be 1. But in any triangle, the smallest side must be greater than the difference of the other two sides. So, the third side must be *greater* than $4 - 3 = 1$. It cannot equal 1. I is false.
  II. Could the perimeter be 12? That is, could the third side be 5? Yes. The three sides could be 3, 4, and 5. In fact, the most common right triangle to appear on the PSAT is a 3-4-5 right triangle. II is true.
  III. Could the perimeter be 16? If it were, then the third side would be 9. But in any triangle, the largest side must be less than the sum of the other two sides. So, the third side must be less than $4 + 3 = 7$. It cannot equal 9. III is false.
- Only statement II is true. The answer is B.

Quantitative Comparison Questions

Of the forty mathematics questions on the PSAT, twelve of them are quantitative comparisons. Unless you have already taken a PSAT, or studied for one, it is very likely that you have never seen such questions before, so read this explanation very carefully.

In these questions there are two quantities in boxes, one in Column A and one in Column B, and it is your job to compare these quantities. There are *only four possible answers* to quantitative comparison questions: A, B, C, and D. The correct answer to a quantitative comparison question is

A   if the quantity in Column A is greater *all the time, no matter what*

B   if the quantity in Column B is greater *all the time, no matter what*

C   if the two quantities are equal *all the time, no matter what*

D   if the answer is not A, B, or C

In some of the questions, information concerning one or both of the quantities is centered above the two boxes. This information *must* be taken into consideration when comparing the two quantities. If a symbol appears in both columns, it represents the same thing in each column.

In Chapter 10 you will learn some important strategies for handling quantitative comparisons. Here, let's examine a few examples to make sure that you understand the concepts involved.

	Column A	Column B
EXAMPLE 5	2^5	5^2

- Evaluate each column: $2^5 = 2 \times 2 \times 2 \times 2 \times 2 = 32$, whereas $5^2 = 5 \times 5 = 25$.
- Compare the quantities. Since $32 > 25$, the quantity in Column A is greater.
- The answer is A.

	Column A	Column B
EXAMPLE 6	$a + b = 100$	
	The average (arithmetic mean) of a and b	50

- The quantity in Column A is the average of a and b: $\dfrac{a+b}{2}$. Since $a + b = 100$, the quantity in Column A is
  $$\frac{a+b}{2} = \frac{100}{2} = 50$$
- Therefore, the quantities in Columns A and B are equal.
- The answer is C.

NOTE: We cannot determine the value of either a or b; all we know is that their sum is 100. Perhaps $a = 75$ and $b = 25$, or $a = 0$ and $b = 100$, or $a = -40$ and $b = 140$. *It doesn't matter.* The average of 75 and 25 is 50; the average of 0 and 100 is 50; and the average of −40 and 140 is 50. Since $a + b = 100$, the average of a and $b = 50$, *all the time, no matter what.* Therefore, the answer is C.

	Column A	Column B
EXAMPLE 7	$(m + n)^2$	$m^2 + n^2$

- If $m = 1$ and $n = 2$, then $(m + n)^2 = (1 + 2)^2 = 3^2 = 9$, whereas $m^2 + n^2 = 1^2 + 2^2 = 1 + 4 = 5$. *In this case*, the quantity in Column A is greater.
- This means that the answer to this problem *cannot* be B or C.
- Why? The answer can be B only if the quantity in Column B is larger *all the time, no matter what*. But it isn't—not when $m = 1$ and $n = 2$.
- Similarly, the answer can be C only if the two quantities are equal *all the time.* But this time they're not.
- Then is the answer A? Maybe. For the answer to be A, the quantity in Column A would have to be greater *all the time, no matter what*. Is it? No. If $m = 1$ and $n = -2$, $(m + n)^2 = (1 + -2)^2 = (-1)^2 = 1$, whereas $m^2 + n^2 = 1^2 + (-2)^2 = 1 + 4 = 5$. *In this case*, the quantity in Column B is greater.
- Therefore, the answer is D.

Grid-in Questions

Eight of the forty mathematics questions on the PSAT are what the College Board calls Student-Produced Response Questions. Since the answers to these questions are entered on a special grid, they are usually referred to as *grid-in* questions. Except for the method of entering your answer, this type of question is probably the one with which you are most familiar. In your math class, most of your homework problems and test questions require you to determine an answer and write it down, and this is what you will do on the grid-in problems. The only difference is that once you have figured out an answer, it must be recorded on a special grid such as the one shown, so that it can be read by a computer. Here is a typical grid-in question.

EXAMPLE 8

John has a rectangular garden in his backyard. He decides to enlarge it by increasing its length by 20% and its width by 30%. If the area of the new garden is *a* times the area of the original garden, what is the value of *a*?

Solution. From the wording of the question, it is clear that the answer does not depend on the actual original dimensions. Therefore, pick an easy value. For example, assume that the original garden is a square whose sides are 10; then the new garden is a 12 by 13 rectangle. Therefore, the area of the original garden is 100, and the area of the new garden is 156. So 156 = a(100), and a = 1.56.

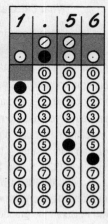

To enter this answer, you write 1.56 in the four spaces at the top of the grid and blacken in the appropriate oval under each space. In the first column, under the 1, blacken the oval marked 1; in the second column, under the decimal point, blacken the oval with the decimal point; in the third column, under the 5, blacken the oval marked 5; and finally, in the fourth column, under the 6, blacken in the oval marked 6.

Note that the only symbols that appear in the grid are the digits from 0 to 9, a decimal point, and a fraction bar (/). The grid does not have a minus sign, so *answers to grid-in problems can never be negative.* In Chapter 7, you will read suggestions for the best way to fill in grids. You will also learn the special rules concerning the proper way to grid in fractions, mixed numbers, and decimals that won't fit in the grid's four columns.

THE USE OF CALCULATORS ON THE PSAT

There isn't a single question on the PSAT for which a calculator is required. In fact, for most questions a calculator is completely useless. There are several questions, however, for which a calculator *could* be used, and since calculators are permitted, you should definitely bring one with you when you take the PSAT. As you go through the hundreds of practice math questions in this book, you should have available the calculator you intend to take to the test, and you should use it whenever you think it is appropriate. You will probably use it more at the beginning of your review because, as you go through this book, you will learn more and more strategies to help you solve problems easily without doing tedious calculations.

If you forget to bring a calculator to the actual test, you will not be able to use one, since none will be provided, and you will not be allowed to share one with a friend. For exactly the same reason, be sure that you have new batteries in your calculator or that you bring a spare, because if your calculator fails during the test, you will have to finish without one.

What Calculator Should You Use?

Almost any four-function, scientific, or graphic calculator is acceptable. Since you don't "need" a calculator at all, you don't "need" any particular type. There is absolutely no advantage to having a graphic calculator, but we do recommend a scientific calculator, since it is occasionally useful to have parentheses keys, ( ); a reciprocal key, $\frac{1}{x}$; and an exponent key, y^x or $\wedge$. All scientific calculators have these features. If you tend to make mistakes working with fractions, you might want to get a calculator that can do fractional arithmetic. With such a calculator, for example, you can add $\frac{1}{3}$ and $\frac{1}{5}$ by entering 1/3 + 1/5; the readout will be 8/15, not the decimal 0.5333333. Some, but not most, scientific calculators have this capability.

CAUTION: Do not buy a new calculator right before you take the PSAT. If you don't have one or want to get a different one, *buy it now* and become familiar with it. Do all the practice exams in this book with the same calculator you intend to bring to the test.

When Should Calculators Be Used?

If you have strong math skills and are a good test-taker, you will probably use your calculator infrequently, if at all, since, for one thing, strong math students can do a lot of basic arithmetic just as accurately, and faster, in their heads or on paper than with a calculator. A less obvious, but more important point is that students who are good test-takers will realize that many problems can be solved without doing any calculations at all (mental, written, or with a calculator); they will solve those problems in less time than it takes to pick a calculator up. On the other hand, if you are less confident about your mathematical ability or your test-taking skills, you will probably find your calculator a useful tool.

NOTE: Throughout this book, this icon will be placed next to a problem where the use of a calculator is recommended. As you will see, this judgment is very subjective. Sometimes a question can be answered in a few seconds, with no calculations whatsoever, *if* you see the best approach. In that case, the use of a calculator would *not* be recommended. If you don't see the easy way, however, and have to do some arithmetic, you may prefer to use a calculator.

Let's look at a few sample questions when some students would use calculators more frequently, others less frequently, and still others not at all.

EXAMPLE 1
    If $16 \times 25 \times 36 = (4a)^2$, what is the value of a?
    (A) 6   (B) 15   (C) 30   (D) 36   (E) 60

(i) Heavy calculator use: WITH A CALCULATOR Multiply: $16 \times 25 \times 36 =$ 14400. Observe that $(4a)^2 = 16a^2$, and so $16a^2 = 14{,}400$. WITH A CALCULATOR divide: $a^2 = 14{,}400 \div 16 = 900$. Finally, WITH A CALCULATOR take the square root: $a = \sqrt{900} = 30$. The answer is C.

(ii) Light calculator use: Immediately notice that you can "cancel" the 16 on the left-hand side with the 4^2 on the right-hand side. WITH A CALCULATOR Multiply $25 \times 36 = 900$, and WITH A CALCULATOR take the square root of 900.

(iii) No calculator use: Cancel the 16 and the 4^2. Notice that $25 = 5^2$ and $36 = 6^2$, so $a^2 = 5^2 \times 6^2 = 30^2$, and $a = 30$.

EXAMPLE 2 (GRID-IN)

    If the length of a diagonal of a rectangle is 15, and if one of the sides is 9, what is the perimeter?

    Whether or not you intend to use your calculator, the first thing to do is to draw a diagram.

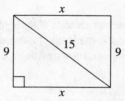

(i) Heavy calculator use: By the Pythagorean theorem, $x^2 + 9^2 = 15^2$. Observe that $9^2 = 81$, and WITH A CALCULATOR evaluate: $15^2 = 225$. Then WITH A CALCULATOR subtract: $225 - 81 = 144$. So, $x^2 = 144$. Hit the square root key on your calculator to get $x = 12$. Finally, WITH A CALCULATOR add to find the perimeter: $9 + 12 + 9 + 12 = 42$.

(ii) Light calculator use: Everything is the same as in (i) except *some* of the calculations can be done mentally: finding the square root of 144 and adding to find the perimeter.

(iii) No calculator use: *All of the calculations* are done mentally, or, better yet, *no calculations are done at all*, because you immediately see that each half of the rectangle is a 9-12-15 right triangle (a 3-4-5 right triangle in which each side was multiplied by 3), and you add up the sides in your head.

	Column A	Column B
EXAMPLE 3	$197 + 298 + 399$	$201 + 302 + 403$

(i) Using a calculator: Calculate each sum, and compare the answers: 894 versus 906. Column B is greater.

(ii) No calculator use: Just notice that each number in Column B is greater than the corresponding number in Column A.

Here are three final comments on the use of calculators:

1. The reason that calculators are of limited value on the PSAT is that no calculator can *do* mathematics. *You* have to know the mathematics and the way to apply it. A calculator cannot tell you whether to multiply or divide or that on a particular question you should use the Pythagorean theorem.

2. No PSAT problem ever requires tedious calculations. However, if you don't see how to avoid calculating, just do it—*don't spend a lot of time looking for a shortcut that will save you a little time!*

3. Most students use calculators more than they should, but if you can solve a problem with a calculator that you might otherwise miss, use the calculator.

WRITING SKILLS

The writing skills section consists of thirty-nine questions to be answered in thirty minutes. A typical test is made up of nineteen identifying sentence errors questions, fourteen improving sentence questions, and six improving paragraph questions.

Identifying Sentence Error

The identifying sentence error questions test your ability to spot faults in usage and sentence structure.

The sentences in this section may contain errors in grammar, usage, choice of words, or idioms. There is either just one error per sentence or the sentence is correct. Some words or phrases are underlined and lettered; everything else in the sentence is correct.

If an underlined word or phrase is incorrect, choose that letter; if the sentence is correct, select <u>No error</u>. Then blacken the appropriate space on your Answer Sheet.

EXAMPLE: SAMPLE ANSWER:

Ⓐ Ⓑ ● Ⓓ Ⓔ

The region has a climate <u>so severe that</u> plants
                                          A

<u>growing there</u> rarely <u>had been</u> more than twelve
        B   C

inches <u>high</u>. <u>No error</u>
         D   E

---

1. Despite the fact that some states have resisted, the Congress have passed
        A   B   C
    legislation permitting highway speed limits to 65 miles per hour on rural
                    D
    interstates. No error
                    E

2. Mohandas Gandhi, to who the title "Father of Passive Resistance"
                            A
    may be given, bravely led the nationalist movement in India against
            B   C   D
    British rule. No error
                    E

3. Joe DiMaggio, whose style was one of quiet excellence, was consistently the
                        A   B
    New York Yankees' outstanding player during his thirteen years on the team.
                            C   D
    No error
      E

4. When Ms. Rivera was truly happy, she does not constantly complain that she
                        A   B   C   D
    has no purpose in life. No error
                              E

Answer Explanations

1. **(C)** Error in subject-verb agreement. The antecedent, *Congress*, is singular. Change *have passed* to *has passed*.
2. **(A)** Error in case. Change *who* to *whom*. It is the object of the preposition *to*.
3. **(E)** Sentence is correct.
4. **(A)** Error in sequence of tenses. The sentence should read: *When Ms. Rivera is truly happy, she does not complain.*

Improving Sentence Questions

The improving sentence questions test your ability to select the wording that makes the strongest sentence—the clearest, the smoothest, the most compact.

Some or all parts of the following sentences are underlined. The first answer choice, (A), simply repeats the underlined part of the sentence. The other four choices present four alternate ways to phrase the underlined part. Select the answer that produces the most effective sentence, one that is clear and exact, and blacken the appropriate space on your answer sheet. In selecting your choice, be sure that it is standard written English, and that it expresses the meaning of the original sentence.

EXAMPLE:

The first biography of author Eudora Welty came out in 1998 <u>and she was eighty-nine years old at the time.</u>

(A) and she was eighty-nine years old at the time
(B) at the time when she was eighty-nine
(C) upon becoming an eighty-nine year old
(D) when she was eighty-nine
(E) at the age of eighty-nine years old

SAMPLE ANSWER:

---

5. <u>More than any animal</u>, the wolverine exemplifies the unbridled ferocity of "nature red in tooth and claw."

   (A) More than any animal
   (B) More than any other animal
   (C) More than another animal
   (D) Unlike any animal
   (E) Compared to other animals

6. The reviewer knew that Barbara Cartland had written several Gothic <u>novels, she didn't remember any of their titles.</u>

   (A) novels, she didn't remember any of their titles
   (B) novels, however she didn't remember any of their titles
   (C) novels, their titles, however, she didn't remember
   (D) novels without remembering any of their titles
   (E) novels, but she remembered none of their titles

7. I think the United States will veto the resolution imposing sanctions against Israel regardless of the desires of the Arab nations for strong action.

(A) regardless of the desires of the Arab nations
(B) irregardless of the Arab nations' desires
(C) regardless of the Arab nations desires
(D) irregardless of the Arab nation's desires
(E) mindful of the desires of the Arab nations

Answer Explanations

5. (B) Choice B includes the necessary word *other*, which makes the comparison correct. Choice D changes the meaning of the sentence by its implication that the wolverine is *not* an animal.

6. (E) Choices A, B, and C are run-on sentences. Choice D changes the meaning of the sentence by implying that it was Barbara Cartland who could not remember the titles.

7. (A) *Irregardless* in Choices B and D is incorrect. Also, in Choices C and D, the case of *nations* is incorrect. The correct form of the plural possessive case of *nation* is *nations'*. Choice E changes the meaning of the sentence; in fact, it reverses it.

Improving Paragraph Questions

The improving paragraph questions test your ability to polish an essay by combining sentences or manipulating sentence parts. You may need to arrange sentences to improve the essay's logical organization, or to pick evidence to strengthen the writer's argument.

The passage below is the unedited draft of a student's essay. Some of the essay needs to be rewritten to make the meaning clearer and more precise. Read the essay carefully.

The essay is followed by six questions about changes that might improve all or part of its organization, development, sentence structure, use of language, appropriateness to the audience, or its use of standard written English. Choose the answer that most clearly and effectively expresses the student's intended meaning. Indicate your choice by filling in the corresponding space on the answer sheet.

[1] As people grow older, quite obviously, the earth does too. [2] And with the process of the earth aging, we must learn to recycle. [3] The idea of using things over and over again to conserve our supply of natural resources is a beautiful one. [4] Those who don't see how easy it is to recycle should be criticized greatly.

[5] As we become more aware of the earth's problems, we all say "Oh, I'd like to help." [6] However, so few really do get involved. [7] Recycling is a simple, yet effective place to start. [8] Taking aluminum cans to the supermarket to be recycled is an ingenious idea. [9] It attracts those who want the money (5 cents a can), and it is also a convenient place to go to. [10] In addition, in almost every town, there is a Recycling Center. [11] I know that there are separate bins for paper, bottles, cans, etc. [12] This is a convenient service to those who recycle. [13] It is so easy to drive a few blocks to a center to drop off what needs to be recycled. [14] This is just another simple example of how easy it really is to recycle and to get involved. [15] Those who don't see its simplicity should be criticized for not doing their part to help make the world a better place.

[16] When I go to other people's houses and see aluminum cans in the garbage, I can honestly say I get enraged. [17] Often I say, "Why don't you just recycle those cans instead of throwing them out?" [18] What makes me even more angry is when they say "We have no time to recycle them." [19] Those people, I feel, should be criticized for not recycling in the past and should be taught a lesson about our earth and how recycling can conserve it.

8. Which of the following most effectively expresses the underlined portion of sentence 2 below?

And <u>with the process of the earth aging</u>, we must learn to recycle.

(A) with the aging process of the earth

(B) the process of the earth's aging

(C) as the earth ages

(D) with the aging earth's process

(E) as the process of the earth's aging continues

9. Considering the essay as a whole, which of the following best explains the main purpose of the second paragraph?

(A) To explain the historical background of the topic

(B) To provide a smooth transition between the first and third paragraphs

(C) To define terms introduced in the first paragraph

(D) To give an example of an idea presented in the first paragraph

(E) To present a different point of view on the issue being discussed

10. Which of the sentences below most effectively combines sentences 10, 11, and 12?

(A) Recycling centers offer recyclers convenience by providing separate bins for paper, bottles, and cans and by being located in almost every town.

(B) Recycling centers, located in almost every town, serve recyclers by providing convenient bins to separate paper, bottles, and cans.

(C) Almost every town has a recycling center with separate bins for paper, bottles, and cans, and this is a convenient service for people who want to recycle.

(D) People who want to recycle will find recycling centers in almost every town, providing a convenient separation of paper, bottles, and cans into bins.

(E) For the convenience of recyclers, separate bins for paper, bottles, and cans are provided by almost every town's recycling center.

Answer Explanations

8. (C) This question asks you to find an alternative to a rather awkward group of words, composed of two phrases, *with the process* and *of the earth aging*. The second is graceless and ungrammatical. It should have read *of the earth's aging*, because in standard usage, nouns and pronouns modifying gerunds are usually written as possessives. Knowing what it should have been, however, is not much help in answering the question. You still must select from the five alternatives the one best way to express the essay writer's idea. In the context of the whole sentence, two of the choices, B and D, make no sense at all. A also borders on incomprehensibility. Left with C and E, the better choice is C because it is more concise and it expresses exactly what the writer intended.

9. (D) To answer this question you need to have read the whole essay. You also need to know the way individual paragraphs function in an essay—any essay. Here, all five choices describe legitimate uses of a paragraph, but they don't all apply to this particular essay. Choices A, C, and E can be quickly discarded. Choice B is a possibility because in a unified essay every paragraph (except the first and last) in some sense serves as a bridge between paragraphs. Because the second paragraph is the longest in the essay, however, its main function is probably more than transitional. In fact, it develops by example an idea originating in the first paragraph—how easy it is to recycle. Therefore, D is the best choice.

10. (B) In a series of short sentences, every idea carries equal weight. By combining short sentences, writers may emphasize the important ideas and subordinate the others. To answer this question, then, you have to decide which idea expressed by the three sentences ought to be emphasized.

Since two of the sentences (11 and 12) refer to the convenient arrangement of recycling centers, that's the point to stress. In the context of the whole essay, the other sentence (10), which pertains to the location of recycling centers, contains less vital information. Usually, the main point of a sentence is contained in the main, or independent, clause, and secondary ideas are found in subordinate, or dependent, clauses.

With that principle in mind, read each of the choices. A and C give equal weight to the location and convenience of recycling centers. D stresses the location rather than the convenience. E subordinates properly but changes the meaning. Therefore, B is the correct answer. In B, information about the location of recycling centers is contained in a subordinate clause included parenthetically inside the main clause.

AFTER THE PSAT/NMSQT

After the scores of the PSAT/NMSQT are received, you, your parents, and your guidance counselor can begin to make plans for college. Here are some Barron's reference books that will be very helpful to you.

BARRON'S HOW TO PREPARE FOR THE SAT I, by Sharon Weiner Green and Ira K. Wolf. *This classic of college entrance examinations includes a diagnostic test as well as seven complete simulated exams that enable you to practice under exact* SAT I *format and test conditions; all model tests have answer keys and answer explanations. Verbal Reasoning practice includes selected and graded word lists, definitions and vocabulary tests. Mathematical Reasoning practice reviews necessary math from arithmetic through high school algebra and geometry, and features the quantitative comparison and grid-in questions included on the* SAT I. *Testing tactics and strategies are featured.* 2001, 21st Edition.

SAT I—MATH WORKBOOK, by Lawrence Leff. *All-new workbook is geared to today's test-takers' needs. Practice exercises contain hundreds of multiple-choice questions, quantitative comparisons, and grid-in questions with answers. Lesson topics include calculators, the new Student-Produced Response Question type, and a wide array of math subjects related to the* SAT I. 2000, 2nd Edition.

SAT I—VERBAL WORKBOOK, by Mitchel Weiner and Sharon Weiner Green. *A companion to the Math Workbook—it provides hundreds of practice exercises and diagnostic tests for intensive review of vocabulary, sentence completion, word relationships, and reading comprehension. Suggested study plan and 1000 questions plus 10 complete model verbal aptitude tests prepare students to score high on college boards, admission, placement, and scholarship examinations where word usage and understanding are tested.* 2001, 10th Edition.

BARRON'S PROFILES OF AMERICAN COLLEGES. *Searching studies of more than 1600 regionally accredited four-year American colleges and universities that will give the prospective student a preview of his or her relationship to a particular* college—based on its facilities, outstanding features and programs, admission requirements, costs, available financial aid, extracurricular activities, programs and major offerings, degrees awarded, enrollment, religious affiliation, housing facilities, social or honorary societies, religious or other regulations for student life. The comprehensive and detailed information on each college will be of tremendous help to guidance counselors, college-bound students, and their families. 2002, 25th Edition.

BASIC WORD LIST, by Samuel C. Brownstein, Mitchel Weiner, and Sharon Weiner Green. *This effective vocabulary builder presents more than 2,000 words that all students should know to prepare for the SAT I, ACT, and other standardized college entrance and college level exams. Each new word is defined and placed in a model sentence. Practice vocabulary exercises and a review of word prefixes and roots.* 1997, 3rd Edition.

ESSAYS THAT WILL GET YOU INTO COLLEGE, by Daniel Kaufman, Chris Dowhan, and Amy Burnham. *Seventy model essays that have worked for the applicants, with advice, discussion, and commentary that reveal the secrets of successful essay writing.* 1998.

HOT WORDS FOR THE SAT I, by Linda Carnevale. *Hundreds of words focused on preparing students for the SAT I, with definitions, samples, and explanations, along with quizzes.* 2001.

2 How to Approach the PSAT/NMSQT

TEST TAKING TACTICS

What Tactics Can Help Me When I Take the PSAT?

1. Memorize the directions given in this book for each type of question. These are only slightly different from the exact words you'll find on the PSAT you'll take. During the test, do not waste even a few seconds reading any directions or sample questions.

2. Know the test. The number and kinds of questions break down as follows:

   52 Verbal Questions (2 Sections, 25 minutes each)
   13 sentence completion questions
   13 analogy questions
   26 critical reading questions

   40 Math Questions (2 Sections, 25 minutes each)
   20 standard multiple-choice questions
   12 quantitative comparison questions
   8 student-produced response (grid-in) questions

   39 Writing Skills Questions (1 Section, 30 minutes)
   19 identifying sentence errors questions
   14 improving sentence questions
   6 improving paragraph questions

3. Expect easy questions at the beginning of each set of the same question type. Within each set (except for the critical reading and writing skills questions), the questions progress from easy to difficult. In other words, the first analogy question in a set will be easier than the last analogy in that set; the first quantitative comparison question will be easier than the last quantitative comparison question.

4. Take advantage of the easy questions to boost your score. Remember, each question is worth the same number of points. Whether it was easy or difficult, whether it took you ten seconds or two minutes to answer, you get the same number of points for each question you

answer correctly. Your job is to answer as many questions as you possibly can without rushing ahead so fast that you make careless errors or lose points for failing to give some questions enough thought. So take enough time to get those easy questions right!

5. *First* answer all the easy questions; *then* tackle the hard ones if you have time. You know that the questions in each segment of the test get harder as you go along (except for the critical reading questions). But there's no rule that says you have to answer the questions in order. You're allowed to skip. So, if the last three analogy questions are driving you crazy, move on to the reading passages right away. Likewise, don't let yourself get bogged down on a difficult quantitative comparison question when only three questions away the easy grid-in questions begin. Test-wise students know when it's time to move on.

6. Eliminate as many wrong answers as you can. Deciding between two choices is easier than deciding among five. Whenever you guess, every answer you eliminate improves your chances of guessing correctly.

7. Change answers only if you have a reason for doing so. Don't give in to last-minute panic. It's usually better for you not to change your answers on a sudden hunch or whim.

8. Because calculators are permitted in the test room, bring along a calculator that you are comfortable using. No question on the test will *require* the use of a calculator, but it may be helpful for some questions. Almost any standard calculator will do: four-function, scientific, and graphing calculators all are allowed.

9. Be careful not to make any stray marks on your answer sheet. This test is graded by a machine, and a machine cannot tell the difference between an accidental mark and a filled-in answer. When the machine sees two marks instead of one, the answer is marked wrong.

10. Check frequently to make sure you are answering the questions in the right spots. No machine is going to notice that you made a mistake early in the test, answered question 4 in the space for question 5, and all your following answers are in the wrong place. One way to avoid this problem is to mark your answers in your test booklet and transfer them to your answer sheet by blocks.

11. Line up your test book with your answer sheet. Whether you choose to fill in the answers question by question or in blocks, you will do so most efficiently if you keep your test book and your answer sheet aligned.

12. Be particularly careful in marking the student-produced responses on the math grid. Before you fill in the appropriate blanks in the grid,

write your answer at the top of the columns. Then go down each column, making sure you're filling in the right spaces.

13. Don't get bogged down on any one question. By the time you get to the actual PSAT, you should have a fair idea of how much time to spend on each question. If a question is taking too long, leave it and go on to the next question. This is no time to try to show the world that you can stick to a job no matter how long it takes. All the machine that grades the test will notice is that after a certain point you didn't have any correct answers.

REDUCING ANXIETY

How Can I Prevent PSAT Anxiety from Setting In?

1. The best way to prepare for any test you ever take is to get a good night's sleep before the test so that you are well rested and alert.

2. Eat breakfast for once in your life. You have a full morning ahead of you; you should have a full stomach as well.

3. Allow plenty of time for getting to the test site. Taking a test is pressure enough. You don't need the extra tension that comes from worrying about whether you will get there on time.

4. Be aware of the amount of time the test is going to take. There are five sections. They will take two hours and ten minutes total. Add to that a five-minute break after the second section, a one-minute break after the fourth, plus thirty minutes for paper pushing. If the test starts at 8:00 A.M., don't make a dentist appointment for 11:00. You can't possibly get there on time, and you'll just spend the last half-hour of the test worrying about it.

5. The College Board tells you to bring two sharpened No. 2 pencils to the test. Bring four. They don't weigh much, and this might be the one day in the decade when two pencil points decide to break. And bring full-size pencils, not little stubs. They are easier to write with, and you might as well be comfortable.

6. Speaking of being comfortable, wear comfortable clothes. This is a test, not a fashion show. Aim for the layered look. Wear something light, but bring a sweater. The test room may be hot, or it may be cold. You can't change the room, but you can put on the sweater.

7. Bring an accurate watch. You need one. The room in which you take the test may not have a clock, and some proctors are not very good about posting the time on the blackboard. Don't depend on them.

Each time you begin a test section, write down in your booklet the time according to your watch. That way you will always know how much time you have left.

8. Smuggle in some quick energy in your pocket—trail mix, raisins, a candy bar. Even if the proctors don't let you eat in the test room, you can still grab a bite en route to the rest rooms during the five-minute break. Taking the test can leave you feeling drained and in need of a quick pickup—bring along your favorite comfort food.

9. There will be a break after the second section. Use this period to clear your thoughts. Take a few deep breaths. Stretch. Close your eyes and imagine yourself floating or sunbathing. In addition to being under mental pressure, you're under physical pressure from sitting so long in an uncomfortable seat with a No. 2 pencil clutched in your hand. Anything you can do to loosen up and get the kinks out will ease your body and help the oxygen get to your brain.

10. Most important of all, remember: very little, if anything, is riding on the result of this test. If you do poorly, no one will know; your PSAT scores are not reported to the colleges to which you plan to apply. So relax!

GUESSING

If you don't know the answer to a question on the PSAT, should you guess?

There is a lot of controversy surrounding the issue of guessing, and if you ask several people for advice, you will surely get conflicting answers. However, the answer to the above question is very simple: In general, *it pays to guess*. To understand why this is so and why so many people are confused about it, you must understand how the PSAT is scored.

On each portion of the PSAT, every question is worth exactly the same amount: one point. A correct answer to a reading comprehension question for which you might have to reread a whole paragraph is worth no more than a correct answer to a verbal analogy that you can answer in a few seconds. You get no more credit for a correct answer to the hardest math question than you do for the easiest. For each question that you answer correctly, you receive one raw score point. Your total raw scores on the math, verbal, and writing skills sections are then converted to scaled scores between 20 and 80. (**Note:** On the SAT I the scaled scores range from 200 to 800, so when most students discuss their PSAT scores they affix a 0 at the end of each number; for example, instead of saying, "I got a 55 on the verbal and a 60 on the math," they would say, "I got a 550 and a 600," or, adding their two scores, might just say, "I scored 1150.")

Consider the following scenario. Suppose that working very slowly and carefully you answer only twenty-seven of the fifty-two verbal questions on the PSAT, but get each of them correct. Your raw score would be 27, and that would be converted to a scaled score of about 52—an above-average score, even though you left out nearly half of the questions. If that were the whole story, then you should take the last minute of the test and quickly fill in an answer to each of the other twenty-five questions. Since each question has five choices, you should get about one-fifth of them right. Surely, you would get *some* of them right—most likely between 4 and 6. Say you get five of them right. Then your raw score would go from 27 to 32, and your scaled score would now be about 57. Your verbal score would increase five points (50 SAT I points) due to one minute of wild guessing! Clearly, this is not what the College Board wants to happen. To counter this, there is a so-called *guessing penalty,* which adjusts your scores for wrong answers, and makes it unlikely that you will profit from wild guessing.

The penalty for each incorrect answer on the verbal sections is a reduction of $\frac{1}{4}$ of a point. What effect would this penalty have in the example just discussed? Recall that by wildly guessing at twenty-five questions, you got five right and twenty wrong. Those five extra right answers caused your raw score to go up by five points. But now you lose $\frac{1}{4}$ of a point for each of the twenty problems you missed—a total reduction of $\frac{20}{4}$ = 5 points. So you broke even: you gained five points and lost five points. Your raw score, and hence your scaled score, didn't change at all.

Notice that the *guessing penalty* didn't actually penalize you. It prevented you from making a big gain that you didn't deserve, but it didn't punish you by lowering your score. It's not a very harsh penalty after all.

Educated guessing, on the other hand, can have an enormous effect on your score; it can increase it dramatically! Let's look at what we mean by educated guessing and see how it can improve your score on the PSAT.

Consider the following sentence completion question.

In Victorian times, countless Egyptian mummies were ground up to produce dried mummy powder, hailed by quacks as a near-magical ----, able to cure a wide variety of ailments.

(A) toxin   (B) diagnosis   (C) symptom   (D) panacea   (E) placebo

Clearly, what is needed is a word such as *medicine*—something capable of curing ailments. Let's assume that you know that *toxin* means poison, so you immediately eliminate A. You also know that although *diagnosis* and *symptom* are medical terms, neither means a medicine or a cure, so you eliminate B and C. You now know that the correct answer must be D or E, but unfortunately you have no idea what *panacea* or *placebo* means. You *could* guess, but you don't want to be wrong; after all, there's that penalty for incorrect answers. So, should you leave it out? Absolutely not. *You must guess!* We'll explain why and how in a moment, but first let's look at one more example, this time a math one.

From 1990 to 1995 the number of students participating in a school's community service program increased by 25%. If the number of participants in 1995 was P, how many students participated in 1990?

(A) 0.75P (B) 0.80P (C) 1.20P (D) 1.25P (E) 1.50P

Even if you are not very good at percent problems (especially when they involve letters!) you should realize that since participation in the program increased, the number of students who participated in 1990 must be *less than P*. So you know the answer must be A or B. What do you do? Do you guess and risk incurring the guessing penalty, or do you leave it out because you have no idea which answer is correct? *You must guess!*

Suppose that you are still working slowly and carefully on the verbal sections, and that of the fifty-two questions, you are sure of the answers to twenty-seven of them; in fifteen of them you are able to eliminate three of the choices, but you have no idea which of the remaining two choices is correct; and the remaining ten questions you don't even look at. You already know what would happen if you guessed wildly on the last ten questions—you would probably break even. But what about the fifteen questions you narrowed down to two choices? If you guess on those, you should get about half right and half wrong. Is that good or bad? *It's very good!* Assume you got seven right and eight wrong. For the seven correct answers you would receive seven points, and for the eight incorrect answers, you would lose $\frac{3}{4}$ = 2 points. This is a net gain of five raw score points, for which your verbal PSAT score would go from 52 to 57 (that's 50 SAT points!). It would be a shame to throw away those points just because you were afraid of the guessing penalty.

Occasionally, you can even eliminate four of the five choices! Suppose that in the sentence completion above, you realize that you do know what *placebo* means, and that it can't be the answer. You still have no idea about *panacea,* so you may be hesitant to answer a question with a word you never heard of, but you *must.* If in the math question above, only one of the choices were smaller than P, it would have to be correct. Don't leave it out because you can't verify the answer directly. You must choose the only answer you haven't eliminated.

What if you can't eliminate three or four of the choices? You should guess if you can eliminate even one choice. Remember, guessing wildly—when you can't eliminate anything—you break even. If you can eliminate anything at all, you come out ahead by guessing.

3 The Sentence Completion Question

The sentence completion questions ask you to choose the best way to complete a sentence from which one or two words have been omitted. These questions test a combination of reading comprehension skills and vocabulary. You must be able to recognize the logic, style, and tone of the sentence so that you can choose the answer that makes sense in this context. You must also be able to recognize the way words are normally used. At some time or another, you have probably had a vocabulary assignment in which you were asked to define a word and use it in a sentence of your own. In these questions, you have to fit words into sentences. Once you understand the implications of the sentence, you should be able to choose the answer that will make the sentence clear, logical, and stylistically consistent.

The sentences cover a wide variety of topics—music, art, science, literature, history. However, this is not a test of your general knowledge. You may feel more comfortable if you are familiar with the topic the sentence is discussing, but you should be able to handle any of the sentences using your understanding of the English language.

Tips for Handling Sentence Completion Questions

1. Before you look at the answer choices, read the sentence and think of words that might make sense in the context. You may not come up with the exact word, but you *may* come up with a synonym.
2. Don't be hasty in picking an answer. Test each answer choice, substituting it for the missing word. That way you can satisfy yourself that you have selected the answer that best fits.
3. In double-blank sentences, eliminate answer pairs by testing their first words. Read through the entire sentence. Then insert the first word of each answer pair in the first blank of the sentence. Ask yourself whether this particular word makes sense in this blank. If the initial word of an answer pair makes no sense in the sentence, you can eliminate that answer pair.
4. If you're having vocabulary trouble, look for familiar parts—prefixes, suffixes, and roots—in unfamiliar words.
5. Watch out for negative words and words telling how long something lasts. Only a small change makes these two sentences very different in meaning:

> They were not lovers.
> They were not often lovers.

6. Look for words or phrases that indicate a contrast between one idea and another—words like *although, however, despite,* or *but.* In such cases an antonym or near-antonym for another word in the sentence may provide the correct answer.

7. Look for words or phrases that indicate similarities—words like *in the same way, in addition,* and *also.* In such cases, a synonym or near-synonym for another word in the sentence may provide the correct answer.

8. Look for words or phrases that indicate that one thing causes another—words like *because, since, therefore,* or *thus.*

EXAMPLE 1

See how the first tip works in dealing with the following sentence:

The psychologist set up the experiment to test the rat's ----; he wished to see how well the rat adjusted to the changing conditions it had to face.

Even before you look at the answer choices, you can figure out what the answer *should* be.

Look at the sentence. A psychologist is trying to test some particular quality or characteristic of a rat. What quality? How do you get the answer?

Look at the second part of the sentence, the part following the semicolon (the second clause, in technical terms). This clause defines or clarifies what the psychologist is trying to test. He is trying to see how well the rat *adjusts.* What words does this suggest to you? *Flexibility* possibly, or *adaptability* comes to mind. Either of these words could logically complete the sentence's thought.

Here are the five answer choices given:

(A) reflexes   (B) communicability   (C) stamina   (D) sociability
(E) adaptability

The best answer clearly is *adaptability,* Choice E.

EXAMPLE 2

When you're racing the clock, you feel like marking down the first correct-sounding answer you come across. *Don't.* You may be going too fast.

Because the enemy had a reputation for engaging in sneak attacks, we were ---- on the alert.

(A) frequently   (B) furtively   (C) evidently   (D) constantly
(E) occasionally

A hasty reader might be content with Choice A, *frequently,* but *frequently* is not the best fit. The best answer is Choice D, *constantly,* because "frequent" periods of alertness would not be enough to provide the necessary protection against sneak attacks that could occur at any time. "Constant" vigilance is called for: the troops would have to be always on the alert.

EXAMPLE 3

Dealing with double-blank sentences can be tricky. It helps to test the first word of each answer pair when you're narrowing things down.

The opossum is ---- venom of snakes in the rattlesnake subfamily and thus views the reptiles not as ---- enemies but as a food source.

(A) vulnerable to . . natural   (B) indicative of . . mortal
(C) impervious to . . lethal   (D) sensitive to . . deadly
(E) defenseless against . . potential

Look at the first word of each answer pair. Do any of these words make no sense in the context? The sentence is talking about the way opossums react to rattlesnake poison. What words seem possible? Opossums could be *vulnerable* to this poison, capable of being hurt by it. They could be *sensitive* to it, excessively affected by it. They could be *defenseless* against it, wholly unable to protect themselves from the poison. They could even be *impervious* to it, unaffected by it. But *indicative* of it? The word makes no sense. You can eliminate Choice B.

Now examine the second half of the sentence. Opossums look on rattlesnakes as a food source; they eat rattlers. What makes it possible for them to do so? They can do so *because* they're *impervious* to the poison (that is, unharmed by it). That's the reason they can treat the rattlesnake as a potential source of food and not as a *lethal* or deadly enemy. The correct answer is Choice C.

Note the cause-and-effect signal *thus*. The nature of the opossum's response to the venom explains why it can look on a dangerous snake as an easy prey.

EXAMPLE 4

After a tragedy, many people claim to have had a ---- of disaster.

(A) taste   (B) dislike   (C) presentiment   (D) context   (E) verdict

Use your knowledge of word parts to enable you to deal with unfamiliar words in sentence completion questions.

Take the unfamiliar word *presentiment*. Break it down into parts. A sentiment is *a feeling* (the root *sens* means *feel*). *Pre-* means *before*. A *presentiment* is something *you feel before* it happens, a foreboding. Your best answer is Choice C.

EXAMPLE 5

Watch out for *not:* it's easy to overlook, but it's a key word.

Madison was not ---- person and thus made few public addresses; but those he made were memorable, filled with noble phrases.

(A) a reticent (B) a stately (C) an inspiring (D) an introspective
(E) a communicative

What would happen if you overlooked *not* in this question? Probably you'd wind up choosing Choice A: Madison was a *reticent* (quiet; reserved) man. *For this reason* he made few public addresses.

Unfortunately, you'd have gotten things backward. The sentence isn't telling you what Madison was like. It's telling you what he was not like. And he was not a *communicative* person; he didn't express himself freely. However, when he did get around to speaking in public, he had valuable things to say.

EXAMPLE 6

We expected him to be jubilant over his victory, but he was ---- instead.

(A) triumphant (B) adult (C) morose (D) talkative (E) culpable

Watch for words that indicate contrast: *although, however, despite,* or *but.*

But suggests that the winner's expected reaction contrasts with his actual one. Instead of being *jubilant* (extremely joyful), he is sad. The correct answer is Choice C, *morose.*

EXAMPLE 7

The simplest animals are those whose bodies are least complex in structure and which do the things done by all animals, such as eating, breathing, moving, and feeling, in the most ---- way.

(A) haphazard (B) bizarre (C) advantageous (D) primitive
(E) unique

The transition word *and* signals you that the writer intends to develop the concept of simplicity introduced in the sentence. You should know from your knowledge of biology that *primitive* life forms were simple in structure and that the more complex forms evolved later. Choice C may seem possible. However, to secure the most *advantageous* way of conducting the activities of life, the animal would have to become specialized and complex. Thus, Choice D *(primitive)* is best, because it is the only choice that develops the idea of simplicity.

EXAMPLE 8

Because his delivery was ----, the effect of his speech on the voters was nonexistent.

(A) halting (B) plausible (C) moving (D) respectable (E) audible

Watch for words that show a cause-and-effect relationship: *because, since, therefore,* or *thus.*

What sort of delivery would cause a speech to have no effect? Obviously, you would not expect a moving or eloquent delivery to have such a sorry result. A *halting* or stumbling speech, however, would normally have little or no effect. Thus, Choice A is best.

Practice Exercise   Answers given on page 45.

Each of the following sentences contains one or two blanks; these blanks indicate that a word or set of words has been left out. Below the sentence are five words or phrases, lettered A through E. Select the word or set of words that best completes the sentence.

1. Although the play was not praised by the critics, it did not ---- thanks to favorable word-of-mouth comments.

   (A) succeed (B) translate (C) function (D) close (E) continue

2. Perhaps because something in us instinctively distrusts such displays of natural fluency, some readers approach John Updike's fiction with ----.

   (A) indifference (B) suspicion (C) veneration (D) recklessness
   (E) bewilderment

3. We lost confidence in him because he never ---- the grandiose promises he had made.

   (A) forgot about (B) reneged on (C) tired of (D) delivered on
   (E) retreated from

4. Because the hawk is ---- bird, farmers try to keep it away from their chickens.

   (A) a migratory (B) an ugly (C) a predatory (D) a reclusive
   (E) a huge

5. We were amazed that a man who had been heretofore the most ---- of public speakers could, in a single speech, electrify an audience and bring them cheering to their feet.

(A) enthralling   (B) accomplished   (C) pedestrian   (D) auspicious
(E) masterful

6. If you are trying to make a strong impression on your audience, you cannot do so by being understated, tentative, or ---- .

(A) hyperbolic   (B) restrained   (C) argumentative   (D) authoritative
(E) passionate

7. Despite the mixture's ---- nature, we found that by lowering its temperature in the laboratory we could dramatically reduce its tendency to vaporize.

(A) resilient   (B) volatile   (C) homogeneous   (D) insipid   (E) acerbic

8. No other artist rewards the viewer with more sheer pleasure than Miró: he is one of those blessed artists who combine profundity and ----.

(A) education   (B) wisdom   (C) faith   (D) fun   (E) depth

9. Some Central Intelligence Agency officers have ---- their previous statements denying any involvement on their part with the rebel network and are now revising their earlier testimony.

(A) justified   (B) recanted   (C) repeated   (D) protracted   (E) heeded

10. New concerns about growing religious tension in northern India were ---- this week after at least fifty people were killed and hundreds were injured or arrested in rioting between Hindus and Moslems.

(A) lessened   (B) invalidated   (C) restrained   (D) dispersed   (E) fueled

11. In a happy, somewhat boisterous celebration of the origins of the United States, the major phase of the Constitution's Bicentennial got off to ---- start on Friday.

(A) a slow   (B) a rousing   (C) a reluctant   (D) an indifferent   (E) a quiet

12. In a revolutionary development in technology, several manufacturers now make biodegradable forms of plastic: some plastic six-pack rings, for example, gradually ---- when exposed to sunlight.

(A) harden   (B) stagnate   (C) inflate   (D) propagate   (E) decompose

13. To alleviate the problem of contaminated chicken, the study panel recommends that the federal government shift its inspection emphasis from cursory bird-by-bird visual checks to a more ---- random sampling for bacterial and chemical contamination.

(A) rigorous   (B) perfunctory   (C) symbolic   (D) discreet   (E) dubious

14. To the dismay of the student body, the class president was ---- berated by the principal at a school assembly.

(A) ignominiously   (B) privately   (C) magnanimously   (D) fortuitously
(E) inconspicuously

15. Although Barbara Tuchman never earned a graduate degree, she nonetheless ---- a scholarly career as a historian noted for her vivid style and ---- erudition.

(A) interrupted . . deficient
(B) relinquished . . immense
(C) abandoned . . capricious
(D) pursued . . prodigious
(E) followed . . scanty

16. When Frazer's editors at Macmillan tried to ---- his endless augmentations, he insisted on a type size so small and a page so packed as to approach illegibility; and if that proved ----, thinner paper.

(A) protract . . unwarranted
(B) expurgate . . satisfactory
(C) reprimand . . irrelevant
(D) restrict. . insufficient
(E) revise. . idiosyncratic

17. Baldwin's brilliant *The Fire Next Time* is both so eloquent in its passion and so searching in its ---- that it is bound to ---- any reader.

(A) bitterness . . embarrass
(B) romanticism . . appall
(C) candor . . unsettle
(D) indifference . . disappoint
(E) conception . . bore

18. Unlike other examples of ---- verse, Milton's *Lycidas* does more than merely mourn for the death of Edward King; it also denounces corruption in the Church in which King was ordained.

(A) satiric   (B) elegiac   (C) free   (D) humorous   (E) didactic

19. We now know that what constitutes practically all of matter is empty space: relatively enormous ---- in which revolve infinitesimal particles so small that they have never been seen or photographed.

(A) crescendos   (B) enigmas   (C) conglomerates   (D) abstractions
(E) voids

20. The officers threatened to take ---- if the lives of their men were ---- by the conquered natives.

(A) liberties . . irritated
(B) measures . . enhanced
(C) pains . . destroyed
(D) reprisals . . endangered
(E) affront . . enervated

21. Despite his ---- appearance, he was chosen by his employer for a job that required neatness and polish.

(A) unkempt (B) impressive (C) prepossessing (D) aloof (E) tardy

22. The ---- remarks of the speaker annoyed the audience because they were lengthy as well as meaningless.

(A) lugubrious (B) sarcastic (C) pithy (D) inane (E) pungent

23. He was so ---- in meeting the payments on his car that the finance company threatened to seize the automobile.

(A) dilatory (B) mercenary (C) solvent (D) diligent (E) compulsive

24. Although the earthquake created some damage, the tidal wave that followed was more devastating because it completely ---- many villages.

(A) bypassed (B) absorbed (C) desiccated (D) congested
(E) inundated

25. The insurance company rejected his application for accident insurance because his ---- occupation made him a poor risk.

(A) desultory (B) haphazard (C) esoteric (D) hazardous
(E) peripatetic

26. Since we had been promised a definite answer to our proposal, we were ---- by his ---- reply.

(A) pleased . . equivocal
(B) vexed . . negative
(C) annoyed . . noncommittal
(D) delighted . . dilatory
(E) baffled . . decided

27. Because she had a reputation for ---- we were surprised and pleased when she greeted us so ----.

(A) insolence . . informally
(B) insouciance . . cordially
(C) graciousness . . amiably
(D) arrogance . . disdainfully
(E) querulousness . . affably

28. The child was so spoiled by her indulgent parents that she pouted and became ---- when she did not receive all of their attention.

(A) discreet   (B) suspicious   (C) elated   (D) sullen   (E) tranquil

29. Just as disloyalty is the mark of the renegade, ---- is the mark of the ----.

(A) timorousness . . hero
(B) temerity . . coward
(C) avarice . . philanthropist
(D) cowardice . . craven
(E) vanity . . flatterer

30. Because Inspector Morse could not contain his scorn for the police commissioner, he was imprudent enough to make ---- remarks about his superior officer.

(A) ambiguous   (B) dispassionate   (C) unfathomable   (D) interminable
(E) scathing

31. Modern architecture has discarded ---- trimming on buildings and has concentrated on an almost Greek simplicity of line.

(A) flamboyant   (B) austere   (C) inconspicuous   (D) aesthetic
(E) derivative

32. Though she was theoretically a friend of labor, her voting record in Congress ---- that impression.

(A) implied   (B) created   (C) confirmed   (D) belied   (E) maintained

33. The young man was quickly promoted when his employers saw how ---- he was.

(A) indigent   (B) indifferent   (C) assiduous   (D) lethargic   (E) cursory

34. Shy and hypochondriacal, Madison was uncomfortable at public gatherings; his character made him a most ---- lawmaker and practicing politician.

(A) conscientious   (B) unlikely   (C) fervent   (D) gregarious
(E) effective

35. The tapeworm is an example of ---- organism, one that lives within or on another creature, deriving some or all of its nutriment from its host.

(A) a hospitable   (B) an exemplary   (C) a parasitic   (D) an autonomous
(E) a protozoan

Answer Key

1. **D**	8. **D**	15. **D**	22. **D**	29. **D**
2. **B**	9. **B**	16. **D**	23. **A**	30. **E**
3. **D**	10. **E**	17. **C**	24. **E**	31. **A**
4. **C**	11. **B**	18. **B**	25. **D**	32. **D**
5. **C**	12. **E**	19. **E**	26. **C**	33. **C**
6. **B**	13. **A**	20. **D**	27. **E**	34. **B**
7. **B**	14. **A**	21. **A**	28. **D**	35. **C**

4 The Analogy Question

In the PSAT/NMSQT, the analogy question presents a pair of words followed by five additional pairs of words. You must select the pair of words from among the five choices which best matches the relationship existing between the first two words.

These are the questions that people seem to think of most often when they think about the PSAT. Analogies may well be the most difficult kind of question on the test, but they aren't impossible, and at least some of them will be fairly easy. Questions of this kind test your understanding of the relationships among words and ideas. You are given one pair and must choose another pair that is related in the same way. Many relationships are possible. The two terms in the pair can be synonyms; one term can be a cause, the other the effect; one can be a tool, the other the user.

Tips for Handling Analogy Questions

1. Consider the first pair in each question carefully, and try to make a clear sentence using the two terms. Then look at the other pairs. It should be possible to substitute the correct answer (and only the correct answer) into your sentence and still have the sentence make sense.

2. Do not be misled if the choices are from different fields or areas, or seem to deal with different items, from the given pair. Study the capitalized words until you see the connection between them; then search for the same relationship among the choices.

   BOTANIST:MICROSCOPE::carpenter:hammer, even though the two workers may have little else in common besides their use of tools.

3. If more than one answer choice fits, try making your sentence more specific.

   Example:

   MITTEN:HAND:: (A) bracelet:wrist (B) belt:waist
   (C) muffler:neck (D) ring:finger (E) sandal:foot

   You make up the sentence, "You wear a mitten on your hand." Unfortunately, *all* the answer choices will fit that sentence, so you say to yourself, "Why do you wear a mitten? You wear a mitten to keep your hand warm." Now when you try to substitute, only Choice C works, so you have your answer.

4. Beware of words that can have more than one meaning. A simple word like *lie* can mean either recline or fib. If you get one meaning fixed too firmly in your mind, you may miss the point of the analogy.

5. Be particularly careful of words that have different meanings when they are pronounced differently. Suppose you are given the analogy SOW:SEED. If you keep thinking of *sow* as a female pig, the analogy makes no sense. But if you change your pronunciation, you will remember that *sow* also means to plant. Try to keep flexible.

6. Be guided by what you know about parts of speech. If the capitalized words are a noun and a verb, each of your answer pairs will be a noun and a verb. If the capitalized words are an adjective and a noun, each of your answer pairs will be an adjective and a noun. Even if you don't recognize the parts of speech of the capitalized words, you can still work things out; if you can recognize the parts of speech in a single answer pair, you know the parts of speech of all the other answer pairs, and of the original pair as well. This information can help you recognize analogy types and spot the use of unfamiliar or secondary meanings of words.

7. Watch out for errors caused by eye-catchers. These are incorrect answer choices *designed* to catch your eye. Eye-catchers grab your attention because they somehow remind you of one of the capitalized words. For example, if the original pair of words is ARMOR:BODY (armor *protects* the body), a good eye-catcher would be helmet:steel (a helmet *is made of* steel).

8. Eliminate answer choices whose terms are only casually linked. In your capitalized pair of words (and in your correct answer choice), the words are always clearly linked:

   Armor *protects* the body.
   A shepherd is *someone who* herds sheep.
   A chapter is *a division of* a book.

   In the answer pairs, the relationship between the words can be pretty vague. There's a clear dictionary relationship between *chapter* and *book*. There's no necessary relationship between *chapter* and *pencil*.

9. Watch out for errors stemming from grammatical reversals. Ask yourself *who* is doing what to whom. FUGITIVE:FLEE is not the same as laughingstock:mock. A fugitive is the person who flees. A laughingstock is the person who *is mocked*.

10. Remember that the test-makers usually place more difficult analogies toward the end of the analogy section. Therefore, if one of the final analogy questions in a set looks simple, *suspect a trap*.

11. Be familiar with the whole range of common analogy types. Know the usual ways in which pairs of words on the PSAT are linked.

Common Analogy Types

Synonyms
DAUNTLESS:COURAGEOUS
Dauntless (fearless) and *courageous* are synonyms.

Synonym Variant
DAUNTLESS:COURAGE
Someone *dauntless* shows *courage*.

Antonyms
DAUNTLESS:COWARDLY
Dauntless and *cowardly* are antonyms.

Antonym Variant
DAUNTLESS:COWARDICE
Someone *dauntless* does not exhibit *cowardice*.

Worker and Work Created
POET:SONNET
A *poet* creates a *sonnet*.

Worker and Tool
PAINTER:BRUSH
A *painter* uses a *brush*.

Tool and Object Worked On
SAW:WOOD
A *saw* cuts *wood*.

Function
CROWBAR:PRY
A *crowbar* is a tool used to *pry*.

Action and Its Significance
NOD:ASSENT
A *nod* is a sign of *assent* (agreement).

Manner
STAMMER:TALK
To *stammer* is to *talk* in a halting manner.

Degree of Intensity
LUKEWARM:BOILING
Lukewarm is less intense than *boiling*.

Class and Member
MAMMAL:WHALE
A *whale* is a member of the class known as *mammal*.

Defining Characteristic
TIGER:CARNIVOROUS
A *tiger* is by definition a *carnivorous* (meat-eating) animal.

Part to Whole
ISLAND:ARCHIPELAGO
An *archipelago* (chain of islands) is made up of many *islands*.

Sex
DOE:STAG
A *doe* is a female deer; a *stag*, a male deer.

Age
DEER:FAWN
A *fawn* is a young *deer*.

Symbol and Abstraction It Represents
DOVE:PEACE
A *dove* is the symbol of *peace*.

Use these tips to help you with the following examples.

EXAMPLE 1

CONSTELLATION:STARS::   (A) prison:bars   (B) assembly:speaker
(C) troupe:actors   (D) mountain:peak   (E) flock:shepherds

A *constellation* is made up of *stars*. A *troupe* (not *troop* but *troupe)* is made up of *actors* (male and female). Choice C is correct.

Note, by the way, the characteristics of the analogy you have just analyzed. The relationship between the words in CONSTELLATION:STARS is built-in: if you look up *constellation* in a dictionary, you will see that a constellation is a group of stars. The words are related *by definition.* The relationship is clear. You can phrase your linking sentence in several ways:

"A *constellation* is made up of *stars.*"
"A *constellation* is a group of *stars.*"
"A *constellation* is composed of *stars.*"
"The specific term for a group of *stars* is *constellation.*"

However, the essential relationship between the words is unchanged.

Your correct answer choice must have the same characteristics as the original pair. The words must have a clear relationship. They must be related by definition. If you substitute them in your linking sentence, they have got to fit—*tight*.

EXAMPLE 2

SKYCAP:AIRPORT::   (A) stenographer:office   (B) cashier:box office
(C) waitress:restaurant   (D) actress:theater   (E) typist:paper

If you word your sentence "A *skycap* works at an *airport*," you will find that Choices A, B, C, and D are all good analogies. At this point, take a second look at the original relationship. A skycap works at an airport, true. What else do you know about a skycap's work? For one, he carries things for people. What's more, when he works at the airport, he relies on tips.

Refine your original sentence to include these additional facts. "A *skycap* carries bags for travelers at the *airport* in the hope of earning tips." Now test the answers. Only one answer fits: "A *waitress* carries food for patrons at a *restaurant* in the hope of earning tips." Choice C is the correct answer.

Your sentence should reflect the relationship between the two capitalized words *exactly*. If it doesn't, try, try again.

EXAMPLE 3

COMPOSER:SYMPHONY::   (A) porter:terminal   (B) writer:plagiarism
(C) coach:team   (D) painter:mural   (E) doctor:stethoscope

A composer creates a symphony. You therefore are looking for a relationship between a worker and a work he or she has created. You can easily eliminate Choices A and E; a porter works *at* a terminal; a doctor works *with* a stethoscope. You can also eliminate Choice C: no coach literally *creates* a team in the same way that a composer creates a symphony.

Writers and painters, however, both create works of art. Which answer is correct, B *or* D?

If you do not know the meanings of *plagiarism* and *mural*, think of a context for one (or both) of them. Someone is "accused of plagiarism." From this you can infer that *plagiarism* is a crime (passing off someone else's work as one's own), not a created work. A *mural* is a picture painted on a wall. The correct answer is Choice D.

EXAMPLE 4

EROSION:ROCKS::   (A) flatness:landscape   (B) fatigue:task
(C) fasting:food   (D) dissipation:character   (E) forgery:signature

The idea of a wearing away of a substance (the *erosion* of *rocks*) is repeated in Choice D. *Dissipation* implies a wasting away of energies, which results in a loss of *character*.

Note that you are dealing with a secondary meaning. *Character* is not used here as a synonym for *nature*. It is used instead with the meaning of a person's *moral constitution*.

EXAMPLE 5

CAMPAIGN:OBJECTIVE::   (A) motivation:goal   (B) misdeed:consequence
(C) victory: triumph   (D) talent:success   (E) voyage:destination

Just as the goal of a *campaign* is defined as its *objective,* the goal of a *voyage* is defined as its *destination*. Choice E is correct.

Note that, while a *misdeed* may have *consequences,* these consequences are not its intended goal.

Practice Exercises   **Answers given on pages 54–56.**

Each of the following questions introduces a pair of words or phrases in capital letters, linked by a colon(:); this colon indicates that these words are related in some way. Following the capitalized pair are five pairs of words or phrases lettered A through E. Select the pair whose relationship is most similar to the relationship illustrated by the capitalized pair.

EXAMPLE:

CLOCK:TIME::   (A) watch:wrist
(B)   pedometer:speed
(C)   thermometer:temperature
(D)   hourglass:sand   (E) radio:sound

ⒶⒷ●ⒹⒺ

Exercise A

1. HELMET:HEAD::   (A) pedal:foot
   (B)   gun:hand   (C) breastplate:chest
   (D)   pendant:neck   (E) knapsack:back

2. GULLIBLE:DUPED::   (A) credible:cheated
   (B)   careful:cautioned   (C) malleable:molded
   (D)   myopic:diagnosed   (E) articulate:silenced

3. FOLLY:SENSE:: (A) insolvency:funds
   (B) plagiarism:books   (C) beauty:beholder
   (D) piety:religion   (E) anxiety:care

4. MOCK:CONTEMPT:: (A) falsify:mimicry
   (B) scold:disapproval   (C) imitate:respect
   (D) anticipate:fear   (E) atone:retribution

5. CONDIMENT:FOOD:: (A) additive:milk
   (B) wit:conversation   (C) tenement:building
   (D) prescription:patient   (E) brochure:book

6. DUNGEON:CONFINEMENT:: (A) church:chapel
   (B) school:truant   (C) asylum:refuge
   (D) hospital:mercy   (E) courthouse:remorse

7. GRIDIRON:FOOTBALL:: (A) net:tennis
   (B) saddle:racing   (C) round:boxing
   (D) puck:hockey   (E) diamond:baseball

8. HERMIT:GREGARIOUS:: (A) miser:penurious
   (B) ascetic:hedonistic   (C) coward:pusillanimous
   (D) scholar:literate   (E) crab:crustacean

9. CLANDESTINE:OVERT:: (A) thorough:complete
   (B) limited:unrestrained   (C) warm:feverish
   (D) circular:oval   (E) vacillating:tentative

10. PINE:YEARN:: (A) amaze:astonish
    (B) whisper:shout   (C) meander:march
    (D) strive:prosper   (E) collect:scatter

11. WINE:VINTNER:: (A) tobacco:smoker
    (B) meat:packer   (C) water:plumber
    (D) beer:brewer   (E) oil:masseur

12. MENDACITY:HONESTY:: (A) courage:cravenness
    (B) truth:beauty   (C) strength:fortitude
    (D) unsophistication:ingenuousness
    (E) hirsuteness:hair

13. PREFACE: BOOK:: (A) prologue:play
    (B) presage:folly   (C) preamble:poem
    (D) appendix:text   (E) couplet:sonnet

14. LAUREL:VICTORY:: (A) black cat:defeat
    (B) fig leaf:license   (C) olive branch:peace
    (D) lantern:caution   (E) flag:triumph

15. PLUCKY:PERSIST::   (A) resentful:forgive
(B) obsequious:fawn   (C) querulous:expect
(D) guilty:confess   (E) stoic:injure

Exercise B

1. DWELL:DENIZEN::   (A) shun:outcast
(B) inherit:heir   (C) squander:miser
(D) obey:autocrat   (E) patronize:protege

2. HAZARDOUS:PERIL::   (A) supercilious:modesty
(B) innovative:novelty   (C) venerable:immaturity
(D) antagonistic:apathy   (E) competitive:pride

3. LAUDABLE:PRAISE::   (A) imperturbable:agitation
(B) fragile:stability   (C) contemptible:scorn
(D) enamored:love   (E) fastidious:taste

4. OPHTHALMOLOGIST:EYES::   (A) podiatrist:feet
(B) cardiologist:brain   (C) bacteriologist:atoms
(D) numismatist:nerves   (E) pediatrician:bones

5. MEANDERING:DIRECT::   (A) menacing:ambitious
(B) affable:permissive   (C) digressive:concise
(D) circuitous:roundabout   (E) aboveboard:open

6. IRON:RUST::   (A) yeast:mold
(B) bronze:patina   (C) cake:icing
(D) stone:gravel   (E) coal:dust

7. EPHEMERAL:LAST::   (A) competitive:contend
(B) indispensable:suffice   (C) perishable:die
(D) insignificant:matter   (E) transient:travel

8. DONOR:GIFT::   (A) prophet:prediction
(B) zealot:detachment   (C) advisee:counsel
(D) braggart:attention   (E) mourner:sympathy

9. ACT:DRAMA::   (A) chapter:essay
(B) aria:opera   (C) platoon:company
(D) grade:course   (E) blueprint:building

10. CEMENT:TROWEL::   (A) lawn:rake
(B) conflagration:match   (C) paint:brush
(D) floor:polish   (E) wallpaper:ladder

11. PIGHEADED:YIELD::   (A) lionhearted:retreat
(B) lilylivered:flee   (C) dogged:pursue
(D) featherbrained:giggle   (E) eagle-eyed:discern

12. UNCTUOUS:SINCERITY::
    (A) fatuous:ambivalence   (B) unclean:impunity
    (C) avuncular:benevolence   (D) frivolous:gravity
    (E) hypocritical:virtue

13. PIRATE:BUCCANEER::   (A) sailor:beachcomber
    (B) puritan:virtuoso   (C) captain:admiral
    (D) wanderer:nomad   (E) cynic:flatterer

14. ALARM:TRIGGER::   (A) prison:escape
    (B) tunnel:dig   (C) criminal:corner
    (D) fright:allay   (E) trap:spring

15. QUOTATION:QUOTATION MARKS::
    (A) remark:colon   (B) sentence:period
    (C) aside:parentheses   (D) clause:semicolon
    (E) interjection:exclamation point

Answer Key

Exercise A

1. **C**	6. **C**	11. **D**
2. **C**	7. **E**	12. **A**
3. **A**	8. **B**	13. **A**
4. **B**	9. **B**	14. **C**
5. **B**	10. **A**	15. **B**

Exercise B

1. **B**	6. **B**	11. **A**
2. **B**	7. **D**	12. **E**
3. **C**	8. **A**	13. **D**
4. **A**	9. **C**	14. **E**
5. **C**	10. **C**	15. **C**

Answer Explanations

Exercise A

1. **(C)** A *helmet* protects one's *head*. A *breastplate*, a piece of armor, protects one's *chest*.
2. **(C)** A person who is *gullible* is easily fooled or *duped*. A person who is *malleable* (impressionable) is easily influenced or *molded*.
3. **(A)** A person engaged in *folly* or foolishness lacks *sense*. A person in a state of *insolvency* or bankruptcy lacks *funds*.
4. **(B)** A person who *mocks* shows *contempt*. A person who *scolds* shows *disapproval*.
5. **(B)** A *condiment* enhances *food*. *Wit* enhances *conversation*.
6. **(C)** A *dungeon* by definition is a place of *confinement*. An *asylum* by definition is a place of *refuge*.
7. **(E)** People play *football* on a field called a *gridiron*. People play *baseball* on a field called a *diamond*.
8. **(B)** A *hermit,* who chooses to live alone, is by definition not *gregarious* (companionable and outgoing). An *ascetic,* who chooses a life of self-denial, is by definition not *hedonistic* (devoted to pleasure).
9. **(B)** An activity which is *clandestine* (secret) is not *overt* or unconcealed. An activity which is *limited* (within boundaries) is not *unrestrained* or free of restrictions.
10. **(A)** To *pine* (to long for or to languish) means to *yearn*. To *amaze* (to astound) means to *astonish*.
11. **(D)** A *vintner* is a person who makes *wine*. A *brewer* is a person who makes *beer*.
12. **(A)** *Mendacity* or untruthfulness is the opposite of *honesty*. *Courage* is the opposite of *cravenness* or cowardice.
13. **(A)** A *preface* is an introduction at the beginning of a *book*. A *prologue* is an introduction at the beginning of a *play*.
14. **(C)** A wreath made from the *laurel* tree symbolizes *victory*. An *olive branch* symbolizes *peace*.
15. **(B)** Someone *plucky* (brave and determined) by definition *persists* or perseveres; someone *obsequious* (groveling; servile) by definition *fawns* or grovels.

Exercise B

1. **(B)** A *denizen* (resident) by definition *dwells* or resides in a region. An *heir* by definition *inherits* or receives a legacy from someone who has died.

2. **(B)** Something *hazardous* (dangerous) is characterized by *peril* (danger). Something *innovative* (new in form or design) is characterized by *novelty* (newness, originality).

3. **(C)** *Laudable* means praiseworthy or deserving *praise*. *Contemptible* means despicable or deserving *scorn*.

4. **(A)** An *ophthalmologist* specializes in the care of the *eyes*. A *podiatrist* specializes in the care of the *feet*.

5. **(C)** *Meandering* (proceeding by an indirect course) and *direct* are antonyms. *Digressive* (departing from the main subject) and *concise* (keeping brief and to the point) are antonyms.

6. **(B)** The covering of *iron* caused by oxidation is called *rust*. The covering of *bronze* is called a *patina*.

7. **(D)** Something *ephemeral* by definition does not *last*. Something *insignificant* by definition does not *matter*.

8. **(A)** A *donor* or benefactor makes a *gift*. A *prophet* or seer makes a *prediction*.

9. **(C)** A *drama* or play is divided into *acts*. A military *company* is divided into platoons.

10. **(C)** *Cement* is applied with a *trowel*. *Paint* is applied with a *brush*.

11. **(A)** Someone *pigheaded* or stubborn is disinclined to *yield* (give in). Someone *lionhearted* or brave is disinclined to *retreat*.

12. **(E)** An *unctuous* or excessively pious manner is affected, having a false appearance of *sincerity*. A *hypocritical* or dissembling manner is feigned, having a false appearance of *virtue*.

13. **(D)** *Pirate* and *buccaneer* are synonyms, as are *wanderer* and *nomad*.

14. **(E)** To *trigger* an *alarm* is to release it or set it off. To *spring* a *trap* is to release it or set it off.

15. **(C)** The beginning and the end of a *quotation* (group of words repeated from a book or speech) are indicated by *quotation marks*. The beginning and the end of an *aside* (parenthetical remark; temporary digression from the main subject) are indicated by *parentheses*.

5 Improving Critical Reading Comprehension

Now more than ever, doing well on the critical reading questions can make the difference between success and failure on the PSAT. The last questions in each verbal section, they are also the most time-consuming and the ones most likely to bog you down. However, you can handle them, and this chapter will show you how.

Long-Range Strategy

Read, Read, Read!
Just do it.

There is no substitute for extensive reading as a preparation for the PSAT and for college work. The only way to build up your proficiency in reading is by reading books of all kinds. As you read, you will develop speed, stamina, and the ability to comprehend the printed page. But if you want to turn yourself into the kind of reader the colleges are looking for, you must develop the habit of reading—closely and critically—every day.

Challenge yourself. Don't limit your reading to light fiction or popular biographies. Branch out a bit. Try to develop an interest in as many fields as you can. Sample some of the serious magazines: *The New Yorker, Smithsonian, Natural History, National Geographic, Newsweek, Time, The New York Review of Books, Harper's Magazine.* In these magazines you'll find articles on literature, music, science, philosophy, history, the arts—the whole range of fields touched on by the PSAT. If you take time to acquaint yourself with the contents of these magazines, you won't find the subject matter of the reading passages on the examination so strange.

Tips for Handling Critical Reading Questions

1. Build on what you already know. Tackle passages with familiar subjects before passages with unfamiliar ones. It is hard to concentrate when you read about something wholly unfamiliar to you. Give yourself a break. In each section, first tackle the reading passage that interests you or deals with topics in which you are well grounded. Then move on to the other passage. You'll do better that way.
2. Try *all* the questions about each passage. If you are stumped by a tough reading question, do not skip the other questions on that passage. The critical reading questions following each passage are

not arranged in order of difficulty. They tend to be arranged sequentially: questions on paragraph 1 come before questions on paragraph 2. So try all the questions on the passage. That tough question may be just one question away from one that's easy for you.

3. First read the passage; then read the questions. Reading the questions before you read the passage will not save you time. It will cost you time. If you read the questions first, when you turn to the passage you will have a number of question words and phrases dancing around in your head. You will be so involved in trying to spot the places they occur in the passage that you will not be able to concentrate on comprehending the passage as a whole.

4. Don't rush-read. Read as rapidly as you can with understanding, but do not force yourself. Do not worry about the time element. If you worry about not finishing the test, you will begin to take shortcuts and miss the correct answer in your haste.

5. Be an active reader. As you read the italicized introductory material preceding the passage and tackle the passage's opening sentences, try to anticipate what the passage will be about. Ask yourself who or what the author is talking about.

6. Map out the passage as you read. As you continue reading, try to identify what *kind* of writing this is, what *techniques* are being used, who its intended *audience* may be, and what *feeling* (if any) the author has toward his subject. Try to retain names, dates, and places for quick reference later. In particular, try to remember where in the passage the author makes *major points*. Then, when you start looking for the phrase or sentence that will justify your choice of answer, you may be able to save time by going back to that section of the passage immediately without having to reread the entire selection.

7. Read any footnotes to clarify terms that appear in the passage. Use this information to answer the questions.

8. When you tackle the questions, *go back to the passage* to verify each answer choice. Do not rely on your memory alone, and, above all, do not ignore the passage and just answer questions on the basis of other things you've read. Remember, the questions are asking you about what *this* author has to say about the subject, not about what some other author you once read said about it in another book.

9. Use the line references in the questions to be sure you've gone back to the correct spot in the passage. The reading passages on the PSAT tend to be long. Fortunately, the lines are numbered, and the questions often refer you to specific lines in the passage by number. It takes less time to locate a line number than to spot a word or phrase. Use the line numbers to orient yourself in the text.

10. Tackle the double passages one at a time. The questions are organized sequentially: questions about Passage 1 come before questions about Passage 2. So, do things in order. *First* read Passage 1; then jump straight to the questions and answer all those based on Passage 1. *Next* read Passage 2; then answer all the questions based on Passage 2. *Finally*, tackle the two or three questions that refer to *both* passages. Go back to both passages as needed.

    Occasionally a couple of questions referring to *both* passages will precede the questions focusing on Passage 1. Do not let this minor hitch throw you. Use your common sense. You've just read the first passage. Skip the one or two questions on both passages, and head for those questions about Passage 1. Answer them. Then read Passage 2. Answer the questions on Passage 2. Finally, go back to those questions you skipped and answer them and any other questions at the end of the set that refer to *both* passages. Remember, however: whenever you skip from question to question, or from passage to passage, *be sure you're filling in the right spaces on your answer sheet.*

11. Expect ideas to be worded in alternate ways. When the questions ask about specific information in the passage, do not expect to find it stated in exactly the same words. If the question is

    According to the passage, widgets are

    (A) good   (B) bad   (C) indifferent

    (D) pink   (E) purple

    Ⓐ Ⓑ Ⓒ Ⓓ Ⓔ

    do not expect to find a sentence in the passage that says, "Widgets are bad." However, you may well find a sentence that says, "Widgets are wholly undesirable and have a strongly negative influence." That is close enough to tell you that the answer must be B.

12. When you read, watch for key words that indicate how a passage is being developed.

    Equality or continuity of ideas (one idea is equal in importance to another, or continues a thought expressed earlier): *again, also, and, another, as well as, besides, first, furthermore, likewise, moreover, in addition*

    Contrast or change of topic: *although, despite, in spite of, instead of, notwithstanding, regardless, nevertheless, on the other hand, however*

    Conclusion: *accordingly, as a result, hence, in conclusion, in short, therefore, thus, consequently*

13. Be on the lookout for *all-inclusive words*, such as *always, at all times,* and *entirely,* and for negative or limiting words, such as *only, never, no, none, except,* and *but.*

Practice Exercises   Answers given on page 70.

Many of the following passages are shorter than the actual passages you will encounter on the PSAT. Use these short passages as your opportunity to tackle a wide range of the question types that appear on the test.

On the following pages are five groups of reading exercises. The passages tend to get somewhat more difficult as you go along. You will find the correct answers at the end of the chapter.

EXERCISE A

The chief characteristic of art today, if we are to judge by the reactions of the common man, is its obscurity. Everybody complains about obscurity in poetry, in painting, in music. I do not suggest that in some
Line cases the complaint is unjustified. But we should remember that the
(5) really original work of art in any age seems obscure to the general public. From a certain point of view it would be true to say that no great work of art finds an appreciative public waiting for it. The work creates its own public, slowly and painfully. A work of art is born as an intellectual foundling. What is interesting to notice is that often the art
(10) specialists themselves are caught napping. It was Andre Gide, you remember, who first saw Proust's great novel while he was working as a reader for a firm of publishers. He turned it down without hesitation. Perhaps you remember Leigh Hunt's verdict on Blake as "an unfortunate madman whose mildness alone prevented him from being locked up."
(15) Wordsworth also thought Blake mad, and yet it was he who wrote: "Every great and original writer, in proportion as he is great and original, must himself create the taste by which he is judged."

1. The passage indicates that critics often

(A) discover unknown geniuses
(B) add to obscurity in art
(C) create an audience for new works
(D) misjudge a masterpiece
(E) explain a work of art to the public

2. The phrase "are caught napping" (line 10) is best taken to mean that the art specialists

(A) are trapped in their profession
(B) are off their guard
(C) feel a need for rest
(D) find their task captivating
(E) would escape if they were able

3. The word "taste" in line 17 means

(A) detectable flavor
(B) small morsel
(C) individual artwork
(D) aesthetic attitude
(E) slight experience

4. The last four sentences in the passage (lines 10–17) provide

(A) a refutation of the contention made earlier
(B) support for the immediately preceding assertion
(C) examples of the inherent contradictions of an argument
(D) a revision of a previously held position
(E) a return to the author's original thesis

    Intuition is not a quality which everyone can understand. As the unimaginative are miserable about a work of fiction until they discover what flesh-and-blood individual served as the model for the hero or
Line heroine, so even many scientists doubt scientific intuition. They cannot
(5) believe that a blind person can see anything that they cannot see. They rely utterly on the celebrated inductive method of reasoning: the facts are to be exposed, and we are to conclude from them only what we must. This is a very sound rule—for mentalities that can do no better. But it is not certain that the really great steps are made in this plodding
(10) fashion. Dreams are made of quite other stuff, and if there are any left in the world who do not know that dreams have remade the world, then there is little that we can teach them.

5. The primary purpose of this passage is to

(A) denounce the unimaginative snobbery of scientists
(B) correct a misconception about the nature of dreams
(C) argue against the use of inductive reasoning
(D) explain the importance of intuition in science
(E) show how challenging scientific research can be

6. The author's attitude toward those who rely solely on the inductive method of reasoning can best be described as

(A) condescending   (B) approving

(C) indignant   (D) ambivalent

(E) hypocritical

7. The word "exposed" in line 7 means

(A) bared to the elements

(B) laid open to danger

(C) held up to ridicule

(D) unmasked

(E) made known

8. The phrase "the really great steps" (line 9) most likely refers to

(A) extremely large paces

(B) vast distances

(C) grandiose fantasies

(D) major scientific advances

(E) broadly interpreted measures

> Too many parents force their children into group activities. They are
> concerned about the child who loves to do things alone, who prefers a
> solitary walk with a camera to a game of ball. They want their sons to be
> Line "good fellows" and their daughters "social mixers." In such foolish fears
> (5) lie the beginnings of the blighting of individuality, the thwarting of per-
> sonality, the stealing of the wealth of one's capital for living joyously and
> well in a confused world. What America needs is a new army of defense,
> manned by young men and women who, through guidance and confi-
> dence, encouragement and wisdom, have built up values for themselves
> (10) and away from crowds and companies.

9. According to the passage, too many parents push their children to be

(A) unnecessarily gregarious

(B) foolishly timorous

(C) pointlessly extravagant

(D) acutely individualistic

(E) financially dependent

10. The primary point the author wishes to make is that

(A) young people need time to themselves

(B) group activities are harmful to children

(C) parents knowingly thwart their children's personalities

(D) independent thinking is of questionable value

(E) America needs universal military training

11. The author puts quotation marks around the words "good fellows" and "social mixers" to indicate that he

(A) is using vocabulary that is unfamiliar to the reader
(B) intends to define these terms later in the course of the passage
(C) can readily distinguish these terms from one another
(D) prefers not to differentiate roles by secondary factors such as gender
(E) refuses to accept the assumption that these are positive values

12. By "the wealth of one's capital for living joyously and well in a confused world" (lines 6–7), the author most likely means

(A) the financial security that one attains from one's individual professional achievements and overanalyzing it
(B) the riches that parents thrust upon children who would far prefer to be left alone to follow their own inclinations
(C) the hours spent in solitary pursuits that enable one to develop into an independent, confident adult
(D) the happy memories of childhood days spent in the company of true friends
(E) the profitable financial and personal contacts young people make when they engage in group activities

> "Sticks and stones can break my bones,
> But names will never harm me."
>
> No doubt you are familiar with this childhood rhyme; perhaps, when
> _Line_ you were younger, you frequently invoked whatever protection it could
> _(5)_ offer against unpleasant epithets. But like many popular slogans and
> verses, this one will not bear too close scrutiny. For names will hurt you.
> Sometimes you may be the victim, and find yourself an object of scorn,
> humiliation, and hatred just because other people have called you certain
> names. At other times you may not be the victim, but clever speakers
> _(10)_ and writers may, through name calling, blind your judgment so that you
> will follow them in a course of action wholly opposed to your own inter-
> ests or principles. Name calling can make you gullible to propaganda
> which you might otherwise readily see through and reject.

13. The author's primary purpose in quoting the rhyme in lines 1–2 is to

(A) remind readers of their childhood vulnerabilities
(B) emphasize the importance of maintaining one's good name
(C) demonstrate his conviction that only physical attacks can harm us
(D) affirm his faith in the rhyme's ability to shield one from unpleasant epithets
(E) introduce the topic of speaking abusively about others

14. By "this one will not bear too close scrutiny" (line 6), the author means that

   (A) the statement will no longer seem valid if you examine it too closely
   (B) the literary quality of the verse does not improve on closer inspection
   (C) people who indulge in name-calling are embarrassed when they are in the spotlight
   (D) the author cannot stand having his comments looked at critically
   (E) a narrow line exists between analyzing a slogan and over-analyzing it

15. According to the passage, name calling may make you more susceptible to

   (A) poetic language   (B) biased arguments
   (C) physical abuse   (D) risky confrontations
   (E) offensive epithets

16. The author evidently believes that slogans and verses frequently

   (A) appeal to our better nature
   (B) are disregarded by children
   (C) are scorned by unprincipled speakers
   (D) represent the popular mood
   (E) oversimplify a problem

     It takes no particular expert in foods, or even glutton, to know that no meal on the table ever is as good as the meal in the oven's roasting pan or the stove's covered kettle. There is something about the furtive lifting
Line of the lid and the opening of the door that is better than all sauces and
(5) gravies. Call it the surprise appetizer. Call it, also, that one gesture which the proprietor of the kitchen hates above all others, which brings forth the shortest, most succinct sentences with the word "meddling" in them. Yet it is essentially a friendly gesture, one based on good will, and not on its more general misconstruction, curiosity. It is quite proper, to state
(10) the case flatly, to say that a little quiet investigation of what is cooking is simply an attempt to share the good things of life. It is possible to state that, but it will take more than a statement to convince the cook that it is not an act of interference. The kitchen has special laws.

17. The author maintains that cooks

   (A) feel proprietary about their domain
   (B) readily share the good things they create
   (C) avoid making friendly gestures to strangers
   (D) exercise care in lifting hot pan lids
   (E) tend to be unusually laconic

18 We can infer that the tone of the short sentences to which the author refers (line 7) is

(A) admonitory   (B) tentative   (C) nonchalant
(D) cordial   (E) serious

19. The word "flatly" in line 10 means

(A) evenly   (B) horizontally
(C) without animation
(D) without qualification
(E) lacking flavor

20. The author's tone in the concluding sentence can best be described as

(A) bitterly resentful   (B) mildly ironic
(C) thoroughly respectful   (D) openly bewildered
(E) quietly curious

EXERCISE B

　　　For the sad state of criticism the writers must hold themselves much to blame. Literary artists, concerned solely in the creation of a book or story as close to perfection as their powers will permit, are generally
Line　quiet individuals, contemplative, retiring. On occasion they can be
(5)　influenced to anger by some grievous social wrong that calls for desperate remedy. But mostly they are prone to sit in their towers reflecting on the absurdities of a foolish world, asking only to be left alone with their labor. Never aggressive in their own interest, seeking only peace, they lay themselves open to aggression. Thus they do not see the enemy who
(10)　has stolen into the shadows at the rear of their retreat and is slowly scaling the walls. Such has been the course of events. While the artists have slept, the critical dwarfs have appeared. They have evolved a new language, written out a new set of definitions. Black is white, and white is black. The ugly and the nauseous are beautiful; the beautiful is nightmare.

1. According to the passage, literary artists are inclined to

(A) ignore what is happening around them
(B) be perpetually aroused by social injustices
(C) slight the work involved in writing
(D) welcome the onset of aggression
(E) accept criticism gladly

2. Which best captures the meaning of the word "powers" in line 3?

(A) delegated authority   (B) physical energies
(C) written statements   (D) intellectual abilities
(E) political ascendancy

3. The word "retiring" in line 4 means

(A) departing from office
(B) tending toward fatigue
(C) withdrawing from contact
(D) receiving a pension
(E) going to bed

4. Through his comments about the critical dwarfs in lines 12–14, the author wishes to convey the impression that critics

(A) deserve praise for their linguistic originality
(B) lack the intellectual stature of those they criticize
(C) appreciate the fundamental oneness of apparent opposites
(D) are as able as writers to scale the literary heights
(E) are less hostile than the authors who look down upon them

5. According to the passage, the critics' standards of criticism are

(A) a natural outgrowth of former standards
(B) complete reversal of accepted standards
(C) an invaluable guide to the literary artist
(D) a source of suggestions of new topics to write about
(E) the result of the artists' neglect of good writing

> When there is no distance between people, the only way that anyone can keep his or her distance is by a code of etiquette that has acceptance in a community. Manners are the antidote to adjustment to the group.
> *Line* They make social intercourse possible without any forfeit of one's
> *(5)* personal dignity. They are armor against invasion of privacy; they are the advance patrols that report whether one should withdraw or advance into intimacy. They are the friendly but noncommittal gestures of civilized people. The manners of crowded countries are, I believe, always more formal than those of open countries (as they are, for example, in
> *(10)* Europe and Japan), and it may be that we are seeing a rising concern about American manners precisely because we encounter more people in closer quarters than we ever have before. We feel the need to find ways in which to be part of the group without selling out our privacy or our individuality for a mess of adjustment.

6. The title that best expresses the idea of this passage is

(A) The Function of Politeness
(B) Invasions of Privacy
(C) Reasons for Social Relationships
(D) The Need for Complete Privacy
(E) American Manners

7. According to the author, manners serve to

(A) facilitate relationships among people
(B) preserve certain ceremonies
(C) help people to make friends quickly
(D) reveal character traits
(E) assist in pleasing one's friends

8. By stating that manners "are armor against invasion of privacy" (line 5), the author wishes to convey that manners

(A) protect one from physical danger
(B) are a cold, hard barrier separating people
(C) allow us to vent our aggressions safely
(D) shield one from unwanted intrusions
(E) enable us to guard our possessions

9. The author suggests that in Europe good manners are

(A) informal
(B) excessive
(C) essential
(D) ignored
(E) individual

10. In the course of the passage, the author does all of the following EXCEPT

(A) state a possibility
(B) use a metaphor
(C) cite an example
(D) make a parenthetical remark
(E) pose a question

One simple physical concept lies behind the formation of the stars: gravitational instability. The concept is not new; Newton first perceived it late in the seventeenth century.

Line   Imagine a uniform, static cloud of gas in space. Imagine then that the
(5)   gas is somehow disturbed so that one small spherical region becomes a little denser than the gas around it so that the small region's gravitational field becomes slightly stronger. It now attracts more matter to it and its gravity increases further, causing it to begin to contract. As it contracts its density increases, which increases its gravity even more, so that it picks
(10)   up even more matter and contracts even further. The process continues until the small region of gas finally forms a gravitationally bound object.

11. The primary purpose of the passage is to
    (A) demonstrate the evolution of the meaning of a term
    (B) depict the successive stages of a phenomenon
    (C) establish the pervasiveness of a process
    (D) support a theory considered outmoded
    (E) describe a static condition

12. The word "disturbed" in line 5 means
    (A) hindered   (B) perplexed   (C) disarranged
    (D) pestered   (E) thickened

13. It can be inferred from the passage that the author views the information contained within it as
    (A) controversial but irrefutable
    (B) speculative and unprofitable
    (C) uncomplicated and traditional
    (D) original but obscure
    (E) sadly lacking in elaboration

14. The author provides information that answers which of the following questions?
    I. How does the small region's increasing density affect its gravitational field?
    II. What causes the disturbance that changes the cloud from its original static state?
    III. What is the end result of the gradually increasing concentration of the small region of gas?
    (A) I only   (B) II only   (C) I and II only
    (D) I and III only   (E) I, II, and III

15. Throughout the passage, the author's manner of presentation is
    (A) argumentative   (B) convoluted
    (C) discursive   (D) expository
    (E) hyperbolic

       Unlike the carefully weighed and planned compositions of Dante, Goethe's writings have always the sense of immediacy and enthusiasm. He was a constant experimenter with life, with ideas, and with forms of
Line writing. For the same reason, his works seldom have the qualities of
(5) finish or formal beauty which distinguish the masterpieces of Dante and Virgil. He came to love the beauties of classicism, but these were never an essential part of his make-up. Instead, the urgency of the moment, the spirit of the thing, guided his pen. As a result, nearly all his works have serious flaws of structure, of inconsistencies, of excesses and
(10) redundancies and extraneities.

In the large sense, Goethe represents the fullest development of the
romanticist. It has been argued that he should not be so designated
because he so clearly matured and outgrew the kind of romanticism
exhibited by Wordsworth, Shelley, and Keats. Shelley and Keats died
(15) young; Wordsworth lived narrowly and abandoned his early attitudes.
In contrast, Goethe lived abundantly and developed his faith in the spirit,
his understanding of nature and human nature, and his reliance on feelings as man's essential motivating force. The result was an all-encom-
passing vision of reality and a philosophy of life broader and deeper than
(20) the partial visions and attitudes of other romanticists. Yet the spirit of
youthfulness, the impatience with close reasoning or "logic-chopping,"
and the continued faith in nature remained his to the end, together with
an occasional waywardness and impulsiveness and a disregard of artistic or logical propriety which savor strongly of romantic individualism.
(25) Since so many twentieth-century thoughts and attitudes are similarly
based on the stimulus of the Romantic Movement, Goethe stands as
particularly the poet of the modern man as Dante stood for medieval
man and as Shakespeare for the man of the Renaissance.

15. The word "close" in line 21 means

(A) nearby   (B) intimate (C) fitting tightly
(D) strictly logical   (E) nearly even

17. A main concern of the passage is to

(A) describe the history of Romanticism until its decline
(B) suggest that romantic literature is similar to Shakespearean drama
(C) argue that romantic writings are more fully developed than classical works
(D) compare Goethe with twentieth-century writers and poets
(E) explain the ways in which Goethe embodied the romantic spirit

18. A characteristic of romanticism NOT mentioned in this passage is its

(A) elevation of nature
(B) preference for spontaneity
(C) modernity of ideas
(D) unconcern for artistic decorum
(E) simplicity of language

19. It can be inferred from the passage that classicism has which of the following
characteristics?

     I. Sensitivity towards emotional promptings
    II. Emphasis on formal aesthetic standards
    III. Meticulous planning of artistic works

(A) II only   (B) III only   (C) I and II
(D) II and III   (E) I, II, and III

20. The author's attitude towards Goethe's writings is best described as

- (A) unqualified endorsement
- (B) lofty indifference
- (C) reluctant tolerance
- (D) measured admiration
- (E) undisguised contempt

Answer Key

Exercise A

1. **D**	8. **D**	15. **B**
2. **B**	9. **A**	16. **E**
3. **D**	10. **A**	17. **A**
4. **B**	11. **E**	18. **A**
5. **E**	12. **C**	19. **D**
6. **A**	13. **E**	20. **B**
7. **E**	14. **A**	

Exercise B

1. **A**	8. **D**	15. **D**
2. **D**	9. **C**	16. **D**
3. **C**	10. **E**	17. **E**
4. **B**	11. **B**	18. **E**
5. **B**	12. **C**	19. **D**
6. **A**	13. **C**	20. **D**
7. **A**	14. **D**	

6   Building Your Vocabulary

Recognizing the meaning of words is essential to comprehending what you read. The more you stumble over unfamiliar words in a text, the more you have to take time out to look up words in your dictionary, the more likely you are to wind up losing track of what the author has to say.

To succeed in college, you must develop a college-level vocabulary. You must learn to use these words, and re-use them until they become second nature to you. The time you put in now learning vocabulary-building techniques for the PSAT will pay off later on, and not just on the PSAT.

In this chapter you will find a fundamental tool that will help you build your vocabulary: Barron's PSAT High-Frequency Word List. No matter how little time you have before the test, you still can familiarize yourself with the sort of vocabulary you will face on the PSAT. First, look over the words you will find on our list: each of these 300 words, ranging from everyday words such as *ample* and *meek* to less commonly known ones such as *esoteric* and *pervasive* has appeared (as answer choices or as question words) at least four times in PSATs in the past two decades.

Not only will looking over the high-frequency word list reassure you that you *do* know some PSAT-type words; but also it may well help you on the actual day of the test. These words have turned up on recent tests; some of them may appear on the test you take.

PSAT HIGH-FREQUENCY WORD LIST

absolve V. pardon (an offense); free from blame. The father confessor *absolved* him of his sins. absolution, N.

abstract ADJ. theoretical; not concrete; nonrepresentational. To him, hunger was an *abstract* concept; he had never missed a meal.

accessible ADJ. easy to approach; obtainable. We asked our guide whether the ruins were *accessible* on foot.

acclaim V. applaud; announce with great approval. The NBC sportscasters *acclaimed* every American victory in the Olympics and lamented every American defeat. acclamation, acclaim, N.

accommodate V. provide lodgings. Mary asked the room clerk whether the hotel would be able to *accommodate* the tour group on such short notice. accommodations, N.

accommodate V. oblige or help someone; adjust or bring into harmony; adapt. Mitch always did everything possible to *accommodate* his elderly relatives, from driving them to medical appointments to helping them with paperwork. accommodating, ADJ. (secondary meaning)

acknowledge V. recognize; admit. Although Ira *acknowledged* that the Beatles' tunes sounded pretty dated nowadays, he still preferred them to the punk rock songs his nephews played.

acrimony N. bitterness of words or manner. The candidate attacked his opponent with great *acrimony*. acrimonious, ADJ.

adversary N. opponent. "Aha!" cried Holmes. "Watson, I suspect this delay is the work of my old *adversary* Professor Moriarty." adversarial, ADJ.

adverse ADJ. unfavorable; hostile. The recession had a highly *adverse* effect on Father's investment portfolio: he lost so much money that he could no longer afford the butler and the upstairs maid. adversity, N.

aesthetic ADJ. artistic; dealing with or capable of appreciation of the beautiful. The beauty of Tiffany's stained glass appealed to Alice's *aesthetic* sense. aesthete, N.

affable ADJ. easily approachable; warmly friendly. Accustomed to cold, aloof supervisors, Nicholas was amazed by how *affable* his new employer was.

affinity N. kinship; attraction to. She felt an *affinity* with all who suffered; their pains were her pains. Her brother, in contrast, had an *affinity* for political wheeling-and-dealing; he manipulated people shamelessly, not caring who got hurt.

alleviate V. relieve; lessen. This should *alleviate* the pain; if it does not, we will use stronger drugs.

altruistic ADJ. unselfishly generous; concerned for others. The star received no fee for appearing at the benefit; it was a purely *altruistic* act. altruism, N.

ambiguous ADJ. unclear or doubtful in meaning. The proctor's *ambiguous* instructions thoroughly confused us; we didn't know which columns we should mark and which we should leave blank. ambiguity, N.

ambivalence N. having contradictory or conflicting emotional attitudes. Torn between loving her parents one minute and hating them the next, she was confused by the *ambivalence* of her feelings. ambivalent, ADJ.

amenable ADJ. readily managed; willing to give in; agreeable; submissive. A born snob, Wilbur was *amenable* to any suggestions from those he looked up to, but he resented advice from his supposed inferiors. Unfortunately, his incorrigible snobbery was not *amenable* to improvement.

ample ADJ. abundant. Bond had *ample* opportunity to escape. Why did he let us catch him?

antagonism N. hostility; active resistance. Barry showed his *antagonism* toward his new stepmother by ignoring her whenever she tried talking to him. antagonistic, ADJ.

apathy N. lack of caring; indifference. A firm believer in democratic government, she could not understand the *apathy* of people who never bothered to vote. She wondered whether they had ever cared or whether they had always been *apathetic*.

apprehension N. fear; discernment; capture. The tourist refused to drive his rental car through downtown Miami because he felt some *apprehension* that he might be carjacked.

apprenticeship N. time spent as a novice learning a trade from a skilled worker. As a child, Pip had thought it would be wonderful to work as Joe's *apprentice;* now he hated his *apprenticeship* and scorned the blacksmith's trade.

appropriate ADJ. fitting or suitable; pertinent. Madonna spent hours looking for a suit that would be *appropriate* to wear at a summer wedding.

appropriate V. acquire; take possession of for one's own use; set aside for a special purpose. The ranchers *appropriated* lands that had originally been intended for Indian use. In response, Congress *appropriated* additional funds for the Bureau of Indian Affairs.

aristocracy N. hereditary nobility; privileged class. Americans have mixed feelings about hereditary *aristocracy:* we say all men are created equal, but we describe people who bear themselves with grace and graciousness as natural *aristocrats*.

aspire V. seek to attain; long for. Because he *aspired* to a career in professional sports, Philip enrolled in a graduate program in sports management. aspiration, N.

assert V. state strongly or positively; insist on or demand recognition of (rights, claims, etc). When Jill *asserted* that nobody else in the junior class had such an early curfew, her parents *asserted* themselves, telling her that if she didn't get home by nine o'clock she would be grounded for the week. assertion, N.

assumption N. something taken for granted; taking over or taking possession of. The young princess made the foolish *assumption* that the regent would not object to her *assumption* of power. assume, V.

authentic ADJ. genuine. The art expert was able to distinguish the *authentic* van Gogh painting from the forged copy. authenticate, V.

autonomous ADJ. self-governing. This island is a colony; however, in most matters, it is *autonomous* and receives no orders from the mother country. The islanders are an independent lot and would fight to preserve their *autonomy*.

aversion N. firm dislike. Bert had an *aversion* to yuppies; Alex had an *aversion* to punks. Their mutual *aversion* was so great that they refused to speak to one another.

banal ADJ. hackneyed; commonplace; trite; lacking originality. The hack writer's worn-out clichés made his comic sketch seem *banal.* He even resorted to the *banality* of having someone slip on a banana peel!

beneficial ADJ. helpful; advantageous; useful. Tiny Tim's cheerful good nature had a *beneficial* influence on Scrooge's disposition.

benign ADJ. kindly; favorable; not malignant. Though her *benign* smile and gentle bearing made Miss Marple seem a sweet little old lady, in reality she was a tough-minded, shrewd observer of human nature. benignity, N.

betray V. be unfaithful; reveal (unconsciously or unwillingly). The spy *betrayed* his country by selling military secrets to the enemy. When he was taken in for questioning, the tightness of his lips *betrayed* his fear of being caught.

brittle ADJ. easily broken; difficult. My employer's self-control was as *brittle* as an eggshell. Her *brittle* personality made it difficult for me to get along with her.

buoyant ADJ. able to float; cheerful and optimistic. When the boat capsized, her *buoyant* life jacket kept Jody afloat. Scrambling back on board, she was still in a *buoyant* mood, certain that despite the delay she'd win the race. buoyancy, N.

candor N. frankness; open honesty. Jack can carry *candor* too far: when he told Jill his honest opinion of her, she nearly slapped his face. Instead of being so *candid,* try keeping your opinions to yourself.

captivate V. charm; fascinate. Although he was predisposed to dislike Elizabeth, Darcy found himself *captivated* by her charm and wit.

caricature N. distortion; burlesque. The *caricatures* he drew always emphasized a personal weakness of the people he burlesqued. also V.

censor N. inspector overseeing public morals; official who prevents publication of offensive material. Because certain passages in his novel *Ulysses* had been condemned by the *censor,* James Joyce was unable to publish the novel in England for many years.

chronicle V. report; record (in chronological order). The gossip columnist was paid to *chronicle* the latest escapades of the socially prominent celebrities. also N.

circumspect ADJ. prudent; cautious. Investigating before acting, she tried always to be *circumspect.*

cite V. quote; refer to; commend. Because Virginia could *cite* hundreds of biblical passages from memory, her pastor *cited* her for her studiousness. citation, N.

cliché N. phrase dulled in meaning by repetition. High school compositions are often marred by such *clichés* as "strong as an ox."

coalesce V. combine; fuse. The brooks *coalesced* into one large river. When minor political parties *coalesce,* their *coalescence* may create a major coalition.

collaborate V. work together. Two writers *collaborated* in preparing this book.

compliance N. readiness to yield; conformity in fulfilling requirements. Bill was so bullheaded that we never expected his easy *compliance* to our requests. As an architect, however, Bill recognized that his design for the new school had to be in *compliance* with the local building code.

component N. element; ingredient. I wish all the *components* of my stereo system were working at the same time.

composure N. mental calmness. Even the latest work crisis failed to shake her *composure.*

compromise V. adjust or settle by making mutual concessions; endanger the interests or reputation of. Sometimes the presence of a neutral third party can help adversaries *compromise* their differences. Unfortunately, your presence at the scene of the dispute *compromises* our claim to neutrality in this matter. also N.

condone V. overlook voluntarily; forgive. Although she had excused Huck for his earlier escapades, Widow Douglas refused to *condone* his latest prank.

confirm V. corroborate; verify; support. I have several witnesses who will *confirm* my account of what happened.

conformity N. agreement or compliance; actions in agreement with prevailing social customs. In *conformity* with the bylaws of the Country Dance and Song Society, I am submitting a petition nominating Susan Murrow as president of the society. Because Kate had always been a rebellious child, we were surprised by her *conformity* to the standards of behavior prevalent at her new school.

confront V. face someone or something; encounter, often in a hostile way. Fearing his wife's hot temper, Stanley was reluctant to *confront* her about her skyrocketing credit card bills.

congenial ADJ. pleasant; friendly. My father loved to go out for a meal with *congenial* companions.

consistency N. harmony of parts; dependability; uniformity; degree of thickness. Holmes judged puddings and explanations on their *consistency:* he liked his puddings without lumps and his explanations without contradictions or improbabilities. consistent, ADJ.

consolidation N. unification; process of becoming firmer or stronger. The recent *consolidation* of several small airlines into one major company has left observers of the industry wondering whether room still exists for the "little guy" in aviation. consolidate, V.

contentious ADJ. quarrelsome. Disagreeing violently with the referees' ruling, the coach became so *contentious* that they threw him out of the game.

convention N. social or moral custom; established practice. Flying in the face of *convention,* George Sand shocked society by taking lovers and wearing men's clothes.

convoluted ADJ. complex and involved; intricate; winding; coiled. Talk about twisted! The new tax regulations are so *convoluted* that even my accountant can't unravel their mysteries.

corrosion N. destruction by chemical action. The *corrosion* of the girders supporting the bridge took place so gradually that no one suspected any danger until the bridge suddenly collapsed. corrode, V.

curtail V. shorten; reduce. When Elton asked Cher for a date, she said she was really sorry she couldn't go out with him, but her dad had ordered her to *curtail* her social life.

dawdle V. loiter; waste time. At the mall, Mother grew impatient with Jo and Amy because they tended to *dawdle* as they went from store to store.

dearth N. scarcity. The *dearth* of skilled labor compelled the employers to open trade schools.

debilitate V. weaken; enfeeble. Michael's severe bout of the flu *debilitated* him so much that he was too tired to go to work for a week.

decorous ADJ. proper. Prudence's *decorous* behavior was praised by her teachers, who wished they had a classroom full of such polite and proper little girls. decorum, N.

decry V. express strong disapproval of; disparage. The founder of the Children's Defense Fund, Marian Wright Edelman, strongly *decries* the lack of financial and moral support for children in America today.

defamation N. harming a person's reputation. *Defamation* of character may result in a slander suit. If rival candidates persist in *defaming* one another, the voters may conclude that all politicians are crooks.

deference N. courteous regard for another's wish. In *deference* to the minister's request, please do not take photographs during the wedding service.

defiance N. opposition; willingness to resist. In learning to read and write in *defiance* of his master's orders, Frederick Douglass showed exceptional courage. defy, V.

degenerate V. become worse; deteriorate. As the fight dragged on, the champion's style *degenerated* until he could barely keep on his feet.

demean V. degrade; humiliate. Standing on his dignity, he refused to *demean* himself by replying to the offensive letter. If you truly believed in the dignity of labor, you would not think it would *demean* you to work as a janitor.

denounce V. condemn; criticize. The reform candidate *denounced* the corrupt city officials for having betrayed the public's trust. denunciation, N.

depict V. portray. In this sensational exposé, the author *depicts* John Lennon as a drug-crazed neurotic. Do you question the accuracy of this *depiction* of Lennon?

deplete V. reduce; exhaust. We must wait until we *deplete* our present inventory before we order replacements.

deplore V. regret strongly; express grief over. Although Ann Landers *deplored* the disintegration of the modern family, she recognized that not every marriage could be saved.

derision N. ridicule; mockery. Greeting his pretentious dialogue with *derision,* the critics refused to consider his play seriously. deride, V.

derivative ADJ. unoriginal; derived from another source. Although her early poetry was clearly *derivative* in nature, the critics felt she had promise and eventually would find her own voice.

detached ADJ. emotionally removed; calm and objective; indifferent. A psychoanalyst must maintain a *detached* point of view and stay uninvolved with her patients' personal lives. detachment, N. (secondary meaning)

deterrent N. something that discourages; hindrance. Does the threat of capital punishment serve as a *deterrent* to potential killers? deter, V.

didactic ADJ. teaching; instructional. Pope's lengthy poem *An Essay on Man* is too *didactic* for my taste: I dislike it when poets turn preachy and moralize.

diffident ADJ. shy; lacking confidence; reserved. Can a naturally *diffident* person become a fast-talking, successful used car salesman?

digression N. wandering away from the subject. Nobody minded when Professor Renoir's lectures wandered away from their official theme; his *digressions* were always more fascinating than the topic of the day. digress, V.

discernible ADJ. distinguishable; perceivable. The ships in the harbor were not *discernible* in the fog.

disclaimer N. denial of a legal claim or right; disavowal. Though reporter Joe Klein issued a *disclaimer* stating that he was *not* "Anonymous," the author of *Primary Colors,* eventually he admitted that he had written the controversial novel. disclaim, V.

disclose V. reveal. Although competitors offered him bribes, he refused to *disclose* any information about his company's forthcoming product. disclosure, N.

discord N. lack of harmony; conflict; Watching Tweedledum battle Tweedledee, Alice wondered what had caused this pointless *discord.*

discrepancy N. lack of consistency; contradiction; difference. "Observe, Watson, the significant *discrepancies* between Sir Percy's original description of the crime and his most recent testimony. What do these contradictions suggest?"

disgruntled ADJ. discontented; sulky and dissatisfied. The numerous delays left the passengers feeling *disgruntled.* disgruntle, V.

disinterested ADJ. unprejudiced. Given the judge's political ambitions and the lawyers' financial interest in the case, the only *disinterested* person in the courtroom may have been the court reporter.

dismiss V. put away from consideration; reject. Believing in John's love for her, she *dismissed* the notion that he might be unfaithful. (secondary meaning)

disparage V. belittle. A doting mother, Emma was more likely to praise her son's crude attempts at art than to *disparage* them.

disparate ADJ. basically different; unrelated. Unfortunately, Tony and Tina have *disparate* notions of marriage: Tony sees it as a carefree extended love affair, while Tina sees it as a solemn commitment to build a family and a home.

dispatch N. speediness; prompt execution; message sent with all due speed. Young Napoleon defeated the enemy with all possible *dispatch;* he then sent a *dispatch* to headquarters, informing his commander of the great victory. also V.

dispel V. scatter; cause to vanish. The bright sunlight eventually *dispelled* the morning mist.

disperse V. scatter. The police fired tear gas into the crowd to *disperse* the protesters.

dissent V. disagree. In the recent Supreme Court decision, Justice O'Connor *dissented* from the majority opinion. also N.

dissipate V. squander; waste; scatter. He is a fine artist, but we fear he may *dissipate* his gifts if he keeps wasting his time doodling on napkins.

distinction N. honor; contrast; discrimination. A holder of the Medal of Honor, George served with great *distinction* in World War II. He made a *distinction,* however, between World War II and Vietnam, which he considered an immoral conflict.

divulge V. reveal. No lover of gossip, Charlotte would never *divulge* anything that a friend told her in confidence.

docile ADJ. obedient; easily managed. As *docile* as he seems today, that old lion was once a ferocious, snarling beast.

doctrine N. teachings, in general; particular principle (religious, legal, etc.) taught. He was so committed to the *doctrines* of his faith that he was unable to evaluate them impartially.

dogmatic ADJ. opinionated; arbitrary; doctrinal. We tried to discourage Doug from being so *dogmatic,* but never could convince him that his opinions might be wrong.

eclectic ADJ. composed of elements drawn from disparate sources. His style of interior decoration was *eclectic:* bits and pieces of furnishings from widely divergent periods, strikingly juxtaposed to create a unique decor. eclecticism, N.

eclipse V. darken; extinguish; surpass. The new stock market high *eclipsed* the previous record set in 1995.

elated ADJ. overjoyed; in high spirits. Grinning from ear to ear, Carl Lewis was clearly *elated* by his ninth Olympic gold medal. elation, N.

elicit V. draw out (by discussion); call forth. The camp counselor's humorous remarks finally *elicited* a smile from the shy new camper.

elusive ADJ. evasive; baffling; hard to grasp. Trying to pin down exactly when the contractors would be done remodeling the house, Nancy was frustrated by their *elusive* replies. elude, V.

embellish V. adorn. We enjoyed my mother-in-law's stories about how she came here from Russia, in part because she *embellished* the bare facts of the journey with humorous anecdotes and vivid descriptive details.

endorse V. approve; support. Everyone waited to see which one of the rival candidates for the city council the mayor would *endorse*. endorsement, N. (secondary meaning).

enhance V. increase; improve. You can *enhance* your chances of being admitted to the college of your choice by learning to write well; an excellent essay can *enhance* any application.

enigma N. puzzle; mystery. "What *do* women want?" asked Dr. Sigmund Freud. Their behavior was an *enigma* to him.

entice V. lure; attract; tempt. She always tried to *entice* her baby brother into mischief.

enumerate V. list; mention one by one. Huck hung his head in shame as Miss Watson *enumerated* his many flaws.

ephemeral ADJ. short-lived; fleeting. The mayfly is an *ephemeral* creature: its adult life lasts little more than a day.

erode V. eat away. The limestone was *eroded* by the dripping water until only a thin shell remained. erosion, N.

erratic ADJ. odd; unpredictable. Investors become anxious when the stock market appears *erratic*.

erroneous ADJ. mistaken; wrong. I thought my answer was correct, but it was *erroneous.*

esoteric ADJ. hard to understand; known only to the chosen few. *New Yorker* short stories often included *esoteric* allusions to obscure people and events; the implication was, if you were in the in-crowd, you'd get the reference; if you came from Cleveland, you would not.

espouse V. adopt; support. She was always ready to *espouse* a worthy cause.

esteem V. respect; value; Jill *esteemed* Jack's taste in music, but she deplored his taste in clothes.

excerpt N. selected passage (written or musical). The cinematic equivalent of an *excerpt* from a novel is a clip from a film.

exemplary ADJ. serving as a model; outstanding. At commencement the dean praised Ellen for her *exemplary* behavior as class president.

exonerate V. acquit; exculpate. The defense team feverishly sought fresh evidence that might *exonerate* its client.

expedite V. hasten. Because we are on a tight schedule, we hope you will be able to *expedite* the delivery of our order. expeditious, ADJ.

exploit N. deed or action, particularly a brave deed. Raoul Wallenberg was noted for his *exploits* in rescuing Jews from Hitler's forces.

facilitate V. help bring about; make less difficult. Rest and proper nourishment should *facilitate* the patient's recovery.

fallacious ADJ. false; misleading. Paradoxically, *fallacious* reasoning does not always yield erroneous results: even though your logic may be faulty, the answer you get may nevertheless be correct. fallacy, N.

farce N. broad comedy; mockery. Nothing went right; the entire interview degenerated into a *farce*. farcical, ADJ.

fastidious ADJ. difficult to please; squeamish. Bobby was such a *fastidious* eater that he would eat a sandwich only if his mother first cut off every scrap of crust.

fawning ADJ. seeking favor by cringing and flattering; obsequious. "Stop crawling around like a boot-licker, Uriah! I can't stand your sweet talk and *fawning* ways." fawn, V.

feasible ADJ. practical. Is it *feasible* to build a new stadium for the Yankees on New York's West Side? Without additional funding, the project is clearly unrealistic.

fervor N. glowing ardor; intensity of feeling. At the protest rally, the students cheered the strikers and booed the dean with equal *fervor*. fervent, fervid, ADJ.

flippant ADJ. lacking proper seriousness. When Mark told Mona he loved her, she dismissed his earnest declaration with a *flippant* "Oh, you say that to all the girls!" flippancy, N.

forthright ADJ. outspoken; frank. Never afraid to call a spade a spade, she was perhaps too *forthright* to be a successful party politician.

frail ADJ. weak. The delicate child seemed too *frail* to lift the heavy carton.

frivolous ADJ. lacking in seriousness; self-indulgently carefree; relatively unimportant. Though Nancy enjoyed Bill's *frivolous,* lighthearted companionship, she sometimes wondered whether he could ever be serious. frivolity, N.

garrulous ADJ. loquacious; wordy; talkative. My Uncle Henry can out-talk any three people I know. He is the most *garrulous* person in Cayuga County. garrulity, N.

generate V. cause; produce; create. In his first days in office, President Clinton managed to *generate* a new mood of optimism; we hoped he could *generate* a few new jobs.

genre N. particular variety of art or literature. Both a short story writer and a poet, Langston Hughes proved himself equally skilled in either *genre.*

gluttonous ADJ. greedy for food. The *gluttonous* boy ate all the cookies.

gratify V. please. Amy's success in her new job *gratified* her parents.

gregarious ADJ. sociable. Typically, party-throwers are *gregarious;* hermits are not.

hackneyed ADJ. commonplace; trite. When the reviewer criticized the movie for its *hackneyed* plot, we agreed; we had seen similar stories hundreds of times before.

halting ADJ. hesitant; faltering. Novice extemporaneous speakers often talk in a *halting* fashion as they grope for the right words.

hamper V. obstruct. The new mother didn't realize how much the effort of caring for an infant would *hamper* her ability to keep an immaculate house.

hindrance N. block; obstacle. Stalled cars along the highway are a *hindrance* to traffic that tow trucks should remove without delay. hinder, V.

hostility N. unfriendliness; hatred. Children who have been the sole objects of their parents' attention often feel *hostility* toward a new baby in the family, resenting the newcomer who has taken their place.

hypocritical ADJ. pretending to be virtuous; deceiving. It was *hypocritical* of Martha to say such nice things about my poetry to me and then make fun of my verses behind my back. hypocrisy, N.

hypothetical ADJ. based on assumptions or hypotheses; supposed. Suppose you are accepted by Harvard, Stanford, and Brown. Which one would you choose to attend? Remember, this is only a *hypothetical* situation. hypothesis, N.

iconoclastic ADJ. attacking cherished traditions. Deeply *iconoclastic,* Jean Genet deliberately set out to shock conventional theatergoers with his radical plays.

immutable ADJ. unchangeable. All things change over time; nothing is *immutable.*

impede v. hinder; block; delay. A series of accidents *impeded* the launching of the space shuttle.

imperceptible ADJ. unnoticeable; undetectable. Fortunately, the stain on the blouse was *imperceptible* after the blouse had gone through the wash.

implacable ADJ. incapable of being pacified. Madame Defarge was the *implacable* enemy of the Evremonde family.

implement V. put into effect; supply with tools. The mayor was unwilling to *implement* the plan until she was sure it had the governor's backing. also N.

implication N. something hinted at or suggested. When Miss Watson said she hadn't seen her purse since the last time Jim was in the house, the *implication* was that she suspected Jim had taken it. imply, V.

impromptu ADJ. without previous preparation; off the cuff; on the spur of the moment. The judges were amazed that she could make such a thorough, well-supported presentation in an *impromptu* speech.

incarcerate V. imprison. The civil rights workers were willing to be arrested and even *incarcerated* if by their imprisonment they could serve the cause.

incongruity N. lack of harmony; absurdity. The *incongruity* of his wearing sneakers with formal attire amused the observers. incongruous, ADJ.

inconsequential ADJ. insignificant; unimportant. Brushing off Ali's apologies for having broken the wine glass, Tamara said, "Don't worry about it; it's *inconsequential.*"

inconsistency N. state of being self-contradictory; lack of uniformity or steadiness. How are lawyers different from agricultural inspectors? While lawyers check *inconsistencies* in witnesses' statements, agricultural inspectors check *inconsistencies* in Grade A eggs. inconsistent, ADJ.

incorporate V. introduce something into a larger whole; combine; unite. Breaking with precedent, President Truman ordered the military to *incorporate* blacks into every branch of the armed services. also ADJ.

indict V. charge. The district attorney didn't want to *indict* the suspect until she was sure she had a strong enough case to convince a jury. indictment, N.

indifferent ADJ. unmoved or unconcerned by; mediocre. Because Consuela felt no desire to marry, she was *indifferent* to Edward's constant proposals. Not only was she *indifferent* to him personally, but she felt that, given his general silliness, he would make an *indifferent* husband.

induce V. persuade; bring about. After the quarrel, Tina said nothing could *induce* her to talk to Tony again. inducement, N.

industrious ADJ. diligent; hard-working. Look busy when the boss walks past your desk; it never hurts to appear *industrious.* industry, N.

inept ADJ. lacking skill; unsuited; incompetent. The *inept* glovemaker was all thumbs. ineptitude, ineptness, N.

infallible ADJ. unerring; faultless. Jane refused to believe the pope was *infallible,* reasoning: "All human beings are capable of error. The pope is a human being. Therefore, the pope is capable of error."

ingenious ADJ. clever; resourceful. Kit admired the *ingenious* way that her computer keyboard opened up to reveal the built-in CD-ROM below. ingenuity, N.

ingenuous ADJ. naive and trusting; young; unsophisticated. The woodsman had not realized how *ingenuous* Little Red Riding Hood was until he heard that she had gone off for a walk in the woods with the Big Bad Wolf.

ingrate N. ungrateful person. That *ingrate* Bob sneered at the tie I gave him.

inherent ADJ. firmly established by nature or habit. Katya's *inherent* love of justice caused her to champion anyone she considered treated unfairly by society.

initiate V. begin; originate; receive into a group. The college is about to *initiate* a program in reducing math anxiety among students.

innate ADJ. inborn. Mozart's parents soon recognized young Wolfgang's *innate* talent for music.

innocuous ADJ. harmless. An occasional glass of wine with dinner is relatively *innocuous* and should have no ill effect on you.

inscrutable ADJ. impenetrable; not readily understood; mysterious. Experienced poker players try to keep their expressions *inscrutable*, hiding their reactions to the cards behind a so-called "poker face."

insightful ADJ. discerning; perceptive. Sol thought he was very *insightful* about human behavior, but he was actually clueless as to why people acted the way they did.

intangible ADJ. not able to be perceived by touch; vague. Though the financial benefits of his Oxford post were meager, Lewis was drawn to it by its *intangible* rewards: prestige, intellectual freedom, the fellowship of his peers.

integrity N. uprightness; wholeness. Lincoln, whose personal *integrity* has inspired millions, fought a civil war to maintain the *integrity* of the Republic, that these United States might remain undivided for all time.

intricacy N. complexity; knottiness. Philip spent many hours designing mazes of such great *intricacy* that none of his classmates could solve them. intricate, ADJ.

introspective ADJ. looking within oneself. Though young Francis of Assisi led a wild and worldly life, even he had *introspective* moments during which he examined his soul.

irony N. hidden sarcasm or satire; use of words that seem to mean the opposite of what they actually mean. Gradually his listeners began to realize that the excessive praise he was lavishing on his opponent was actually *irony;* he was in fact ridiculing the poor fool.

judicious ADJ. sound in judgment; wise. At a key moment in his life, he made a *judicious* investment that was the foundation of his later wealth.

languid ADJ. weary; feeble; listless; apathetic. The chronic invalid's most recent siege of illness left her *languid* and drooping. languor, N. languish, V.

larceny N. theft. Because of the prisoner's long record of thefts, the district attorney refused to reduce the charge from grand *larceny* to petty *larceny.*

lethargic ADJ. drowsy; dull. The stuffy room made her *lethargic:* she felt as if she was about to nod off.

loathe V. detest. Booing and hissing, the audience showed how much they *loathed* the wicked villain.

malice N. hatred; spite. Jealous of Cinderella's beauty, her wicked stepsisters expressed their *malice* by forcing her to do menial tasks.

meek ADJ. quiet and obedient; spiritless. Can Lois Lane see through Superman's disguise and spot the superhero masquerading as the *meek,* timorous Clark Kent?

meticulous ADJ. excessively careful; painstaking; scrupulous. Martha Stewart is a *meticulous* housekeeper, fussing about each and every detail that goes into making up her perfect home.

misconception N. misunderstanding; misinterpretation. I'm afraid you are suffering from a *misconception,* Mr. Collins: I do not want to marry you at all.

misrepresent V. give a false or incorrect impression, usually intentionally. The ad "Lovely Florida building site with water view" *misrepresented* the property, which was actually ten acres of bottomless swamp.

mock V. ridicule; imitate, often in derision. It is unkind to *mock* anyone; it is stupid to *mock* anyone significantly bigger than you. mockery, N.

monarchy N. government under a single ruler. Though England today is a *monarchy,* there is some question whether it will be one in 20 years, given the present discontent at the prospect of Prince Charles as king.

monotony N. sameness leading to boredom. What could be more deadly dull than the *monotony* of punching numbers into a computer hour after hour?

mutability N. ability to change in form; fickleness. Going from rags to riches, and then back to rags again, the bankrupt financier was a victim of the *mutability* of fortune.

naiveté N. quality of being unsophisticated; simplicity; artlessness; gullibility. Touched by the *naiveté* of sweet, convent-trained Cosette, Marius pledges himself to protect her innocence. naive, ADJ.

nocturnal ADJ. relating to, occurring, or active in the night. Mr. Jones obtained a watchdog to prevent the *nocturnal* raids on his chicken coops.

nonchalance N. indifference; lack of concern; composure. Cool, calm, and collected under fire, James Bond shows remarkable *nonchalance* in the face of danger.

nostalgia N. homesickness; longing for the past. My grandfather seldom spoke of life in the old country; he had little patience with *nostalgia.* nostalgic, ADJ.

notorious ADJ. disreputable; widely known; scandalous. To the starlet, any publicity was good publicity: if she couldn't have a good reputation, she'd settle for being *notorious.* notoriety, N.

nurture V. nourish; educate; foster. The Head Start program attempts to *nurture* pre-kindergarten children so that they will do well when they enter public school. also N.

obnoxious ADJ. offensive; objectionable. A sneak and a tattletale, Sid was an *obnoxious* little brat.

obscure ADJ. dark; vague; unclear. Even after I read the poem a fourth time, its meaning was still *obscure*. obscurity, N.

obscure V. darken; make unclear. At times he seemed purposely to *obscure* his meaning, preferring mystery to clarity.

opaque ADJ. not transparent; impenetrable to light. The *opaque* window shade kept the sunlight out of the room. opacity, N.

optimist N. person who looks on the good side. The pessimist says the glass is half-empty; the *optimist* says it is half-full.

orator N. public speaker. The abolitionist Frederick Douglass was a brilliant *orator* whose speeches brought home to his audience the evils of slavery.

ostentatious ADJ. showy; pretentious; trying to attract attention. Trump's latest casino in Atlantic City is the most *ostentatious* gambling palace in the East: it easily outglitters its competitors. ostentation, N.

outmoded ADJ. no longer stylish; old-fashioned. Unconcerned about keeping in style, Lenore was perfectly happy to wear *outmoded* clothes as long as they were clean and unfrayed.

pacifist N. one opposed to force; antimilitarist. Shooting his way through the jungle, Rambo was clearly not a *pacifist*.

pacify V. soothe; make calm or quiet; subdue. Dentists criticize the practice of giving fussy children sweets to *pacify* them.

paradox N. something apparently contradictory in nature; statement that looks false but is actually correct. Richard presents a bit of a *paradox,* for he is a card-carrying member of both the National Rifle Association and the relatively pacifist American Civil Liberties Union.

patronize V. support; act superior toward; be a customer of. Penniless artists hope to find some wealthy art lover who will *patronize* them. If a wine steward *patronized* me because he saw I knew nothing about fine wine, I'd refuse to *patronize* his restaurant.

pedantic ADJ. showing off learning; bookish. Leavening his decisions with humorous, down-to-earth anecdotes, Judge Walker was not at all the *pedantic* legal scholar. pedant, N.

perjury N. false testimony while under oath. Rather than lie under oath and perhaps be indicted for *perjury,* the witness chose to take the Fifth Amendment, refusing to answer any questions on the grounds that he might incriminate himself.

perpetual ADJ. everlasting. Ponce de Leon hoped to find the legendary fountain of *perpetual* youth. perpetuity, N.

pervasive ADJ. pervading; spread throughout every part. Despite airing them for several hours, she could not rid her clothes of the *pervasive* odor of mothballs that clung to them. pervade, V.

pessimism N. belief that life is basically bad or evil; gloominess. Considering how well you have done in the course so far, you have no real reason for such *pessimism* about your final grade.

petulant ADJ. touchy; peevish. If you'd had hardly any sleep for three nights and people kept on phoning and waking you up, you'd sound pretty *petulant,* too.

phenomena N. Pl. observable facts or events. We kept careful records of the *phenomena* we noted in the course of these experiments.

philanthropist N. lover of mankind; doer of good. In his role as *philanthropist* and public benefactor, John D. Rockefeller, Sr., donated millions to charity; as an individual, however, he was a tight-fisted old man.

plagiarize V. steal another's ideas and pass them off as one's own. The teacher could tell that the student had *plagiarized* parts of his essay; she could recognize whole paragraphs straight from *Barron's Book Notes.*

potency N. power; effectiveness; influence. Looking at the expiration date on the cough syrup bottle, we wondered whether the medication still retained its *potency.* potent, ADJ.

pragmatic ADJ. practical (as opposed to idealistic); concerned with the practical worth or impact of something. This coming trip to France should provide me with a *pragmatic* test of the value of my conversational French class.

precedent N. something preceding in time that may be used as an authority or guide for future action. If I buy you a car for your sixteenth birthday, your brothers will want me to buy them cars when they turn sixteen, too; I can't afford to set such an expensive *precedent.*

predator N. creature that seizes and devours another animal; person who robs or exploits others. Not just cats, but a wide variety of *predators*—owls, hawks, weasels, foxes—catch mice for dinner. A carnivore is by definition *predatory,* for it *preys* on weaker creatures.

premise N. assumption; postulate. Based on the *premise* that there's no fool like an old fool, P. T. Barnum hired a 90-year-old clown for his circus.

premonition N. forewarning. We ignored these *premonitions* of disaster because they appeared to be based on childish fears.

presumptuous ADJ. taking liberties; overstepping bounds; nervy. I thought it was *presumptuous* of Mort to butt into Bishop Tutu's talk with Mrs. Clinton and ask them for their autographs; I wouldn't have had the nerve.

prevail V. triumph; predominate; prove superior in strength, power, or influence; be current. A radical committed to social change, Reed had no patience with the conservative views that *prevailed* in the America of his day. prevalent, ADJ., prevailing, ADJ.

prey N. target of a hunt; victim. In S*talking the Wild Asparagus*, Euell Gibbons has as his *prey* not wild beasts but wild plants. also V.

profound ADJ. deep; not superficial; complete. Freud's remarkable insights into human behavior caused his fellow scientists to honor him as a *profound* thinker. profundity, N.

proliferation N. rapid growth; spread; multiplication. Times of economic hardship inevitably encourage the *proliferation* of countless get-rich-quick schemes. proliferate, V.

prolific ADJ. abundantly fruitful. My editors must assume I'm a *prolific* writer: they expect me to revise six books this year!

prologue N. introduction (to a poem or play). In the *prologue* to *Romeo and Juliet*, Shakespeare introduces the audience to the feud between the Montagues and the Capulets.

prominent ADJ. conspicuous; notable; sticking out. Have you ever noticed that Prince Charles's *prominent* ears make him resemble the big-eared character in *Mad* comics?

promote V. help to flourish; advance in rank; publicize. Founder of the Children's Defense Fund, Marian Wright Edelman ceaselessly *promotes* the welfare of young people everywhere.

prophetic ADJ. foretelling the future. I have no magical *prophetic* powers; when I predict what will happen, I base my predictions on common sense. prophesy, V.

prosperity N. good fortune; financial success; physical well-being. Promising to stay together "for richer, for poorer," the newlyweds vowed to be true to one another in *prosperity* and hardship alike.

provocative ADJ. arousing anger or interest; annoying. In a typically *provocative* act, the bully kicked sand into the weaker man's face.

prudent ADJ. cautious; careful. A miser hoards money not because he is *prudent* but because he is greedy. prudence, N.

ramble V. wander aimlessly (physically or mentally). Listening to the teacher *ramble*, Shelby wondered whether he'd ever get to the point. also N.

random ADJ. without definite purpose, plan, or aim; haphazard. Although the sponsor of the raffle claimed all winners were chosen at *random,* people had their suspicions when the grand prize went to the sponsor's brother-in-law.

recluse N. hermit; loner. Disappointed in love, Miss Emily became a *recluse;* she shut herself away in her empty mansion and refused to see another living soul. reclusive, ADJ.

refute V. disprove. The defense called several respectable witnesses who were able to *refute* the false testimony of the prosecution's only witness.

rejuvenate V. make young again. The charlatan claimed that his elixir would *rejuvenate* the aged and weary.

relinquish V. give up something with reluctance; yield. Once you get used to fringe benefits like expense account meals and a company car, it's very hard to *relinquish* them.

renown N. fame. For many years an unheralded researcher, Barbara McClintock gained international *renown* when she won the Nobel Prize in Physiology and Medicine.

reprehensible ADJ. deserving blame. Shocked by the viciousness of the bombing, politicians of every party uniformly condemned the terrorists' *reprehensible* deed.

repudiate V. disown; disavow. On separating from Tony, Tina announced that she would *repudiate* all debts incurred by her soon-to-be ex-husband.

reserved ADJ. self-controlled; careful in expressing oneself. They made an odd couple: she was outspoken and uninhibited; he was cautious and *reserved*. (secondary meaning)

resignation N. patient submissiveness; statement that one is quitting a job. If Bob Cratchit had not accepted Scrooge's bullying with such *resignation*, he might have gotten up the nerve to hand in his *resignation*. resigned, ADJ.

resolution N. determination. Nothing could shake his *resolution* to succeed despite all difficulties. resolved, ADJ.

resolve V. decide; settle; solve. "I have *resolved*, Watson, to travel to Bohemia to *resolve* the dispute between Irene Adler and the King. In my absence, do your best to *resolve* any mysteries that arise."

restraint N. moderation or self-control; controlling force; restriction. Control yourself, young lady! Show some *restraint!*

retain V. keep; employ. Fighting to *retain* his seat in Congress, Senator Foghorn *retained* a new manager to head his reelection campaign.

reticent ADJ. reserved; uncommunicative; inclined to be silent. Fearing his competitors might get advance word about his plans from talkative staff members, Hughes preferred *reticent* employees to loquacious ones.

reverent ADJ. respectful; worshipful. Though I bow my head in church and recite the prayers, sometimes I don't feel properly *reverent*. revere, V.

ruthless ADJ. pitiless; cruel. Captain Hook was a dangerous, *ruthless* villain who would stop at nothing to destroy Peter Pan.

satirize V. mock. Cartoonist Gary Trudeau often *satirizes* contemporary politicians; through the comments of the *Doonesbury* characters, Trudeau ridicules political corruption and folly. satirical, ADJ.

scrutinize V. examine closely and critically. Searching for flaws, the sergeant *scrutinized* every detail of the private's uniform.

seclusion N. isolation; solitude. One moment she loved crowds; the next, she sought *seclusion*.

serenity N. calmness; placidity. The *serenity* of the sleepy town was shattered by a tremendous explosion.

sever V. cut; separate. Dr. Guillotin invented a machine that could neatly *sever* an aristocratic head from its equally aristocratic body.

severity N. harshness; intensity; austerity; rigidity. The *severity* of Jane's migraine attack was so great that she took to her bed for a week.

singular ADJ. unique; extraordinary; odd. Though the young man tried to understand Father William's *singular* behavior, he still found it odd that the old man incessantly stood on his head. singularity, N.

skeptical ADJ. doubting; suspending judgment until having examined the evidence supporting a point of view. I am *skeptical* about this project; I want some proof that it can work. skepticism, N.

steadfast ADJ. loyal; unswerving. Penelope was *steadfast* in her affections, faithfully waiting for Ulysses to return from his wanderings.

stoic ADJ. impassive; unmoved by joy or grief. I wasn't particularly *stoic* when I had my flu shot; I squealed like a stuck pig. also N.

stratagem N. deceptive scheme. Though Wellington's forces seemed to be in full retreat, in reality their withdrawal was a *stratagem* intended to lure the enemy away from its sheltered position.

subdued ADJ. less intense; quieter. Bob liked the *subdued* lighting at the restaurant because he thought it was romantic. I just thought it was dimly lit.

subversive ADJ. tending to overthrow or destroy. At first glance, the notion that Styrofoam cups may actually be more ecologically sound than paper cups strikes most environmentalists as *subversive.*

superficial ADJ. trivial; shallow. Since your report gave only a *superficial* analysis of the problem, I cannot give you more than a passing grade.

superfluous ADJ. excessive; unnecessary. Please try not to include so many *superfluous* details in your report; just give me the bare facts. superfluity, N.

suppress V. crush; subdue; inhibit. Too polite to laugh in anyone's face, Roy did his best to *suppress* his amusement at Ed's inane remark.

surpass V. exceed. Her PSAT scores *surpassed* our expectations.

susceptible ADJ. impressionable; easily influenced; having little resistance, as to a disease; receptive to. Said the patent medicine man to the extremely *susceptible* customer: "Buy this new miracle drug, and you will no longer be *susceptible* to the common cold."

suspend V. defer or postpone; expel or eject; halt or discontinue; hang from above. When the judge *suspended* his sentence, Bill breathed a sigh of relief. When the principal *suspended* her from school, Wanda tried to look as if she didn't care. When the trapeze artist broke her arm, she had to *suspend* her activities: she no longer could be *suspended* from her trapeze.

sustain V. experience; support; nourish. Stuart *sustained* such a severe injury that the doctors feared he would be unable to work to *sustain* his growing family.

symmetry N. arrangement of parts so that balance is obtained; congruity. Something lopsided by definition lacks *symmetry*.

synthesis N. combining parts into a whole. Now that we have succeeded in isolating this drug, our next problem is to plan its *synthesis* in the laboratory. synthesize, V.

taciturn ADJ. habitually silent; talking little. The stereotypical cowboy is a *taciturn* soul, answering lengthy questions with a "Yep" or "Nope."

tedious ADJ. boring; tiring. The repetitious nature of work on the assembly line made Martin's job very *tedious*. tedium, N.

temper V. moderate; tone down or restrain; toughen (steel). Not even her supervisor's grumpiness could *temper* Nancy's enthusiasm for her new job.

temperament N. characteristic frame of mind; disposition; emotional excess. Although the twins look alike, they differ markedly in *temperament:* Todd is calm, but Rod is excitable. Racket-throwing tennis star John McEnroe was famed for his displays of *temperament*.

termination N. end. Though the time for *termination* of the project was near, we still had a lot of work to finish before we shut up shop.

thwart V. baffle; frustrate. He felt that everyone was trying to *thwart* his plans and prevent his success.

toxic ADJ. poisonous. We must seek an antidote for whatever *toxic* substance he has eaten. toxicity, N.

transcendent ADJ. surpassing; exceeding ordinary limits; superior. Standing on the hillside watching the sunset through the Golden Gate was a *transcendent* experience for Lise: it was so beautiful it surpassed her wildest dreams.

transparent ADJ. easily detected; permitting light to pass through freely. Bobby managed to put an innocent look on his face; to his mother, however, his guilt was *transparent*.

trepidation N. fear; nervous apprehension. As she entered the office of the dean of admissions, Sharon felt some *trepidation* about how she would do in her interview.

turbulence N. state of violent agitation. Warned of approaching *turbulence* in the atmosphere, the pilot told the passengers to fasten their seat belts.

urbane ADJ. suave; refined; elegant. The courtier was *urbane* and sophisticated. urbanity, N.

utopia N. ideal place, state, or society. Fed up with this imperfect universe, Don would have liked to run off to Shangri-la or some other fictitious *utopia*. utopian, ADJ.

vacillate V. waver; fluctuate. Uncertain which suitor she ought to marry, the princess *vacillated,* saying now one, now the other. vacillation, N.

versatile ADJ. having many talents; capable of working in many fields. She was a *versatile* athlete, earning varsity letters in basketball, hockey, and track.

volatile ADJ. changeable; explosive; evaporating rapidly. The political climate today is extremely *volatile:* no one can predict what the electorate will do next. Maria Callas's temper was extremely *volatile:* the only thing you could predict was that she was sure to blow up. Ethyl chloride is an extremely *volatile* liquid: it evaporates instantly.

voracious ADJ. ravenous. The wolf is a *voracious* animal, its hunger never satisfied.

wary ADJ. very cautious. The spies grew *wary* as they approached the sentry.

7 The Mathematics Sections: Strategies, Tips, and Practice

The College Board considers the PSAT to be "a test of general reasoning abilities." It attempts to use basic concepts of arithmetic, algebra, and geometry as a method of testing your ability to think logically. The Board is not testing whether you know how to calculate an average, find the area of a circle, use the Pythagorean theorem, or read a bar graph. *It assumes you can.* In fact, because the Board is not even interested in testing your memory, most of the formulas you will need are listed at the beginning of each math section. In other words, the College Board's objective is to use your familiarity with numbers and geometric figures as a way of testing your *logical thinking skills*.

Most of the arithmetic that you need to know for the PSAT is taught in elementary school, and much of the other material is taught in middle school or junior high school. The only high school math that you need is some elementary algebra and a little basic geometry. To do well on the PSAT, you must know this basic material. But that's not enough. You have to be able to use these concepts in ways that may be unfamiliar to you. That's where the test-taking tactics come in.

THE USE OF CALCULATORS ON THE PSAT

There isn't a single question on any section of the PSAT for which a calculator is required. In fact, on most questions a calculator is completely useless. There are several questions, however, for which a calculator *could* be used; and since calculators are permitted, you should definitely bring one with you when you take the PSAT.

If you forget to bring a calculator to the actual test, you will not be able to use one, since none will be provided and you will not be allowed to share one with a friend. For the same reason, be sure that you have new batteries in your calculator or that you bring a spare, because if your calculator fails during the test, you will have to finish without one.

What Calculator Should You Use?

Almost any four-function, scientific, or graphic calculator is acceptable. Since you don't "need" a calculator at all, you don't "need" any particular type. There is absolutely no advantage to having a graphic calculator; but we do recommend a scientific calculator, since it is occasionally useful to have parentheses keys, ( ); a reciprocal key, $\frac{1}{x}$; and an exponent key, y^x or ^. All scientific calculators have these features. If you tend to make mistakes in working with fractions, you may want to get a calculator that can do fractional arithmetic. With such a calculator, for example, you can add $\frac{1}{3}$ and $\frac{1}{5}$ by entering 1 / 3 + 1 / 5; the readout will be 8/15, not the decimal 0.5333333. Some, but not most, scientific calculators have this capability.

When Should Calculators Be Used?

If you have strong math skills and are a good test-taker, you will probably use your calculator infrequently, if at all.

On the other hand, if you are less confident about your mathematical ability or your test-taking skills, you will probably find your calculator a useful tool.

Throughout this book, the icon 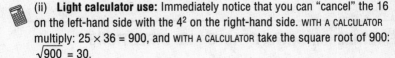 will be placed next to a problem where the use of a calculator is recommended. As you will see, this judgment is very subjective. Sometimes a question can be answered in a few seconds, with no calculations whatsoever, if you see the best approach. In that case, the use of a calculator is not recommended. If you don't see the easy way, however, and have to do some arithmetic, you may prefer to use a calculator.

Let's look at a few sample questions on which some students would use calculators a lot, others a little, and still others not at all.

Example 1.

If $16 \times 25 \times 36 = (4a)^2$, what is the value of a?

(A) 6   (B) 15   (C) 30   (D) 36   (E) 60

(i) **Heavy calculator use:** WITH A CALCULATOR multiply: $16 \times 25 \times 36 = 14,400$. Observe that $(4a)^2 = 16a^2$, and so $16a^2 = 14,400$. WITH A CALCULATOR divide: $a^2 = 14,400 \div 16 = 900$. Finally, WITH A CALCULATOR take the square root: $a = \sqrt{900} = 30$. The answer is **C**.

(ii) **Light calculator use:** Immediately notice that you can "cancel" the 16 on the left-hand side with the 4^2 on the right-hand side. WITH A CALCULATOR multiply: $25 \times 36 = 900$, and WITH A CALCULATOR take the square root of 900: $\sqrt{900} = 30$.

(iii) **No calculator use:** "Cancel" the 16 and the 4^2. Notice that $25 = 5^2$ and $36 = 6^2$, so $a^2 = 5^2 \times 6^2 = 30^2$, and $a = 30$.

Example 2 (Grid-in).

If the length of a diagonal of a rectangle is 13, and if one of the sides is 5, what is the perimeter?

Whether you intend to use your calculator a lot, a little, or not at all, the first thing to do is to draw a diagram.

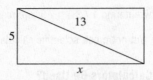

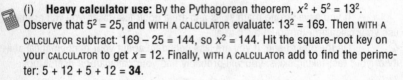

(i)   **Heavy calculator use:** By the Pythagorean theorem, $x^2 + 5^2 = 13^2$. Observe that $5^2 = 25$, and WITH A CALCULATOR evaluate: $13^2 = 169$. Then WITH A CALCULATOR subtract: $169 - 25 = 144$, so $x^2 = 144$. Hit the square-root key on your CALCULATOR to get $x = 12$. Finally, WITH A CALCULATOR add to find the perimeter: $5 + 12 + 5 + 12 = \textbf{34}$.

(ii)   **Light calculator use:** The steps are the same as in (i) except that *some of the calculations* are done mentally: taking the square root of 144 and adding at the end.

(iii)   **No calculator use:** *All calculations* are done mentally. Better yet, *no calculations are done at all,* because you immediately see that each half of the rectangle is a 5-12-13 right triangle, and you add the sides mentally.

	Column A	Column B
Example 3.	$(-15)(-43)$	$(-4)(-9)(-18)$

(i)   **Using a calculator.** Do both multiplications, making sure to enter the negative signs on the CALCULATOR. Compare the answers: 645 versus –648. Column **A** is greater.

(ii)   **No calculator use:** Column A is positive since it is the product of two negative numbers, whereas Column B, which is the product of three negative numbers, is negative.

MEMORIZE IMPORTANT FACTS AND DIRECTIONS

On the first page of each mathematics section of the PSAT, you will see the following mathematical facts (see page 95), though in a slightly different arrangement.

The College Board's official guide, *Taking the SAT I Reasoning Test*, offers the following tip:

> The test doesn't require you to memorize formulas. Commonly used formulas are provided in the test booklet at the beginning of each mathematical section.

If you interpret this to mean "Don't bother memorizing the formulas provided," this is terrible advice. It may be reassuring to know that, if you should forget a basic geometry fact, you can look it up in the box headed "Reference Information," but you should decide right now that you will never have to do that. During the test, you don't want to spend any precious time looking up facts that you can learn now. All of these "commonly used formulas" and other important facts are listed in this chapter. As you learn and review these facts, you should commit them to memory.

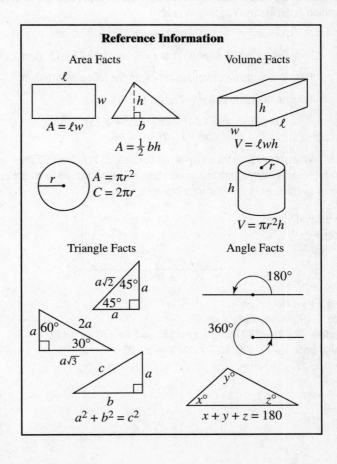

Also in this chapter you will learn the instructions for the three types of mathematics questions on the PSAT. *They will not change.* They will be exactly the same on the test you take.

Helpful Hint

As you prepare for this test, memorize the directions for each section. *When you take the PSAT, do not waste even one second reading directions.*

AN IMPORTANT SYMBOL

Throughout the book, the symbol "$\Rightarrow$" is used to indicate that one step in the solution of a problem follows *immediately* from the preceding one, and that no explanation is necessary. You should read:

$$2x = 12 \Rightarrow x = 6$$

as $2x = 12$ *implies* (or *which implies*) *that* $x = 6$, or, *since* $2x = 12$, then $x = 6$.

Here is a sample solution, using $\Rightarrow$, to the following problem:

What is the value of $3x^2 - 7$ when $x = -5$?

$$x = -5 \Rightarrow x^2 = (-5)^2 = 25 \Rightarrow 3x^2 = 3(25) = 75 \Rightarrow$$
$$3x^2 - 7 = 75 - 7 = \textbf{68}.$$

When the reason for a step is not obvious, $\Rightarrow$ is not used: rather, an explanation is given. In many solutions, some steps are explained, while others are linked by the $\Rightarrow$ symbol, as in the following example:

In the diagram at the right, if $w = 10$, what is z?

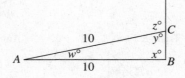

- $w + x + y = 180$.
- Since $\triangle ABC$ is isosceles, $x = y$.
- Therefore, $w + 2y = 180 \Rightarrow 10 + 2y = 180 \Rightarrow 2y = 170 \Rightarrow y = 85$.
- Finally, since $y + z = 180$, $85 + z = 180 \Rightarrow z = \textbf{95}$.

IMPORTANT DEFINITIONS, FACTS, FORMULAS, AND STRATEGIES

1. **Sum:** the result of an addition: 8 is the sum of 6 and 2

2. **Difference:** the result of a subtraction: 4 is the difference of 6 and 2

3. **Product:** the result of a multiplication: 12 is the product of 6 and 2

4. **Quotient:** the result of a division: 3 is the quotient of 6 and 2

5. **Remainder:** when 15 is divided by 6, the quotient is 2 and the remainder is 3: $15 = 6 \times 2 + 3$

6. **Integers:** $\{\ldots, -3, -2, -1, 0, 1, 2, 3, \ldots\}$

7. **Factor** or **Divisor:** any integer that leaves no remainder (i.e., a remainder of 0) when it is divided into another integer: 1, 2, 5, 10 are the factors (or divisors) of 10

8. **Multiple:** the product of one integer by a second integer: 7, 14, 21, 28, ... are multiples of 7 ($7 = 1 \times 7$, $14 = 2 \times 7$, and so on)

9. **Even integers:** the multiples of 2: $\{\ldots, -4, -2, 0, 2, 4, \ldots\}$

10. **Odd integers:** the non-multiples of 2: $\{\ldots, -3, -1, 1, 3, 5, \ldots\}$

11. **Consecutive integers:** two or more integers, written in sequence, each of which is 1 more than the preceding one. For example:

$$7, 8, 9 \qquad -2, -1, 0, 1, 2 \qquad n, n+1, n+2$$

12. **Prime number:** a positive integer that has exactly two divisors. The first few primes are 2, 3, 5, 7, 11, 13, 17. (*not* 1)

13. **Exponent:** a number written as a superscript: the 3 in 7^3. On the SAT I, the only exponents you need to know about are positive integers: $2^n = 2 \times 2 \times 2 \times \ldots \times 2$, where 2 appears as a factor n times.

14. **Laws of Exponents:**

    For any numbers b and c and positive integers m and n:

    (i) $b^m b^n = b^{m+n}$ (ii) $\dfrac{b^m}{b^n} = b^{m-n}$ (iii) $(b^m)^n = b^{mn}$

    (iv) $b^m c^m = (bc)^m$

15. **Square root of a positive number:** if a is positive, $\sqrt{a}$ is the only positive number whose square is a: $(\sqrt{a})^2 = \sqrt{a} \times \sqrt{a} = a$

16. The product and the quotient of two positive numbers or two negative numbers are positive; the product and the quotient of a positive number and a negative number are negative.

17. • The product of an *even* number of negative factors is positive.
    • The product of an *odd* number of negative factors is negative.

18. For any positive numbers *a* and *b*:

$$\sqrt{ab} = \sqrt{a} \times \sqrt{b} \quad \text{and} \quad \sqrt{\frac{a}{b}} = \frac{\sqrt{a}}{\sqrt{b}}$$

19. For any real numbers *a*, *b*, and *c*:

    • $a(b + c) = ab + ac$ • $a(b - c) = ab - ac$

    and, if a ≠ 0,

    • $\dfrac{b+c}{a} = \dfrac{b}{a} + \dfrac{c}{a}$ • $\dfrac{b-c}{a} = \dfrac{b}{a} - \dfrac{c}{d}$

20. To compare two fractions, use your calculator to convert them to decimals.

21. To multiply two fractions, multiply their numerators and multiply their denominators:

$$\frac{3}{5} \times \frac{4}{7} = \frac{3 \times 4}{5 \times 7} = \frac{12}{35}$$

22. To divide any number by a fraction, multiply that number by the reciprocal of the fraction.

$$\frac{3}{5} \div \frac{2}{3} = \frac{3}{5} \times \frac{3}{2} = \frac{9}{10}$$

23. To add or subtract fractions with the same denominator, add or subtract the numerators and keep the denominator:

$$\frac{4}{9} + \frac{1}{9} = \frac{5}{9} \quad \text{and} \quad \frac{4}{9} - \frac{1}{9} = \frac{3}{9} = \frac{1}{3}$$

24. To add or subtract fractions with different denominators, first rewrite the fractions as equivalent fractions with the same denominator:

$$\frac{1}{6} + \frac{3}{4} = \frac{2}{12} + \frac{9}{12} = \frac{11}{12}$$

25. **Percent:** a fraction whose denominator is 100:

$$15\% = \frac{15}{100} = .15$$

26. The *percent increase* of a quantity is

$$\frac{\text{actual increase}}{\text{original amount}} \times 100\%.$$

    The *percent decrease* of a quantity is

$$\frac{\text{actual decrease}}{\text{original amount}} \times 100\%.$$

27. **Ratio:** a fraction that compares two quantities that are measured in the same units. The ratio *2 to 3* can be written $\frac{2}{3}$ or 2:3.

28. In any ratio problem, write the letter x after each number and use some given information to solve for x.

29. **Proportion:** an equation that states that two ratios (fractions) are equal. Solve proportions by cross-multiplying: if $\dfrac{a}{b} = \dfrac{c}{d}$, then $ad = bc$.

30. **Average of a set of n numbers:** the sum of those numbers divided by n:

$$\text{average} = \frac{\text{sum of the } n \text{ numbers}}{n} \quad \text{or simply}$$

$$A = \frac{\text{sum}}{n}$$

31. If you know the average, A, of a set of n numbers, multiply A by n to get their sum: sum = nA.

32. To multiply two binomials, use the FOIL method: multiply each term in the first parentheses by each term in the second parentheses and simplify by combining terms, if possible.

$$(2x - 7)(3x + 2) = (2x)(3x) + (2x)(2) + (-7)(3x) + (-7)(2) =$$
First terms   Outer terms   Inner terms   Last terms

$$6x^2 + 4x - 21x - 14 = 6x^2 - 17x - 14$$

33. The three most important binomial products on the PSAT are these:
    - $(x - y)(x + y) = x^2 - y^2$
    - $(x - y)^2 = (x - y)(x - y) = x^2 - 2xy + y^2$
    - $(x + y)^2 = (x + y)(x + y) = x^2 + 2xy + y^2$

34. All distance problems involve one of three variations of the same formula:

$$\text{distance} = \text{rate} \times \text{time} \qquad \text{rate} = \frac{\text{distance}}{\text{time}}$$

$$\text{time} = \frac{\text{distance}}{\text{rate}}$$

35.

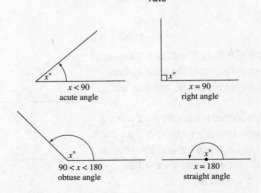

$x < 90$
acute angle

$x = 90$
right angle

$90 < x < 180$
obtuse angle

$x = 180$
straight angle

36. If two or more angles form a straight angle, the sum of their measures is 180°.

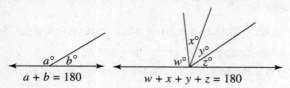

$a + b = 180$ $w + x + y + z = 180$

37. The sum of all the measures of all the angles around a point is 360°.

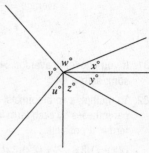

$u + v + w + x + y + z = 360$

38.

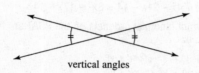

vertical angles

39. Vertical angles have equal measures.

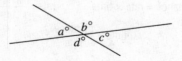

$a = c$ and $b = d$.

40. If a pair of parallel lines is cut by a transversal that is *not* perpendicular to the parallel lines:
   - Four of the angles are acute, and four are obtuse.
   - All four acute angles are equal: $a = c = e = g$.
   - All four obtuse angles are equal: $b = d = f = h$.
   - The sum of any acute angle and any obtuse angle is 180°: for example, $d + e = 180$, $c + f = 180$, $b + g = 180$, ...

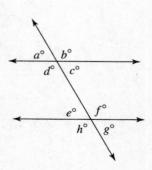

41. In any triangle, the sum of the measures of the three angles is 180°: $x + y + z = 180$.

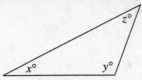

42. The measure of an exterior angle of a triangle is equal to the sum of the measures of the two opposite interior angles.

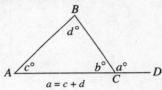

$$a = c + d$$

43. In any triangle:
   - the longest side is opposite the largest angle;
   - the shortest side is opposite the smallest angle;
   - sides with the same length are opposite angles with the same measure.

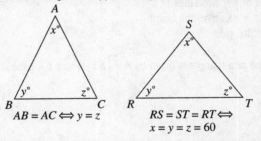

$AB = AC \Longleftrightarrow y = z$

$RS = ST = RT \Longleftrightarrow$
$x = y = z = 60$

44. In any right triangle, the sum of the measures of the two acute angles is 90°.

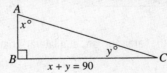

$$x + y = 90$$

45.

Pythagorean theorem
$$a^2 + b^2 = c^2$$

46. In a 45-45-90 right triangle, the sides are x, x, and $x\sqrt{2}$.

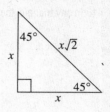

47. In a 30-60-90 right triangle the sides are x, $x\sqrt{3}$, and $2x$.

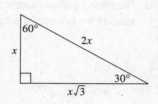

48. The sum of the lengths of any two sides of a triangle is greater than the length of the third side.

    The difference between the lengths of any two sides of a triangle is less than the length of the third side.

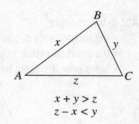

$$x + y > z$$
$$z - x < y$$

49. The area of a triangle is given by $A = \frac{1}{2}bh$, where b = base and h = height.

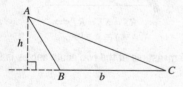 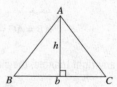

50. If A represents the area of an equilateral triangle with side s, then $A = \dfrac{s^2\sqrt{3}}{4}$.

51. In any quadrilateral, the sum of the measures of the four angles is 360°.

52. A ***parallelogram*** is a quadrilateral in which both pairs of opposite sides are parallel. A ***rectangle*** is a parallelogram in which all four angles are right angles. A ***square*** is a rectangle in which all four sides have the same length.

53. In any parallelogram:
    - Opposite sides are equal: $AB = CD$ and $AD = BC$.
    - Opposite angles are equal: $a = c$ and $b = d$.
    - Consecutive angles add up to 180°: $a + b = 180$, $b + c = 180$, and so on.
    - The two diagonals bisect each other: $AE = EC$ and $BE = ED$.

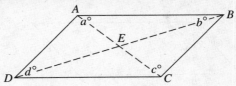

54. In any rectangle:
    - The measure of each angle in a rectangle is 90°.
    - The diagonals of a rectangle have the same length: $AC = BD$.

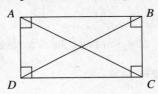

55. In any square:
    - All four sides have the same length.
    - Each diagonal divides the square into two 45-45-90 right triangles.
    - The diagonals are perpendicular to each other: $AC \perp BD$.

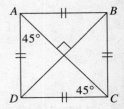

56. Formulas for perimeter and area:

- For a parallelogram: $A = bh$ and $P = 2(a + b)$.
- For a rectangle: $A = \ell w$ and $P = 2(\ell + w)$.
- For a square: $A = s^2$ or $A = \frac{1}{2}d^2$ and $P = 4s$.

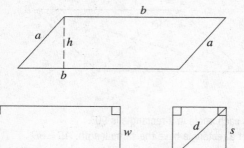

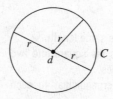

57. Let r be the radius, d the diameter, C the circumference, and A the area of a circle, then

$$d = 2r \quad C = \pi d = 2\pi r \quad A = \pi r^2$$

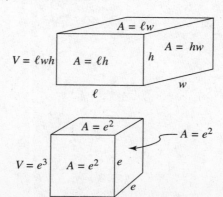

58. The formula for the volume of a rectangular solid is $V = \ell wh$.

In a cube, all the edges are equal. Therefore, if e is the edge, the formula for the volume is $V = e^3$.

59. The formula for the surface area of a rectangular solid is $A = 2(\ell w + \ell h + wh)$. The formula for the surface area of a cube is $A = 6e^2$.

60. The formula for the volume, V, of a cylinder is $V = \pi r^2 h$. The surface area, A, of the side of the cylinder is $A = 2\pi rh$. The area of the top and bottom are each πr^2.

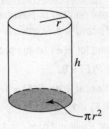

61. The distance, d, between two points, $A(x_1, y_1)$ and $B(x_2, y_2)$, can be calculated using the distance formula:

$$d = \sqrt{(x_2 - x_1)^2 + (y_2 - y_1)^2}$$

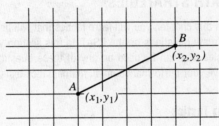

62. The slope of the line is given by:

$$\text{slope} = \frac{y_2 - y_1}{x_2 - x_1}$$

63. • The slope of any horizontal line is 0.
    • The slope of any line that goes up as you move from left to right is positive.
    • The slope of any line that goes down as you move from left to right is negative.

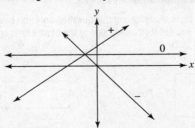

64. **The Counting Principle:** If two jobs need to be completed and there are *m* ways to do the first job and *n* ways to do the second job, then there are $m \times n$ ways to do one job followed by the other. This principle can be extended to any number of jobs.

65. If *E* is any event, the **probability** that *E* will occur is given by

$$P(E) = \frac{\text{number of favorable outcomes}}{\text{total number of possible outcomes}},$$

assuming that all of the possible outcomes are equally likely.

66.–69. Let *E* be an event, and let $P(E)$ be the probability that it will occur.

66. If *E* is *impossible,* then **$P(E) = 0$**.

67. If it is *certain* that *E* will occur, then **$P(E) = 1$**.

68. In all other cases, **$0 < P(E) < 1$**.

69. The probability that event *E* will *not* occur is **$1 - P(E)$**.

70. If an experiment is done 2 (or more) times, the probability that first one event will occur, and then a second event will occur, is the product of the probabilities.

GENERAL MATH STRATEGIES

Later in this chapter, you will learn tactics that will help you with the three specific types of math questions on the PSAT. In this section you will learn several important strategies that can be used on any of these questions. Mastering these tactics will improve your performance on all mathematics tests.

Testing Tactics

1. Draw a Diagram.

On any geometry question for which a figure is not provided, draw one (as accurately as possible) in your test booklet.

Let's consider some examples.

Example 1.

What is the area of a rectangle whose length is twice its width and whose perimeter is equal to that of a square whose area is 1?

Solution. Don't even think of answering this question until you have drawn a square and a rectangle and labeled each of them: each side of the square is 1; and if the width of the rectangle is *w*, its length is 2*w*.

Now, write the required equation and solve it:

$$6w = 4 \Rightarrow w = \frac{4}{6} = \frac{2}{3} \Rightarrow 2w = \frac{4}{3}$$

The area of the rectangle = $lw = \left(\frac{4}{3}\right)\left(\frac{2}{3}\right) = \frac{8}{9}$.

Drawings should not be limited, however, to geometry questions; there are many other questions on which drawings will help.

Example 2.

A jar contains 10 red marbles and 30 green ones. How many red marbles must be added to the jar so that 60% of the marbles will be red?

Solution. Draw a diagram and label it. From the diagram it is clear that there are now $40 + x$ marbles in the jar, of which $10 + x$ are red. Since we want the fraction of red marbles to be

$60\% \left(= \frac{3}{5}\right)$, we have $\frac{10 + x}{40 + x} = \frac{3}{5}$.

x	Red
30	Green
10	Red

Cross-multiplying, we get:

$$50 + 5x = 120 + 3x \Rightarrow 2x = 70 \Rightarrow x = \mathbf{35}.$$

Of course, you could have set up the equation and solved it without the diagram, but the drawing makes the solution easier and you are less likely to make a careless mistake.

2. If a Diagram Is Drawn to Scale, Trust It, and Use Your Eyes.

Remember that every diagram that appears on the PSAT has been drawn as accurately as possible *unless* you see "<u>Note</u>: Figure not drawn to scale" written below it.

For figures that are drawn to scale, the following are true: line segments that appear to be the same length *are* the same length; if an angle clearly looks obtuse, it *is* obtuse; and if one angle appears larger than another, you may assume that it *is* larger.

Example 3.

In the figure at the right, what is the sum of the measures of all of the marked angles?

(A) 360°   (B) 540°
(C) 720°   (D) 900°
(E) 1080°

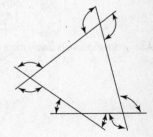

Solution. Make your best estimate of each angle, and add up the values. The five choices are so far apart that, even if you're off by 15° or more on some of the angles, you'll get the right answer. The sum of the estimates shown is 690°, so the correct answer *must* be 720° **(C)**.

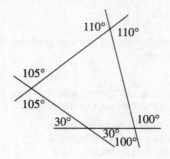

Column A	Column B

Example 4.

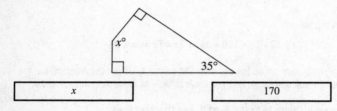

x	170

Solution. Since the diagram is drawn to scale, trust it. Look at x: it appears to be *about* 90 + 50 = 140; it is *definitely* less than 170.

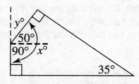

Also, y, drawn above is clearly more than 10, so x is less than 170. Choose **B**.

3. If a Diagram Is *Not* drawn to Scale, Redraw It to Scale, and Then Use Your Eyes.

For figures that have not been drawn to scale, you can make *no* assumptions. Lines that look parallel may not be; an angle that appears to be obtuse may, in fact, be acute; two line segments may have the same length even though one looks twice as long as the other.

Example 5.

In △*ACB*, what is the value of *x*?

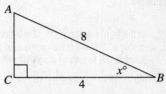

Note: Figure not drawn to scale

   (A) 75   (B) 60   (C) 45   (D) 30   (E) 15

Solution. In what way is this figure not drawn to scale? *AB* = 8 and *BC* = 4, but in the figure *AB* is *not* twice as long as *BC*. Redraw the triangle so that *AB is* twice as long as *BC*. Now, just look: *x* is about **60 (B)**.

In fact, *x* is exactly 60. If the hypotenuse of a right triangle is twice the length of one of the legs, you have a 30-60-90 triangle, and the angle formed by the hypotenuse and that leg is 60°.

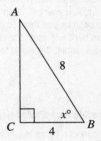

Example 6.

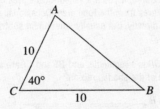

Note: Figure not drawn to scale

AB

10

Solution. In the given diagram, *AB* is longer than *AC*, which is 10, but *we cannot trust the diagram*. Actually, there are two things wrong: ∠*C* is labeled 40°, but looks much more like 60° or 70°, and *AC* and *BC* are each labeled 10, but *BC* is drawn much longer. Use TACTIC 3. Redraw the triangle with a 40° angle and two sides of the same length. Now, it's clear that *AB* < 10. Choose **B**.

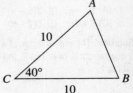

4. Add a Line to a Diagram.

Occasionally, after staring at a diagram, you still have no idea how to solve the problem to which it applies. It looks as though there isn't enough given information. When this happens, it often helps to draw another line in the diagram.

Example 7.

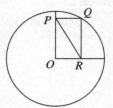

In the figure at the right, Q is a point on the circle whose center is O and whose radius is r, and $OPQR$ is a rectangle. What is the length of diagonal PR?

(A) r　(B) r^2　(C) $\dfrac{r^2}{\pi}$　(D) $\dfrac{r\sqrt{2}}{\pi}$

(E) It cannot be determined from the information given.

Solution. If, after staring at the diagram and thinking about rectangles, circles, and the Pythagorean theorem, you're still lost, don't give up. Ask yourself, "Can I add another line to this diagram?" As soon as you think to draw in OQ, the other diagonal, the problem becomes easy: the two diagonals are equal, and, since OQ is a radius, it is equal to **r (A)**.

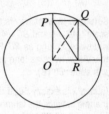

5. Subtract to Find Shaded Regions.

Whenever part of a figure is white and part is shaded, the straightforward way to find the area of the shaded portion is to find the area of the entire figure and then subtract from it the area of the white region. Of course, if you are asked for the area of the white region, you can, instead, subtract the shaded area from the total area. Occasionally, you may see an easy way to calculate the shaded area directly, but usually you should subtract.

Example 8.

In the figure below, $ABCD$ is a rectangle, and BE and CF are arcs of circles centered at A and D. What is the area of the shaded region?

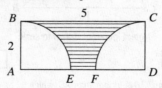

(A) $10 - \pi$　(B) $2(5 - \pi)$　(C) $2(5 - 2\pi)$
(D) $6 + 2\pi$　(E) $5(2 - \pi)$

Solution. The entire region is a 2×5 rectangle whose area is 10. Since each white region is a quarter-circle of radius 2, the combined area of these regions is that of a semicircle of radius 2:

$$\frac{1}{2}\pi(2)^2 = 2\pi.$$

Therefore, the area of the shaded region is $10 - 2\pi = \mathbf{2(5 - \pi)}$ **(B)**.

6. Don't Do More Than You Have To.

Look for shortcuts. Since a problem can often be solved in more than one way, you should always look for the easiest method. Consider the following examples.

Example 9.

If $5(3x - 7) = 20$, what is $3x - 8$?

It's not difficult to solve for x:

$$5(3x - 7) = 20 \Rightarrow 15x - 35 = 20 \Rightarrow 15x = 55 \Rightarrow$$

$$x = \frac{55}{15} = \frac{11}{3}$$

But it's too much work. Besides, once you find that $x = \frac{11}{3}$, you still have to multiply to get $3x$: $3\left(\frac{11}{3}\right) = 11$, and then subtract to get $3x - 8$: $11 - 8 = \mathbf{3}$.

Solution. The key is to recognize that you don't need x. Finding $3x - 7$ is easy (just divide the original equation by 5), and $3x - 8$ is just 1 less:

$$5(3x - 7) = 20 \Rightarrow 3x - 7 = 4 \Rightarrow 3x - 8 = \mathbf{3}.$$

<u>Column A</u>   <u>Column B</u>

Example 10.

Zach worked from 9:47 A.M. until 12:11 P.M.
Sam worked from 9:11 A.M. until 12:47 P.M.

The number of minutes Zach worked	The number of minutes Sam worked

Solution. Don't spend any time calculating how many minutes either boy worked. You need to know only which column is greater; and since Sam started earlier and finished later, he clearly worked longer. The answer is **B**.

7. Pay Attention to Units.

Often the answer to a question must be in units different from those used in the given data. As you read the question, <u>underline</u> exactly what you are being asked. Do the examiners want hours or minutes or seconds, dollars or cents, feet or inches, meters or centimeters? On multiple-choice questions an answer with the wrong units is almost always one of the choices.

Example 11.

At a speed of 48 miles per hour, how many minutes will be required to drive 32 miles?

(A) $\frac{2}{3}$ (B) $\frac{3}{2}$ (C) 40 (D) 45 (E) 2400

Solution. This is a relatively easy question. Just be attentive. Since $\dfrac{32}{48} = \dfrac{2}{3}$, it will take $\dfrac{2}{3}$ of an *hour* to drive 32 miles. Choice A is $\dfrac{2}{3}$; but that is *not* the correct answer because you are asked how many *minutes* will be required. (Did you underline the word "minutes" in the question?) The correct answer is $\dfrac{2}{3}(60) = $ **40 (C)**.

8. Systematically Make Lists.

When a question asks "how many," often the best strategy is to make a list of all the possibilities. It is important that you make the list in a *systematic* fashion so that you don't inadvertently leave something out. Often, shortly after starting the list, you can see a pattern developing and can figure out how many more entries there will be without writing them all down.

Example 12.

The product of three positive integers is 300. If one of them is 5, what is the least possible value of the sum of the other two?

Solution. Since one of the integers is 5, the product of the other two is 60 ($5 \times 60 = 300$). Systematically, list all possible pairs, (a, b), of positive integers whose product is 60, and check their sums. First, let $a = 1$, then 2, and so on.

a	b	$a + b$
1	60	61
2	30	32
3	20	23
4	15	19
5	12	17
6	10	16

The answer is **16**.

Example 13.

A palindrome is a number, such as 93539, that reads the same forward and backward. How many palindromes are there between 100 and 1000?

Solution. First, write down the numbers in the 100's that end in 1:

101, 111, 121, 131, 141, 151, 161, 171, 181, 191

Now write the numbers beginning and ending in 2:

202, 212, 222, 232, 242, 252, 262, 272, 282, 292

By now you should see the pattern: there are 10 numbers beginning with 1, and 10 beginning with 2, and there will be 10 beginning with 3, 4, ..., 9 for a total of $9 \times 10 = $ **90** palindromes.

9. Handle Strange Symbols Properly.

On the PSAT a few questions use symbols, such as: $\oplus$, $\square$, $\odot$, $\circledast$, and $\clubsuit$, that you have never before seen in a mathematics problem. How can you answer such a question? Don't panic! It's easy; you are always told exactly what the symbol means! All you have to do is follow the directions carefully.

Example 14.

If $a \odot b = \dfrac{a+b}{a-b}$, what is the value of 25 $\odot$ 15?

Solution. The definition of "$\odot$" tells us that, whenever two numbers surround a "happy face," we are to form a fraction in which the numerator is the sum of the numbers and the denominator is their difference. Here, 25 $\odot$ 15 is the fraction whose numerator is 25 + 15 = 40 and whose denominator is 25 − 15 = 10: $\dfrac{40}{10}$ = **4**.

Sometimes the same symbol is used in two (or even three) questions. In these cases, the first question is easy and involves only numbers; the second is a bit harder and usually contains variables.

Column A   Column B

Examples 15–16 refer to the following definition.

For any real numbers x and y: $x \updownarrow y = x + y^2$

Example 15.

| 1 $\updownarrow$ 3 | | 6 $\updownarrow$ 2 |

Example 16.

| The number of pairs, (x, y), of positive integers that are solutions of $x \updownarrow y = 10$ | | 2 |

Solution 15. Column A: $1 + 3^2 = 1 + 9 = 10$
Column B: $6 + 2^2 = 6 + 4 = 10$
The answer is **C**.

Solution 16. Use TACTIC 8: *systematically* list the solutions of $x \updownarrow y = 10$. Start with $y = 1$ and continue:

$$9 + 1^2 = 10; \quad 6 + 2^2 = 10; \quad \text{and} \quad 1 + 3^2 = 10.$$

There are three solutions, so Column **A** is greater.

Example 17.

For any real numbers c and d, $c \boxplus d = c^d + d^c$. What is the value of $1 \boxplus (2 \boxplus 3)$?

Solution. Remember the correct order of operations: always do first what's in the parentheses.

$$2 \boxplus 3 = 2^3 + 3^2 = 8 + 9 = 17$$
$$\text{and}$$
$$1 \boxplus 17 = 1^{17} + 17^1 = 1 + 17 = 18.$$

Grid-in **18**.

Practice Exercises   Answers given on pages 116–119.

Multiple-Choice Questions

1. In the figure at the right, if the radius of circle O is 10, what is the length of diagonal AC of rectangle $OABC$?

   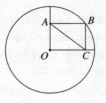

   (A) $\sqrt{2}$ (B) $\sqrt{10}$ (C) $5\sqrt{2}$

   (D) 10   (E) $10\sqrt{2}$

2. In the figure below, $ABCD$ is a square and AED is an equilateral triangle. If $AB = 2$, what is the area of the shaded region?

   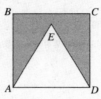

   (A) $\sqrt{3}$ (B) 2   (C) 3   (D) $4 - 2\sqrt{3}$ (E) $4 - \sqrt{3}$

3. If $5x + 13 = 31$, what is the value of $\sqrt{5x + 31}$?

   (A) $\sqrt{13}$ (B) $\sqrt{\dfrac{173}{5}}$ (C) 7   (D) 13   (E) 169

4. At Nat's Nuts a $2\frac{1}{4}$-pound bag of pistachio nuts costs $6.00.

   At this rate, what is the cost, in cents, of a bag weighing 9 ounces?

   (A) 1.5   (B) 24   (C) 150   (D) 1350   (E) 2400

5. In the figure at the right, three circles of radius 1 are tangent to one another. What is the area of the shaded region between the circles?

   (A) $\dfrac{\pi}{2} - \sqrt{3}$ (B) 1.5   (C) $\pi - \sqrt{3}$

   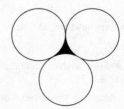

   (D) $\sqrt{3} - \dfrac{\pi}{2}$ (E) $2 - \dfrac{\pi}{2}$

Quantitative Comparison Questions

	Column A	Column B
6.	The number of odd positive factors of 30	The number of even positive factors of 30

Questions 7–8 refer to the following definition.

{a, b} represents the remainder when a is divided by b.

7.	{$10^3, 3$}	{$10^5, 5$}

c and d are integers with $c < d$.

8.	{c, d}	{d, c}

Grid-in Questions

9. In writing all of the integers from 1 to 300, how many times is the digit 1 used?

10. If $a + 2b = 14$ and $5a + 4b = 16$, what is the average (arithmetic mean) of a and b?

11. A bag contains 4 marbles, 1 of each color: red, blue, yellow, and green. The marbles are removed at random, 1 at a time. If the first marble is red, what is the probability that the yellow marble is removed before the blue marble?

12. The area of circle O in the figure below is 12. What is the area of the shaded sector?

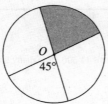

Note: Figure not drawn to scale

Answer Key

1. **D**	3. **C**	5. **D**	7. **A**
2. **E**	4. **C**	6. **C**	8. **A**

9.

10.

or 2.5

11.

	3	/	6

or 1/2 or .5

12.

1	2	/	8

or 3/2 or 1.5

Answer Explanations

1. **D.** Even if you can't solve this problem, don't omit it. Use TACTIC 2: trust the diagram. AC is clearly longer than OC, and very close to radius OE.

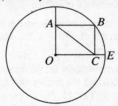

   Therefore, AC must be about 10. Either by inspection or with your calculator, check the choices. They are approximately as follows:

   (A) $\sqrt{2} = 1.4$;   (B) $\sqrt{10} = 3.1$;   (C) $5\sqrt{2} = 7$;

   (D) 10;   (E) $10\sqrt{2} = 14$. The answer must be **10**.

   **The answer *is* 10. The two diagonals are equal, and diagonal OB is a radius.

2. **E.** Use TACTIC 5: subtract to find the shaded area. The area of square $ABCD$ is 4. By Fact 50, the area of $\triangle AED$ is

   $$\frac{2^2\sqrt{3}}{4} = \frac{4\sqrt{3}}{4} = \sqrt{3}.$$ Then the area of the shaded region is $4 - \sqrt{3}$.

3. **C.** Use TACTIC 6: don't do more than you have to. In particular, don't solve for x. Here

   $5x + 13 = 31 \Rightarrow 5x = 18 \Rightarrow 5x + 31 =$
   $18 + 31 = 49 \Rightarrow \sqrt{5x + 31} = \sqrt{49} = 7$.

4. **C.** This is a relatively simple ratio, but use TACTIC 7 and make sure you get the units right. You need to know that there are 100 cents in a dollar and 16 ounces in a pound.

   $$\frac{price}{weight}: \frac{6 \text{ dollars}}{2.25 \text{ pounds}} = \frac{600 \text{ cents}}{36 \text{ ounces}} = \frac{x \text{ cents}}{9 \text{ ounces}}$$

   Now cross-multiply and solve: $36x = 5400 \Rightarrow x = \mathbf{150}$.

5. D. Use TACTIC 4 and add some lines: connect the centers of the three circles to form an equilateral triangle whose sides are 2. Now use TACTIC 5 and find the shaded area by subtracting the area of the three sectors from the area of the triangle,

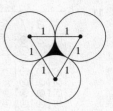

which is $\dfrac{2^2\sqrt{3}}{4} = \sqrt{3}$ (Fact 50). Each sector is $\dfrac{1}{6}$ of a

circle of radius 1. Together the three sectors form $\dfrac{1}{2}$ of such a circle, so their total

area is $\dfrac{1}{2}\pi(1)^2 = \dfrac{\pi}{2}$. Finally, subtract: the area of the shaded region is $\sqrt{3} - \dfrac{\pi}{2}$.

6. C. Use TACTIC 8. Systematically list all the factors of 30, either individually or in pairs: 1, 30, 2, 15, 3, 10, 5, 6. Of the 8 factors, 4 are even and 4 are odd. The columns are equal (C).

7. A. Use TACTIC 9: Follow the directons carefully! Column A: when 10^3 (1000) is divided by 3, the quotient is 333 and the remainder is 1. Column B: 10^5 is divisible by 5, so the remainder is 0. Column A is greater.

8. A. Column A: since $c < d$, the quotient when c is divided by d is 0, and the remainder is c. Column B: when d is divided by c, the remainder must be less than c. Column A is greater.

9. (160) Use TACTIC 8. Systematically list the numbers that contain the digit 1, writing as many as you need to see the pattern. Between 1 and 99 the digit 1 is used 10 times as the units digit (1, 11, 21, …, 91) and 10 times as the tens digit (10, 11, 12, …, 19) for a total of 20 times. From 200 to 299, there are 20 more times (the same 20 but preceded by 2). Finally, from 100 to 199 there are 20 more plus 100 numbers where the digit 1 is used in the hundreds place. The total is 20 + 20 + 20 + 100 = **160**.

10. $\left(\dfrac{5}{2} \text{ or } 2.5\right)$ Use TACTIC 6: don't do more than is necessary. You don't need to solve

this system of equations; you don't need to know the values of a and b, only their average. Adding the two equations gives

$$6a + 6b = 30 \Rightarrow a + b = 5 \Rightarrow \dfrac{a+b}{2} =$$

$$\dfrac{5}{2} \text{ or } \mathbf{2.5}.$$

11. $\left(\dfrac{3}{6} \text{ or } \dfrac{1}{2} \text{ or } .5\right)$ Use TACTIC 8. Systematically list all of the orders in which the marbles

could be drawn. With 4 colors, there would ordinarily have been 24 orders, but since the first marble drawn was red, there are only 6 arrangements for the other 3 colors: BYG, BGY, YGB, YBG, GYB, GBY. In 3 of these 6 the yellow comes before the blue, and in the other 3 the blue comes before the yellow. Therefore, the

probability that the yellow marble will be removed before the blue marble is $\dfrac{3}{6}$ or

$\dfrac{1}{2}$ or **.5**.

12. $\left(\dfrac{12}{8}\text{ or }\dfrac{3}{2}\text{ or }1.5\right)$ The shaded sector is $\dfrac{45}{360} = \dfrac{1}{8}$ of the circle, so its area is $\dfrac{1}{8}$ of 12:

$\dfrac{12}{8}$ or $\dfrac{3}{2}$ or **1.5**.

If you didn't see that, use TACTIC 8-3 and redraw the figure to scale by making the angle as close as possible to 45°. It is now clear that the sector is $\dfrac{1}{8}$ of the circle (or very close to it).

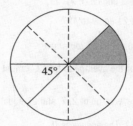

THE MULTIPLE-CHOICE QUESTION

The first mathematics section on the PSAT contains 20 multiple-choice questions. On the first page of this section, you will see the following directions:

In this section *solve each problem,* using any available space on the page for scratchwork. *Then* decide which is the best of the choices given and fill in the corresponding oval on the answer sheet. (Emphasis added.)

The directions are very simple. Basically, they tell you to ignore, at first, the fact that these are multiple-choice questions. Just *solve each problem,* and *then* look at the five choices to see which one is best. As you will learn in this section, however, that is not always the best strategy.

In this section you will learn important strategies you need to help you answer multiple-choice questions on the PSAT. However, as invaluable as these tactics are, use them only when you need them. *If you know how to solve a problem and are confident that you can do so accurately and reasonably quickly, JUST DO IT!*

10. Test the Choices, Starting with C.

TACTIC 10, often called *backsolving,* is useful when you are asked to solve for an unknown and you understand what needs to be done to answer the question, but you want to avoid doing the algebra. The idea is simple: test the various choices to see which one is correct.

NOTE: On the PSAT the answers to virtually all numerical multiple-choice questions are listed in either increasing or decreasing order. Consequently, C is the middle value; and in applying TACTIC 10, *you should always start with C.* For example, assume that choices A, B, C, D, and E are given in increasing order. Try C. If it works, you've found the answer. If C doesn't work, you should now know whether you need to test a larger number or a smaller one, and that information permits you to eliminate two more choices. If C is too small, you need a larger number, so A and B are out; if C is too large, you can eliminate D and E, which are even larger.

Examples 18 and 19 illustrate the proper use of TACTIC 10.

Example 18.

If the average (arithmetic mean) of 2, 7, and x is 12, what is the value of x?

(A) 9   (B) 12   (C) 21   (D) 27   (E) 36

Solution. Use TACTIC 10. Test choice C: $x = 21$.

• Is the average of 2, 7, and 21 equal to 12?

• No: $\dfrac{2+7+21}{3} = \dfrac{30}{3} = 10$, which is *too small.*

• Eliminate C; also, since, for the average to be 12, x must be *greater* than 21, eliminate A and B.

• Try choice D: $x = \mathbf{27}$. Is the average of 2, 7, and 27 equal to 12?

• Yes: $\dfrac{2+7+27}{3} = \dfrac{36}{3} = 12$. The answer is **D**.

Every problem that can be solved using TACTIC 10 can be solved directly, usually in less time. Therefore, we stress: *if you are confident that you can solve a problem quickly and accurately, just do so.*

Example 19.

If the sum of five consecutive odd integers is 735, what is the largest of these integers?

(A) 155   (B) 151   (C) 145   (D) 143   (E) 141

Solution. Use TACTIC 10. Test choice C: 145.

• If 145 is the largest of the five integers, the integers are 145, 143, 141, 139, and 137. Quickly add them on your calculator. The sum is 705.
• Since 705 is too small, eliminate C, D, and E.
• If you noticed that the amount by which 705 is too small is 30, you should realize that each of the five numbers needs to be increased by 6; therefore, the largest is **151 (B)**.
• If you didn't notice, just try 151, and see that it works.

This solution is easy, and it avoids having to set up and solve the required equation:

$$n + (n + 2) + (n + 4) + (n + 6) + (n + 8) = 735.$$

11. Replace Variables with Numbers.

Mastery of TACTIC 11 is critical for anyone developing good test-taking skills. This tactic can be used whenever the five choices involve the variables in the question. There are three steps:

1. Replace each letter with an easy-to-use number.

2. Solve the problem using those numbers.

3. Evaluate each of the five choices with the numbers you picked to see which choice is equal to the answer you obtained.

Examples 20 and 21 illustrate the proper use of TACTIC 11.

Example 20.

If a is equal to b multiplied by c, which of the following is equal to b divided by c?

(A) $\dfrac{a}{bc}$ (B) $\dfrac{ab}{c}$ (C) $\dfrac{a}{c}$ (D) $\dfrac{a}{c^2}$ (E) $\dfrac{a}{bc^2}$

Solution.

- Pick three easy-to-use numbers that satisfy $a = bc$: for example, $a = 6$, $b = 2$, $c = 3$.
- Solve the problem with these numbers: $b \div c = \dfrac{b}{c} = \dfrac{2}{3}$.

- Check each of the five choices to see which one is equal to $\dfrac{2}{3}$:

- (A) $\dfrac{a}{bc} = \dfrac{6}{(2)(3)} = 1$: NO.   (B) $\dfrac{a}{bc} = \dfrac{6(3)}{7} = 6$: NO.

  (C) $\dfrac{a}{c} = \dfrac{6}{3} = 2$: NO.   (D) $\dfrac{a}{c^2} = \dfrac{6}{3^2} = \dfrac{6}{9} = \dfrac{2}{3}$: YES!

  Still check (E): $\dfrac{a}{c^2} = \dfrac{6}{2(3^2)} = \dfrac{6}{18} = \dfrac{1}{3}$: NO.

- The answer is **D**.

Example 21.

If the sum of four consecutive odd integers is s, then, in terms of s, what is the greatest of these integers?

(A) $\dfrac{s-12}{4}$ (B) $\dfrac{s-6}{4}$ (C) $\dfrac{s+6}{4}$ (D) $\dfrac{s+12}{4}$

(E) $\dfrac{s+16}{4}$

Solution.

- Pick four easy-to-use consecutive odd integers: say, 1, 3, 5, 7. Then s, their sum, is 16.
- Solve the problem with these numbers: the greatest of these integers is 7.

- When $s = 10$, the five choices are $\dfrac{s-12}{4} = \dfrac{4}{4}$,

  $\dfrac{s-6}{4} = \dfrac{10}{4}$, $\dfrac{s+6}{4} = \dfrac{22}{4}$, $\dfrac{s+12}{4} = \dfrac{28}{4}$, $\dfrac{s+16}{4} = \dfrac{32}{4}$.

- Only $\dfrac{28}{4}$, choice **D**, is equal to 7.

Of course, Examples 20 and 21 can be solved without using TACTIC 11 *if your algebra skills are good*.

The important point is that, if you are uncomfortable with the correct algebraic solution, you don't want to omit these questions. You can use TACTIC 11 and *always* get the right answer.

Example 22 is somewhat different. You are asked to reason through a word problem involving only variables. Most students find problems like these mind-boggling. Here, the use of TACTIC 11 is essential.

Helpful Hint

Replace the letters with numbers that are easy to use, not necessarily ones that make sense. *It is perfectly OK to ignore reality.* A school can have five students, apples can cost $10 each, trains can go 5 miles per hour or 1000 miles per hour—it doesn't matter.

Example 22.

If a school cafeteria needs *c* cans of soup each week for each student, and if there are *s* students in the school, for how many weeks will *x* cans of soup last?

(A) $\frac{cx}{s}$ (B) $\frac{xs}{c}$ (C) $\frac{s}{cx}$ (D) $\frac{x}{cs}$ (E) csx

Solution.

- Replace *c*, *s*, and *x* with three easy-to-use numbers. If a school cafeteria needs 2 cans of soup each week for each student, and if there are 5 students in the school, how many weeks will 20 cans of soup last?
- Since the cafeteria needs $2 \times 5 = 10$ cans of soup per week, 20 cans will last for 2 weeks.
- Which of the choices equals 2 when $c = 2$, $s = 5$, and $x = 20$?
- The five choices become: $\frac{cx}{x} = 8$, $\frac{xs}{c} = 50$, $\frac{x}{cs} = \frac{1}{8}$, $\frac{x}{cs} = 2$, $csx = 200$.

The answer is **D**.

12. Choose an Appropriate Number.

TACTIC 12 is similar to TACTIC 11 in that we pick convenient numbers. However, here no variable is given in the problem. TACTIC 12 is especially useful in problems involving fractions, ratios, and percents.

Helpful Hint

In problems involving fractions, the best number to use is the least common denominator of all the fractions. In problems involving percents, the easiest number to use is 100.

Example 23.

At Central High School each student studies exactly one foreign language. Three-fifths of the students take Spanish, and one-fourth of the remaining students take Italian. If all of the others take French, what <u>percent</u> of the students take French?

(A) 10   (B) 15   (C) 20   (D) 25   (E) 30

Solution. The least common denominator of $\frac{3}{5}$ and $\frac{1}{4}$ is 20, so assume that there are 20 students at Central High. (Remember that the numbers you choose don't have to be realistic.) Then the number of students taking Spanish is 12 $\left(\frac{3}{5} \text{ of } 20 \right)$. Of the remaining 8 students, 2 $\left(\frac{1}{4} \text{ of } 8 \right)$ take Italian. The other 6 take French. Finally, 6 is **30%** of 20. The answer is **E**.

Example 24.

From 1994 to 1995 the sales of a book decreased by 80%. If the sales in 1996 were the same as in 1994, by what percent did they increase from 1995 to 1996?

(A) 80%   (B) 100%   (C) 120%   (D) 400%   (E) 500%

Solution. Use TACTIC 12, and assume that 100 copies were sold in 1994 (and 1996). Sales dropped by 80 (80% of 100) to 20 in 1995 and then increased by 80, from 20 back to 100, in 1996. The percent increase was

$$\frac{\text{actual increase}}{\text{original amount}} \times 100\% = \frac{80}{20} \times 100\% = \textbf{400\% (D).}$$

13. Add Equations.

When a question involves two equations, either add them or subtract them. If there are three or more equations, add them.

Helpful Hint

Very often, answering a question does *not* require you to solve the equations. Remember TACTIC 6: *Do not do any more than is necessary.*

Example 25.

If $3x + 5y = 14$ and $x - y = 6$, what is the average of x and y?

(A) 0   (B) 2.5   (C) 3   (D) 3.5   (E) 5

Solution. Add the equations:

$$\begin{array}{r} 3x + 5y = 14 \\ +\quad x - \ y = \ 6 \\ \hline 4x + 4y = 20 \end{array}$$

Divide each side by 4:

$$x + y = 5$$

The average of x and y is their sum divided by 2:

$$\frac{x + y}{2} = \frac{5}{2} = \textbf{2.5}$$

The answer is **B**.

Example 26.

If $a - b = 1$, $b - c = 2$, and $c - a = d$, what is the value of d?

(A) -3 (B) -1 (C) 1 (D) 3
(E) It cannot be determined from the information given.

Solution. Add the three equations:

$$\begin{aligned}a - b &= 1\\ b - c &= 2\\ +\ c - a &= d\\ \hline 0 &= 3 + d \Rightarrow d = -3\end{aligned}$$

The answer is **A**.

14. Eliminate Absurd Choices, and Guess.

When you have no idea how to solve a problem, eliminate all the absurd choices and *guess* from among the remaining ones.

Example 27.

The average of 5, 10, 15, and x is 20. What is x?

(A) 0 (B) 20 (C) 25 (D) 45 (E) 50

Solution. If the average of four numbers is 20, and three of them are less than 20, the other one must be greater than 20. Eliminate A and B and guess. If you further realize that, since 5 and 10 are *a lot* less than 20, x will probably be *a lot* more than 20, you can eliminate C, as well. Then guess either D or E.

Example 28.

If 25% of 220 equals 5.5% of w, what is w?

(A) 10 (B) 55 (C) 100 (D) 110 (E) 1000

Solution. Since 5.5% of w equals 25% of 220, which is surely greater than 5.5% of 220, w must be *greater* than 220. Eliminate A, B, C, and D. The answer *must* be **E**!

Practice Exercises   Answers given on pages 125–127.

1. Judy is now twice as old as Adam but 6 years ago she was 5 times as old as he was. How old is Judy now?

   (A) 10 (B) 16 (C) 20 (D) 24 (E) 32

2. If $a < b$ and c is the sum of a and b, which of the following is the positive difference between a and b?

   (A) $2a - c$ (B) $2b - c$ (C) $c - 2b$
   (D) $c - a + b$ (E) $c - a - b$

3. If w widgets cost c cents, how many widgets can you get for d dollars?

   (A) $\dfrac{100dw}{c}$ (B) $\dfrac{dw}{100c}$ (C) $100cdw$

   (D) $\dfrac{dw}{c}$ (E) cdw

4. If 120% of *a* is equal to 80% of *b*, which of the following is equal to *a* + *b*?

(A) 1.5*a* (B) 2*a* (C) 2.5*a* (D) 3*a* (E) 5*a*

5. In the figure at the right, *WXYZ* is a square whose sides are 12. *AB*, *CD*, *EF*, and *GH* are each 8, and are the diameters of the four semicircles. What is the area of the shaded region?

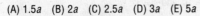

(A) 144 − 128π   (B) 144 − 64π
(C) 144 − 32π   (D) 144 − 16π
(E) 16π

6. What is *a* divided by *a*% of *a*?

(A) $\frac{a}{100}$ (B) $\frac{100}{a}$ (C) $\frac{a^2}{100}$ (D) $\frac{100}{a^2}$ (E) 100*a*

7. On a certain Russian-American committee, $\frac{2}{3}$ of the members are men, and $\frac{3}{8}$ of the men are Americans. If $\frac{3}{5}$ of the committee members are Russian, what fraction of the members are American women?

(A) $\frac{3}{20}$ (B) $\frac{11}{60}$ (C) $\frac{1}{4}$ (D) $\frac{2}{5}$ (E) $\frac{5}{12}$

8. Nadia will be *x* years old *y* years from now. How old was she *z* years ago?

(A) *x* + *y* + *z* (B) *x* + *y* − *z* (C) *x* − *y* − *z*
(D) *y* − *x* − *z* (E) *z* − *y* − *x*

9. If 12*a* + 3*b* = 1 and 7*b* − 2*a* = 9, what is the average (arithmetic mean) of *a* and *b*?

(A) 0.1 (B) 0.5 (C) 1 (D) 2.5 (E) 5

10. If *x*% of *y* is 10, what is *y*?

(A) $\frac{10}{x}$ (B) $\frac{100}{x}$ (C) $\frac{1000}{x}$ (D) $\frac{x}{100}$ (E) $\frac{x}{10}$

Answer Key

1. **B**	3. **A**	5. **C**	7. **A**	9. **B**
2. **B**	4. **C**	6. **B**	8. **C**	10. **C**

1. B. Use TACTIC 10: backsolve, starting with C. If Judy is now 20, Adam is 10; 6 years ago, they would have been 14 and 4, which is less than 5 times as much. Eliminate C, D, and E, and try a smaller value. If Judy is now **16**, Adam is 8; 6 years ago, they would have been 10 and 2. That's it; 10 is 5 times 2.

2. B. Use TACTIC 11. Pick simple values for *a*, *b*, and *c*. Let *a* = 1, *b* = 2, and *c* = 3. Then *b* − *a* = 1. Only **2*b* − *c*** is equal to 1.

3. A. Use TACTIC 11: replaces variables with numbers. If 2 widgets cost 10 cents, then widgets cost 5 cents each; and for 3 dollars, you can get 60 widgets. Which of the choices equals 60 when $w = 2$, $c = 10$, and $d = 3$?

Only $\dfrac{100dw}{c}$.

4. C. Use Tactic 12: choose appropriate numbers. Since 120% of 80 = 80% of 120, let $a = 80$ and $b = 120$. Then $a + b = 200$, and $200 \div 80 = \mathbf{2.5}$.

5. C. If you don't know how to solve this, you must use TACTIC 14: eliminate the absurd choices and guess. Which choices are absurd? Certainly, A and B, both of which are negative. Also, since choice D is about 94, which is much more than half the area of the square, it is much too large. Guess between C (about 43) and E (about 50). If you remember that the way to find shaded areas is to subtract, guess C: $\mathbf{144 - 32\pi}$.

6. B. Use TACTICS 11 and 12: replace a by a number, and use 100 since the problem involves percents.

$$100 \div (100\% \text{ of } 100) = 100 \div 100 = 1.$$

Test each choice; which one equals 1 when

$a = 100$? A and B: $\dfrac{100}{100} = 1$. Eliminate C, D,

and E; and test A and B with another value, 50, for a:

$$50 \div (50\% \text{ of } 50) = 50 \div (25) = 2.$$

Now, only $\dfrac{100}{a}$, works: $\dfrac{100}{50} = 2$.

7. A. Use TACTIC 12: choose appropriate numbers. The LCM of all the denominators is 120, so assume that the committee has 120 members. Then there are

$\dfrac{2}{3} \times 120 = 80$ men and 40 women. Of the 80 men, 30 $\left(\dfrac{3}{8} \times 80\right)$ are

American. Since there are 72 $\left(\dfrac{3}{5} \times 120\right)$ Russians, there are $120 - 72 = 48$

Americans, of whom 30 are men, so the other 18 are women. Finally, the

fraction of American women is $\dfrac{18}{120} = \dfrac{3}{20}$.

8. C. Use TACTIC 11: replace x, y, and z with easy-to-use numbers.

Assume Nadia will be 10 in 2 years. How old was she 3 years ago? If she will be 10 in 2 years, she is 8 now and 3 years ago was 5. Which of the choices equals 5 when $x = 10$, $y = 2$, and $z = 3$? Only $\boldsymbol{x - y - z}$.

9. B. Use TACTIC 13, and add the two equations:

$$10a + 10b = 10 \Rightarrow a + b = 1 \Rightarrow \frac{a+b}{2} = \frac{1}{2} \text{ or } \textbf{0.5}.$$

10. C. Use TACTICS 11 and 12. Since 100% of 10 is 10, let $x = 100$ and $y = 10$. When $x = 100$, choices C and E are each 10. Eliminate A, B, and D, and try some other numbers: 50% of 20 is 10. Of C and E, only $\frac{1000}{x} = 20$ when $x = 50$.

THE QUANTITATIVE COMPARISON QUESTION

In the second mathematics section on the PSAT, the first 12 questions are quantitative comparisons, which, like the multiple-choice questions, proceed from easy to difficult. Since you probably have never seen questions of this type, you are not likely to be familiar with the various strategies for answering them. In this section you will learn the most important tactics. After you master them, you will see that quantitative comparisons are the easiest of the three types of mathematics questions, and you will wish that there were more than just 12 of them.

On the first page of the PSAT section containing the quantitative comparison questions, you will find directions for answering quantitative comparisons and three examples, similar to those shown on the next page.

Before learning the different strategies for answering this type of question, let's clarify the directions. In quantitative comparison questions there are two quantities, one in Column A and one in Column B, and it is your job to compare them. For these questions there are **only four possible answers:** A, B, C, and D. E is **never** the answer to a quantitative comparison question.

The correct answer to a quantitative comparison question is

A if the quantity in Column A is greater **all the time, no matter what;**
B if the quantity in Column B is greater **all the time, no matter what;**
C if the two quantities are equal **all the time, no matter what;**
D if the relationship cannot be determined from the information given; that is, **if the answer is not A, B, or C.**

Directions for Quantitative Comparison Questions

In each of questions 1–15, two quantities appear in boxes: one in Column A and one in Column B. You must compare them. The correct answer to a question is

A   if the quantity in Column A is greater;
B   if the quantity in Column B is greater;
C   if the two quantities are equal;
D   if it is impossible to determine which quantity is greater.

Notes:
- *The correct answer is __never__ E.*
- Sometimes information about one or both of the quantities is centered above the two boxes.
- If the same symbol appears in both columns, it represents the same thing each time.
- All variables represent real numbers.

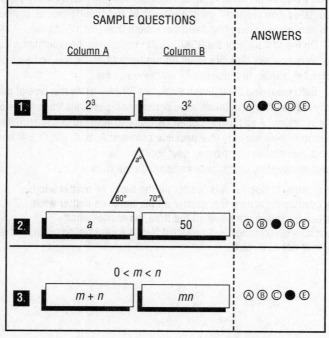

Therefore, *if you can find a single instance* in which the quantity in Column A is greater than the quantity in Column B, you can immediately eliminate two choices: B and C. The answer could be B only if the quantity in Column B were greater **all the time**; but you know of one instance when it isn't. Similarly, the quantities are not equal **all the time**, so the answer can't be C. The correct answer, therefore, *must be* A or D. Even if this is the hardest quantitative comparison on the test, and you have no idea of what to do next, you've narrowed down the correct answer to one of two choices, and you *must* guess. If it turns out that the quantity in Column A *is* greater all the time, then A is the answer; if it isn't, then the answer is D.

Helpful Hint

Right now, memorize the instructions given above for answering quantitative comparison questions. *When you take the PSAT, do not spend even one second reading the directions or looking at the sample problems.*

Testing Tactics

15. Replace Variables with Numbers.

Many problems that are hard to analyze because they contain variables become easy to solve when the variables are replaced by simple numbers.

TACTIC 15 is the most important tactic for quantitative comparison questions. *Be sure to master it!*

Most quantitative comparison questions contain variables. When those variables are replaced by simple numbers such as 0 and 1, the quantities in the two columns become much easier to compare.

Column A	Column B

Example 29.

$$a < b < c < d$$

ab	cd

Solution.

- Replace *a*, *b*, *c*, and *d* with easy-to-use numbers that satisfy the condition $a < b < c < d$: for example, $a = 1$, $b = 2$, $c = 5$, $d = 10$.
- Evaluate the two columns: $ab = (1)(2) = 2$, and $cd = (5)(10) = 50$.
- Therefore, *in this case*, the quantity in Column B is greater.
- Does that mean that B is the correct answer? Not necessarily. The quantity in Column B is greater this time, but will it be greater **every single time, no matter what?**
- What it does mean is that neither A nor C could possibly be the answer: Column A can't be greater **every single time, no matter what,** because it isn't greater *this* time; and the columns aren't equal **every single time, no matter what,** because they aren't equal *this* time.

The correct answer, therefore, is either B or D; and in the few seconds that it took you to plug in 1, 2, 5, and 10 for *a*, *b*, *c*, and *d*, you were able to eliminate two of the four choices. If you could do nothing else, you should now guess.

But, of course, *you can and will do something else*. You will try some other numbers. But *which* numbers? Since the first numbers you chose were positive, try some negative numbers this time.

Let $a = -5$, $b = -3$, $c = -2$, and $d = -1$.

- Evaluate: $ab = (-5)(-3) = 15$ and $cd = (-2)(-1) = 2$.
- Therefore, *in this case*, the quantity in Column A is greater.
- Column B is *not* greater all the time. B is *not* the correct answer.
- The answer is **D**.

Here are some guidelines for deciding which numbers to use when applying TACTIC 15.

1. **The very best numbers to use first are 1, 0, and –1.**

2. **Often, fractions between 0 and 1 are useful.**

3. **Occasionally, "large" numbers such as 10 or 100 can be used.**

4. **If there is more than one variable, it is permissible to replace each with the same number.**

5. **If a variable appears more than once in a problem, it must be replaced by the same number each time.**

6. **Do not impose any conditions not specifically stated.** In particular, do not assume that variables must represent integers. For example, 3 is not the only number that satisfies $2 < x < 4$ (2.1, 3.95, and π all work). The expression $a < b < c < d$ does not mean that *a*, *b*, *c*, *d* are *integers*, let alone *consecutive* integers (which is why we didn't choose 1, 2, 3, and 4 in Example 29), nor does it mean that any or all of these variables are *positive*.

When you replace the variables in a quantitative comparison question with numbers, remember:

If the value in Column A is ever greater:
   eliminate B and C—the answer must be A or D.
If the value in Column B is ever greater:
   eliminate A and C—the answer must be B or D.
If the two columns are ever equal:
   eliminate A and B—the answer must be C or D.

Practice applying TACTIC 15 to these examples.

Column A	Column B

Example 30.

$$m > 0 \text{ and } m \neq 1$$

m^2	m^3

Column A	Column B

Example 31.

$w + 10$	$w - 11$

Solution 30. Use TACTIC 15. Replace m with numbers satisfying $m > 0$ and $m \neq 1$.

	Column A	Column B	Compare	Eliminate
Let $m = 2$.	$2^2 = 4$	$2^3 = 8$	B is greater.	A and C
Let $m = \dfrac{1}{2}$.	$\left(\dfrac{1}{2}\right)^2 = \dfrac{1}{4}$	$\left(\dfrac{1}{2}\right)^3 = \dfrac{1}{8}$	A is greater.	B

The answer is **D**.

Solution 31. Use TACTIC 15. There are no restrictions on w, so use the best numbers: 1, 0, –1.

	Column A	Column B	Compare	Eliminate
Let $w = 1$.	$1 + 10 = 11$	$1 - 11 = -10$	A is greater.	B and C
Let $w = 0$.	$0 + 10 = 10$	$0 - 11 = -11$	A is greater.	
Let $w = -1$.	$-1 + 10 = 9$	$-1 - 11 = -12$	A is greater.	

Guess **A**. We let w be a positive number, a negative number, and 0. Each time Column A was greater. That's not proof, but it justifies an educated guess.

16. Choose an Appropriate Number.

This is just like TACTIC 15. We are replacing a variable with a number, but the variable isn't mentioned in the problem.

Column A	Column B

Example 32.

Every band member is either 15, 16, or 17 years old.
One-third of the band members are 16, and
twice as many band members are 16 as 15.

The number of 17-year-old band members	The total number of 15- and 16-year-old band members

Solution: If the first sentence of Example 32 had been "There are n students in the school band, all of whom are 15, 16, or 17 years old," the problem would have been identical to this one. Using TACTIC 15, you could have replaced n with an easy-to-use number, such as 6, and solved:

$\frac{1}{3}(6) = 2$ are 16 years old; then 1 is 15, and the remaining 3 are 17. The answer is **C**.

Example 33.

Abe, Ben, and Cal divided a cash prize.

Abe took 50% of the money and spent $\frac{3}{5}$ of what he took.

Ben took 40% of the money and spent $\frac{3}{4}$ of what he took.

The amount that Abe spent	The amount that Ben spent

Solution. Use TACTIC 16. Assume the prize was $100. Then Abe took $50 and spent

$\frac{3}{\overset{}{\underset{1}{8}}}(\$\overset{10}{50}) = \$30$. Ben took $40 and spent $\frac{3}{\overset{}{\underset{1}{4}}}(\$\overset{10}{40}) = \$30$.

The answer is **C**.

17. Make the Problem Easier: Do the Same Thing to Each Column.

In solving a quantitative comparison problem, you can always add the same quantity to each column or subtract the same quantity from each column. You can multiply or divide each side of an equation or inequality by the same quantity, *but in the case of _inequalities_ you can do this only if the quantity is positive.* Since you don't know whether the columns are equal or unequal, you cannot multiply or divide by a variable *unless you know that it is positive.* If the quantities in each column are positive, you may square them or take their square roots.

Here are three examples on which to practice TACTIC 17.

Column A	Column B

Example 34.

$\frac{1}{3} + \frac{1}{4} + \frac{1}{9}$	$\frac{1}{9} + \frac{1}{3} + \frac{1}{5}$

Example 35.

a is a negative number

a^2	$-a^2$

Column A   Column B

Example 36.

| $\dfrac{\sqrt{20}}{2}$ | $\dfrac{5}{\sqrt{5}}$ |

Column A   Column B

Solution 34.

Cancel (subtract)
$\frac{1}{3}$ and $\frac{1}{9}$ from

each column: $\dfrac{\cancel{1}}{3} + \dfrac{1}{4} + \dfrac{\cancel{1}}{9}$ $\dfrac{\cancel{1}}{9} + \dfrac{\cancel{1}}{3} + \dfrac{1}{5}$

Since $\frac{1}{4} > \frac{1}{5}$, the answer is **A**.

Solution 35.
Add a^2 to
each column: $a^2 + a^2 = 2a^2$ $-a^2 + a^2 = 0$

Since a is negative, $2a^2$ is positive. The answer is **A**.

Solution 36.
Square each column: $\left(\dfrac{\sqrt{20}}{2}\right)^2 = \dfrac{20}{4} = 5$ $\left(\dfrac{5}{\sqrt{5}}\right)^2 = \dfrac{25}{5} = 5$

The answer is **C**.

18. Ask "Could They Be Equal?" and "Must They Be Equal?"

TACTIC 18 is most useful when one column contains a variable and the other contains a number. In this situation ask yourself, "Could they be equal?" If the answer is "yes," eliminate A and B, and then ask, "Must they be equal?" If the second answer is "yes," then C is correct; if the second answer is "no," then choose D. When the answer to "Could they be equal?" is "no," we usually know right away what the correct answer is.

Let's look at a few examples:

Column A   Column B

Example 37.

The sides of a triangle are 3, 4, and x.

| x | 5 |

Column A   Column B

Example 38.

Bank A has 10 tellers and bank B has 20 tellers.
Each bank has more female tellers than male tellers.

The number of female tellers at bank A	The number of female tellers at bank B

Example 39.

The perimeter of a rectangle whose area is 21	20

Solution 37. Could they be equal? Could $x = 5$? Of course. That's the all-important 3-4-5 right triangle. Eliminate A and B. Must they be equal? Must $x = 5$? The answer is "no." Actually, x can be any number satisfying the inequality $1 < x < 7$.

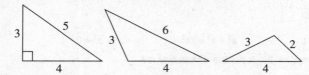

Solution 38. Could they be equal? Could the number of female tellers be the same in both banks? No. More than half (i.e., more than 10) of bank B's 20 tellers are female, but bank A has only 10 tellers in all. The answer is **B**.

Solution 39. Could they be equal? Could a rectangle whose area is 21 have a perimeter of 20? Yes, if its length is 7 and its width is 3: $7 + 3 + 7 + 3 = 20$. Eliminate A and B. Must they be equal? If you're *not* sure, guess between C and D.

There are other possibilities—lots of them; here are a 7×3 rectangle and a few others:

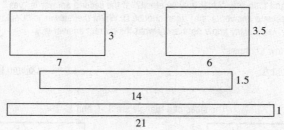

19. Don't Calculate: Compare.

Avoid unnecessary calculations. You don't have to determine the exact values of the quantities in Columns A and B; you just have to compare them.

These are problems on which poor test-takers use their calculators and good test-takers think! Practicing TACTIC 19 will help you become a good test-taker.

Now, test your understanding of TACTIC 19 by solving these problems.

Column A   Column B

Example 40.

| The number of years from 1492 to 1929 | | The number of years from 1429 to 1992 |

Example 41.

| $43^2 + 27^2$ | | $(43 + 27)^2$ |

Example 42.

Howie earned a 75 on each of his first three math tests
and an 80 on the fourth and fifth tests.

| Howie's average after four tests. | | Howie's average after five tests. |

Solution 40. The subtraction is easy enough, but why do it? The dates in Column **B** start earlier and end later. Clearly, they span more years. You don't need to know how many years. The answer is **B**.

Solution 41. For *any* positive numbers a and b, $(a + b)^2 > a^2 + b^2$. You should do the calculations only if you don't know this fact. The answer is **B**.

Solution 42. Remember that you want to know which average is higher, *not* what the averages are. After four tests Howie's average is clearly less than 80, so an 80 on the fifth test had to *raise* his average. The answer is **B**.

Practice Exercises

Answers given on pages 137–138.

<u>Column A</u>　　　　　　　　　　　　　　　　　<u>Column B</u>

$a < 0$

1.　$4a$　　　　　　　　　　　　　　　a^4

$x > 0$

2.　$10x$　　　　　　　　　　　　　　$\dfrac{10}{x}$

$ab < 0$

3.　$(a + b)^2$　　　　　　　　　　　　$a^2 + b^2$

4.　$99 + 299 + 499$　　　　　　　　　$103 + 305 + 507$

5.　The area of a circle whose radius is 17　　　　The area of a circle whose diameter is 35

Line ℓ goes through (1,1) and (5,2).
Line m is perpendicular to ℓ.

6.　The slope of line ℓ　　　　　　　　The slope of line m

---

x, y, and z are three consecutive integers
between 300 and 400.

7.　The average (arithmetic mean) of x and z　　　　The average (arithmetic mean) of x, y, and z

---

$x + y = 5$
$y - x = -5$

8.　y　　　　　　　　　　　　　　　0

Stores A and B sell the same television set.
The regular price at store A is 10% less
than the regular price at store B.

9.　The price of the television set when store A has a 10% off sale　　　　The price of the television set when store B has a 20% off sale

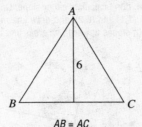

$AB = AC$

<u>Note:</u> Figure not drawn to scale

10. | The area of $\triangle ABC$ | | 3 |

Answer Key

1. **B**	3. **B**	5. **B**	7. **C**	9. **A**
2. **D**	4. **B**	6. **A**	8. **C**	10. **D**

Answer Explanations

1. B. Use TACTIC 15. Replace a with numbers satisfying $a < 0$.

	Column A	Column B	Compare	Eliminate
Let $a = -1$.	$4(-1) = -4$	$(-1)^4 = 1$	B is greater.	A and C
Let $a = -2$.	$4(-2) = -8$	$(-2)^4 = 16$	B is greater.	

Both times, Column B was greater: choose B.

2. D. Use TACTIC 15. When $x = 1$, the columns are equal; when $x = 2$, they aren't.

3. B. Use TACTIC 17.

	Column A	Column B
Expand Column A:	$(a + b)^2 =$	
	$a^2 + 2ab + b^2$	$a^2 + b^2$
Subtract $a^2 + b^2$ from each column:	$2ab$	0

Since it is given that $ab < 0$, then $2ab < 0$.

4. B. This can be solved in less than 30 seconds with a calculator, but in only 5 seconds without one! Use TACTIC 19: don't calculate; compare. Each of the three numbers in Column B is greater than the corresponding number in Column A. Column B is greater.

5. B. Again, use TACTIC 19: don't calculate the two areas; compare them. The circle in Column A has a radius of 17, and so its diameter is 34. Since the circle in Column B has a larger diameter, its area is greater.

6. **A.**   Again, use TACTIC 19: don't calculate either slope. Quickly, make a rough sketch of line ℓ, going through (1,1) and (5,2), and draw line m perpendicular to it. Line ℓ has a positive slope (it slopes upward), whereas line m has a negative slope. Column A is greater.

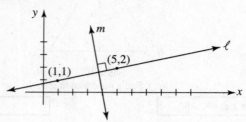

7. **C.**   Use TACTIC 15: replace x, y, and z with three consecutive integers between 300 and 400—say, 318, 319, and 320, and use your calculator to find the averages.

Column A: $\dfrac{318+320}{2} = \dfrac{638}{2} = 319.$

Column B: $\dfrac{318+319+320}{3} = \dfrac{957}{3} = 319.$

8. **C.**   Use TACTIC 18. Could $y = 0$? In each equation, if $y = 0$, then $x = 5$, so y can equal 0. Eliminate A and B, and either guess between C and D or try to continue. Must $y = 0$? Yes; when you have two equations in two variables, there is only one solution, so nothing else is possible.

9. **A.**   Use TACTIC 16: choose an appropriate number. *The best number to use in percent problems is 100*, so assume that the regular price of the television in store B is 100 (the units don't matter). Since 10% of 100 is 10, the regular price in store A is $100 - 10 = 90$.
Column A: 10% of 90 is 9, so the sale price in store A is $90 - 9 = 81$.
Column B: 20% of 100 is 20, so the sale price in store B is $100 - 20 = 80$.

10. **D.**   Use TACTIC 18. Could the area of $\triangle ABC = 3$? Since the height is 6, the area would be 3 only if the base were 1: $\frac{1}{2}(1)(6) = 3$. Could $BC = 1$? Sure (see the figure). Must the base be 1? Of course not. Neither column is *always* greater, and the columns are not *always* equal (D).

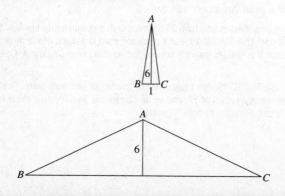

THE GRID-IN QUESTION

On the PSAT, the section that contains the 12 quantitative comparisons has 8 additional questions for which no choices are given. These are the grid-in problems, which represent the type of question with which you are most familiar—you solve a problem and then write the answer on your answer sheet. The only difference is that, on the PSAT, you must enter the answer on a special grid that can be read by a computer.

Your answer sheet will have 8 grids, one for each question. Each one will look like the grid below. After solving a problem, the first step is to write the answer in the four boxes at the top of the grid. You then blacken the appropriate oval under each box. For example, if your answer to a question is 2450, you write 2450 at the top of the grid, one digit in each box, and then in each column blacken the oval that contains the number you wrote at the top of the column. This is not difficult; but there are some special rules concerning grid-in questions, so let's go over them before you practice gridding in some numbers.

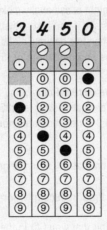

1. The only symbols that appear in the grid are the digits 0 to 9, a decimal point, and a slash (/), used to write fractions. Keep in mind that, since there is no negative sign, *the answer to every grid-in question is a positive number or zero*.

2. Be aware that you will receive credit for a correct answer no matter where you grid it. For example, the answer 17 could be gridded in any of three positions:

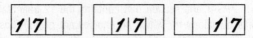

Nevertheless, we suggest that you consistently **write all your answers** the way numbers are usually displayed—**to the right, with blank spaces at the left**.

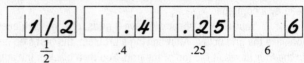

3. **Never round off your answers**. If a decimal answer will fit in the grid and you round it off, your answer will be marked wrong. For example, if the answer is .148 and you correctly round it off to the nearest hundredth and enter .15, you will receive *no credit*. If a decimal answer will not fit in the grid, enter a decimal point in the first column, followed by the first three digits. For example, if your answer is 0.454545..., enter it as .454. You would receive credit if you rounded it to .455, but don't. You might occasionally make a mistake in rounding, whereas you'll *never* make a mistake if you just copy the first three digits. *Note:* If the correct answer has more than two decimal digits, *you must use all four columns of the grid*. You will receive *no credit* for .4 or .5 or .45. (These answers are not accurate enough.)

4. **Never write a 0 before the decimal point.** The first column of the grid doesn't even have a 0 in it. If the correct answer is 0.3333..., you must grid it as .333. You can't grid 0.33, and 0.3 is not accurate enough.

5. **Never reduce fractions**.

   • If your answer is a fraction that will fit in the grid, such as $\frac{2}{3}$ or $\frac{4}{18}$ or $\frac{6}{34}$, just

   enter it. Don't waste time reducing it or converting it to a decimal.

   • If your answer is a fraction that won't fit in the grid, do not attempt to reduce

   it; use your calculator to *convert it to a decimal*. For example, $\frac{24}{65}$ won't fit in a

   grid—it would require five spaces: <u>2 4 / 6 5</u>. Don't waste even a few seconds

   trying to reduce it; just divide on your calculator, and enter .369. Unlike $\frac{24}{65}$, the

   fraction $\frac{24}{64}$ can be reduced—to $\frac{12}{32}$, which doesn't help, or to $\frac{6}{16}$ or $\frac{3}{8}$, both of

   which could be entered. *Don't do it!* Reducing a fraction takes time, and you might make a mistake. You won't make a mistake if you just use your calculator: $24 \div 64 = .375$.

6. ***Be aware that you can never enter a mixed number***. If your answer is $2\frac{1}{2}$, you

   cannot leave a space and enter your answer as 2 1/2. Also, if you enter

   $\boxed{\textbf{2 1 / 2}}$, the machine will read it as $\frac{21}{2}$ and mark it wrong. You must

   enter $2\frac{1}{2}$ as the improper fraction $\frac{5}{2}$ or as the decimal 2.5.

7. Since full credit is given for any equivalent answer, use these guidelines to ***enter***

   your answer in the simplest way. If your answer is $\frac{6}{9}$, you should enter 6/9.

   (However, credit would be given for any of the following: 2/3, 4/6, 8/12, .666, .667.)

8. Sometimes grid-in questions have more than one correct answer. On these questions, ***grid in only one of the acceptable answers***. For example, if a question asked for a positive number less than 100 that was divisible by both 5 and 7, you could enter *either* 35 *or* 70, but not both. Similarly, if a question asked for a number between $\frac{3}{7}$ and $\frac{5}{9}$, you could enter any *one* of hundreds

   of possibilities: fractions such as $\frac{1}{2}$ and $\frac{4}{9}$ or *any* decimal between

   .429 and .554—.43 or .499 or .52, for example.

9. ***Keep in mind that there is no penalty for a wrong answer to a grid-in question***. Therefore, you might as well guess, even if you have no idea what to do. As you will see shortly, there are some strategies for making intelligent guesses.

10. Be sure to ***grid every answer very carefully***. The computer does not read what you have written in the boxes; it reads only the answer in the grid. If the correct answer to a question is 100 and you write 100 in the boxes, but accidentally grid in 200, you get *no* credit.

11. If you know that the answer to a question is 100, can you just grid it in and not bother writing it on top? Yes, you will get full credit, and so some PSAT guides recommend that you don't waste time writing the answer. This is terrible advice. Instead, **write each answer in the boxes**. It takes less than 2 seconds per answer to do this, and it definitely cuts down on careless errors in gridding. More important, if you go back to check your work, it is much easier to read what's in the boxes on top than what's in the grid.

12. Be aware that the smallest number that can be gridded is 0; the largest is 9999. No number greater than 100 can have a decimal point. The largest number less than 100 that can be gridded is 99.9; the smallest number greater than 100 that can be gridded is 101.

Testing Tactics

20. Backsolve.

If you think of a grid-in problem as a multiple-choice question in which the choices accidentally got erased, you can still use TACTIC 10: test the choices. You just have to make up the choices as you go.

Example 43.

If the average (arithmetic mean) of 2, 7, and x is 12, what is the value of x?

Solution. You could start with 10; but if you immediately realize that the average of 2, 7, and 10 is less than 10 (so it can't be 12), you'll try a bigger number, say 20. The average of 2, 7, and 20 is

$$\frac{2+7+20}{3} = \frac{29}{3} = 9\frac{2}{3},$$

which is too small. Try $x = 30$:

$$\frac{2+7+30}{3} = \frac{39}{3} = 13,$$

just a bit too big. Since 12 is closer to 13 than it is to $9\frac{2}{3}$, your next choice should be closer to 30 than 20, surely more than 25. Your third try might well be **27**, which works.

Example 44.

For every positive number $x \neq 20$: $\boxed{x} = 20 + x$ and $\textcircled{x} = 20 - x$.

If $\dfrac{\boxed{x}}{\textcircled{x}} = 4$, what is the value of x?

Solution. In order for $20 - x$ to be positive, x has to be less than 20.

Try $x = 15$: $\dfrac{20+15}{20-15} = \dfrac{35}{5} = 7$. That's too big.

Try $x = 10$: $\dfrac{20+10}{20-10} = \dfrac{30}{10} = 3$. That's too small.

Try $x = 12$: $\dfrac{20+12}{20-12} = \dfrac{32}{8} = 4$. That's it.

21. Choose an Appropriate Number.

This is exactly the same as TACTIC 12. The most appropriate numbers to choose are 100 for percent problems, the LCD (least common denominator) for fraction problems, and the LCM (least common multiple) of the coefficients for problems involving equations. Each of the problems discussed under TACTIC 12 could have been a grid-in, because we didn't even look at the choices until we had the correct answer.

Example 45.

During an Election Day sale, the price of every television set in a store was reduced by $33\frac{1}{3}$%. By what percent must these sale prices be raised so that the TVs now sell for their original prices? (Do not grid the % sign.)

Solution. Since this problem involves percents, you should think about using 100. But the fraction $\frac{1}{3}$ is also involved, so 300 is an even better choice. Assume the original price was $300. Since $33\frac{1}{3}$% of 300 = $\frac{1}{3}$ of 300 = 100, the sale price was $200. To restore the price to $300, it must now be raised by $100. The percent increase is

$$\frac{\text{actual increase}}{\text{original amount}} \times 100\% = \frac{100}{200} \times 100\% = \textbf{50\%}.$$

Practice Exercises   Answers given on pages 145–147.

> Directions: Enter your response to these problems on the grids on page 144.

1. For what number $b > 0$ is it true that b divided by b% of b equals b?

2. Patty has 150 coins, each of which is a dime or a quarter. If she has $27.90, how many quarters does she have?

3. A fair coin is flipped repeatedly. Each time it lands "heads," Ali gets a point, and whenever it lands "tails," Jason gets a point. The game continues until someone gets 5 points. If the score is now 4 to 3 in Ali's favor, and the probability that Ali will win the game is k times the probability that Jason will win the game, what is the value of k?

4. At a certain university, $\frac{1}{4}$ of the applicants failed to meet minimum standards and were rejected immediately. Of those who met the standards, $\frac{2}{5}$ were accepted. If 1200 applicants were accepted, how many applied?

5. More than half of the members of the Key Club are girls. If $\frac{4}{7}$ of the girls and $\frac{7}{11}$ of the boys in the Key Club attended the April meeting, what is the smallest number of members the club could have?

6. Jessica copied a column of numbers and added them. The only mistake she made was that she copied one number as 5095 instead of 5.95. If the sum she got was 8545.05, what should the answer have been?

7. Jerry spent $105 for a tool kit and a box of nails. If the tool kit cost $100 more than the nails, how many boxes of nails could be purchased for the price of the tool kit?

8. Ken is now 3 times as old as his younger sister, but in 7 years he will be only twice as old as she will be then. How old is Ken now?

9. The value of an investment increased 50% in 1992 and again in 1993. In each of 1994 and 1995 the value of the investment decreased by 50%. At the end of 1995 the value of the investment was how many times the value at the beginning of 1992?

10. How many integers between 1 and 1000 are the product of two consecutive integers?

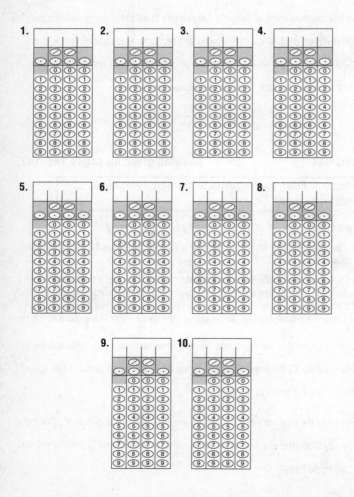

Answer Key

1. $\boxed{1\ 0}$ 2. $\boxed{8\ 6}$ 3. $\boxed{3}$ 4. $\boxed{4\ 0\ 0\ 0}$

5. $\boxed{2\ 5}$ 6. $\boxed{3\ 4\ 5\ 6}$ 7. $\boxed{4\ 1}$ 8. $\boxed{2\ 1}$

9. $\boxed{9\ /\ 1\ 6}$ or $\boxed{.\ 5\ 6\ 2}$ 10. $\boxed{3\ 1}$

Answer Explanations

1. (10) $b \div (b\% \text{ of } b) = b \div \left(\dfrac{b}{100} \times b \right) =$

$b \div \left(\dfrac{b^2}{100} \right) = b \times \dfrac{100}{b^2} = \dfrac{100}{b}.$

Since this value is to equal b, you have $\dfrac{100}{b} = b \Rightarrow b^2 = 100 \Rightarrow b = \mathbf{10}.$

2. (86)   Use TACTIC 20: backsolve. Pick an easy starting value, say $q = 100$. If this gives a value greater than \$27.90, decrease q; if it gives a value less than \$27.90, increase q.

Number of Quarters	Number of Dimes	Value
100	50	\$25.00 + \$5.00 = \$30.00
80	70	\$20.00 + \$7.00 = \$27.00
85	65	\$21.25 + \$6.50 = \$27.75
86	64	\$21.50 + \$6.40 = \$27.90

3. (3) Jason can win only if the next two flips are both tails. The probability of that

happening is $\frac{1}{2} \times \frac{1}{2} = \frac{1}{4}$. Therefore, the probability that Ali wins is $1 - \frac{1}{4} = \frac{3}{4}$.

Since $\frac{3}{4} = 3\left(\frac{1}{4}\right)$ $k = \mathbf{3}$.

4. (4000) Use TACTIC 21: choose an appropriate number. The LCD of $\frac{1}{4}$ and $\frac{2}{5}$

is 20, so *assume* that there were 20 applicants. Then $\frac{1}{4}(20) = 5$ failed to meet

the minimum standards. Of the remaining 15 applicants, $\frac{2}{5}$, or 6, were

accepted, so 6 of every 20 applicants were accepted. Set up a proportion:

$$\frac{6}{20} = \frac{1200}{x} \Rightarrow 6x = 24{,}000 \Rightarrow x = \mathbf{4000}.$$

5. (25) Since $\frac{4}{7}$ of the girls attended the meeting, the number of girls in the club must

be a multiple of 7: 7, 14, 21, ... Similarly, the number of boys in the club
must be a multiple of 11: 11, 22, ... Since there are at least 11 boys and there
are more girls than boys, there must be at least 14 girls. The smallest possible
total is 14 + 11 = **25**.

6. (3456) To get the correct sum, subtract the number Jessica added in error and add
the number she left out:
8545.05 − 5095 + 5.95 = **3456**.

7. (41) The first thing to do is to calculate the prices of the tool kit and the nails. *Be
careful*—they are *not* $100 and $5. You can get the answer algebraically or by trial
and error. If you let x = cost of the nails, then $100 + x$ = cost of the tool kit, and

$$x + (100 + x) = 105 \Rightarrow 2x + 100 = 105 \Rightarrow$$
$$2x = 5 \Rightarrow x = 2.5.$$

Then the nails cost $2.50, and the tool kit $102.50. Finally, 102.50 ÷ 2.50 = **41**.

8. (21) Use TACTIC 21. Pick a value for the sister's age—say, 2. Then Ken is 6. In
7 years, sister and brother will be 9 and 13, respectively. No good; 13 is less than
twice 9. Try a bigger number—5. Then Ken is 15, and in 7 years the two will be
12 and 22. That's closer, but still too small. Try 7. Then Ken is **21**, and in 7 years
his sister and he will be 14 and 28. That's it!

9. $\left(.562 \text{ or } \frac{9}{16}\right)$ Use TACTIC 21. Pick an easy-to-use starting value—$100, say. Then

the value of the investment at the end of each of the 4 years 1992, 1993, 1994,
1995 was $150, $225, $112.50, $56.25, so the final value was .5625 times the
initial value. Note that some initial values would lead to an answer more easily
expressed as a fraction. For example, if you start with $16, the yearly values

would be $24, $36, $18, and $9, and the answer would be $\frac{9}{16}$.

10. (31)   Use TACTIC 8. List the integers systematically: 1×2, 2×3, ... , 24×25, ...
You don't have to multiply and list the products (2, 6, 12, ... , 600, ...); you just
have to know when to stop. The largest product less than 1000 is $31 \times 32 = 992$,
so there are **31** numbers.

SUMMARY OF IMPORTANT TIPS AND TACTICS

1. Whenever you know how to answer a question directly, just do it. The tactics given in this chapter should be used only when you need them.

2. Memorize all the formulas you need to know. Even though some of them are printed on the first page of each math section, during the test you do not want to waste any time referring back to that reference material.

3. Be sure to bring a calculator, but use it only when you need it. Don't use it for simple arithmetic that you can easily do in your head.

4. Remember that no problem requires lengthy or difficult computations. If you find yourself doing a lot of arithmetic, stop and reread the question. You are probably not answering the question asked.

5. Answer every question you attempt. Even if you can't solve it, you can almost always eliminate two or more choices. Often you know that an answer must be negative, but two or three of the choices are positive, or an answer must be even, and some of the choices are odd.

6. Unless a diagram is labeled "<u>Note</u>: Figure not drawn to scale," it is perfectly accurate, and you can trust it in making an estimate.

7. When a diagram has not been provided, draw one, especially on any geometry problem.

8. If a diagram has been provided, feel free to label it, mark it up in any way, including adding line segments, if necessary.

9. Answer any question for which you can estimate the answer, even if you are not sure you are correct.

10. Don't panic when you see a strange symbol in a question, It will always be defined. Getting the correct answer just involves following the directions given in the definition.

11. When a question involves two equations, either add them or subtract them. If there are three or more, just add them.

12. Never make unwarranted assumptions. Do not assume numbers are positive or integers. If a question refers to two numbers, do not assume that they have to be different. If you know a figure has four sides, do not assume that it is a rectangle.

13. Be sure to work in consistent units. If the width and length of a rectangle are 8 inches and 2 feet, respectively, either convert the 2 feet to 24 inches or the 8 inches to two-thirds of a foot before calculating the area or perimeter.

Standard Multiple-Choice Questions

1. Whenever you answer a question by backsolving, start with Choice C.

2. When you replace variables with numbers, choose easy-to-use numbers, whether or not they are realistic.

3. Choose appropriate numbers. The best number to use in percent problems is 100. In problems involving fractions, the best number to use is the least common denominator.

4. When you have no idea how to solve a problem, eliminate all of the absurd choices and guess.

Quantitative Comparison Questions

1. There are only four possible answers to a quantitative comparison question: A, B, C, or D. E can *never* be the correct choice.

2. If the quantity in each column is a number (there are no variables), then the answer cannot be D.

3. Remember that you do not need to calculate the value of each column; you only have to compare them.

4. Replace variables with numbers. The best numbers to try are 1, 0, and −1. Occasionally, fractions between 0 and 1 and large numbers, such as 10 or 100, are useful.

5. Make the problem easier by doing the same thing to each column. You can always add the same number to each column or subtract the same number from each column. You can multiply or divide each column by the same number, if you know that the number is positive.

6. Ask "Could the columns be equal?" and "Must the columns be equal?"

Student-Produced Response (Grid-in) Questions

1. Write your answer in the four spaces at the top of the grid, and *carefully* grid in your answer below. No credit is given for a correct answer if it has been gridded improperly.

2. Remember that the answer to a grid-in question can never be negative.

3. You can never grid in a mixed number—you must convert it to an improper fraction or a decimal.

4. Never round off your answers and never reduce fractions. If a fraction can fit in the four spaces of the grid, enter it. If not, use your calculator to convert it to a decimal (by dividing) and enter a decimal point followed by the first three decimal digits.

5. When gridding a decimal, do not write a 0 before the decimal point.

6. If a question has more than one possible answer, only grid in one of them.

7. There is no penalty for wrong answers on grid-in questions, so you should grid in anything that seems reasonable, rather than leave out a question.

8 Improving Written Expression

The writing skills section on the PSAT greatly resembles the SAT II: Subject Test in Writing most students take in their senior year. You definitely want to study hard when you prepare for the writing skills section: a good score on this section of the test may make all the difference between your becoming a National Merit finalist and your coming out a runner up.

The questions test your ability to recognize clear, correct standard written English, the kind of writing your college professors will expect on the papers you write for them. You'll be expected to know basic grammar, such as subject-verb agreement, pronoun-antecedent agreement, correct verb tense, correct sentence structure, and correct diction. You'll need to know how to recognize a dangling participle and how to spot when two parts of a sentence are not clearly connected. You'll also need to know when a paragraph is (or isn't) properly developed and organized.

IDENTIFYING SENTENCE ERRORS

There are three different kinds of questions on the writing skills section of the PSAT: identifying sentence errors, improving sentences, and improving paragraphs. Almost half of them, nineteen of the thirty-nine, to be exact, are identifying sentence errors questions in which you have to find an error in the underlined section of a sentence. You do not have to correct the sentence or explain what is wrong. Here are the directions.

The sentences in this section may contain errors in grammar, usage, choice of words, or idioms. There is either just one error per sentence or the sentence is correct. Some words or phrases are underlined and lettered; everything else in the sentence is correct.

If an underlined word or phrase is incorrect, choose that letter; if the sentence is correct, select <u>No error</u>. Then blacken the appropriate space on your Answer Sheet.

EXAMPLE:

The fields have soil <u>so rich that</u> corn
A

<u>growing here</u> commonly <u>had stood</u> more
B   C

than six feet <u>tall</u>. <u>No error</u>
D   E

SAMPLE ANSWER:

Ⓐ Ⓑ ● Ⓓ Ⓔ

Tips For Handling Identifying Sentence Error Questions

1. Remember that the error, if there is one, must be in the underlined part of the sentence. You don't have to worry about improvements that could be made in the rest of the sentence. For example, if you have a sentence in which the subject is plural and the verb is singular, you could call either one the error. But if only the verb is underlined, the error for that sentence is the verb.

2. Use your ear for the language. Remember, you don't have to name the error, or be able to explain why it is wrong. All you have to do is recognize that something *is* wrong. On the early, easy questions in the set, if a word or phrase sounds wrong to you, it probably is, even if you don't know why.

3. Look first for the most common errors. Most of the sentences will have errors. If you are having trouble finding mistakes, check for some of the more common ones: subject-verb agreement, pronoun-antecedent problems, misuse of adjectives and adverbs, dangling modifiers. But look for errors only in the underlined parts of the sentence.

4. Remember that not every sentence contains an error. Ten to twenty percent of the time, the sentence is correct as it stands. Do not get so caught up in hunting for errors that you start seeing errors that aren't there. If no obvious errors strike your eye and the sentence sounds natural to your ear, go with Choice E: No error.

EXAMPLE 1

Mr. Brown <u>is</u> one of the commuters who <u>takes</u> the 7:30 train <u>from</u> Brooktown
      A   B   C
<u>every</u> morning. <u>No error</u>
  D   E

Since *who* refers to *commuters*, it is plural, and needs a plural verb. Therefore, the error is Choice B. If you were writing this sentence yourself, you could correct it in any number of other ways. You could say, "Mr. Brown is a commuter who takes . . ." or "Mr. Brown, a commuter, takes . . ." or "Mr. Brown, who is one of the commuters, takes . . ." However, the actual question doesn't offer you any of these possibilities. You have to choose from the underlined choices. Don't waste your time considering other ways to fix the sentence.

EXAMPLE 2

See if you ear helps you with this question.

In my history class I learned why the American colonies opposed the British, how
     A   B   C
they organized the militia, and the work of the Continental Congress. No error
                                       D   E

The last part of this sentence probably sounds funny to you—awkward, strange, wooden. You may not know exactly what it is, but something sounds wrong here. If you followed your instincts and chose Choice D as the error, you would be right. The error is a lack of parallel structure. The sentence is listing three things you learned, and they should all be in the same form. Your ear expects the pattern to be the same. Since the first two items listed are clauses, the third should be too: "In my history class I learned why the American colonies opposed the British, how they organized the militia, and how the Continental Congress worked."

EXAMPLE 3

Marilyn and I ran as fast as we could, but we missed our train, which made us late
              A   B   C   D
for work. No error
        E

Imagine that you have this sentence, and you can't see what is wrong with it. Start at the beginning and check each answer choice. *I* is part of the subject, so it is the right case: after all, you wouldn't say "Me ran fast." *Fast* can be an adverb, so it is being used correctly here. *Which* is a pronoun, and needs a noun for its antecedent. The only available noun is *train*, but that doesn't make sense (the train didn't make us late—*missing* the train made us late.) So there is your error, Choice C.

Once you have checked each answer choice, if you still can't find an error, choose Choice E, "No error." A certain number of questions have no errors.

IMPROVING SENTENCES

The next most numerous set of questions in this section involves spotting the form of a sentence that works best. In these improving sentence questions, you will be presented with five different versions of the same sentence; you must choose the best one. Here are the directions:

Some or all parts of the following sentences are underlined. The first answer choice, (A), simply repeats the underlined part of the sentence. The other four choices present four alternate ways to phrase the underlined part. Select the answer that produces the most effective sentence, one that is clear and exact, and blacken the appropriate space on your answer sheet. In selecting your choice, be sure that it is standard written English, and that it expresses the meaning of the original sentence.

EXAMPLE:

The first biography of author Eudora Welty came out in 1998
<u>and she was eighty-nine years old at the time.</u>

- (A) and she was eighty-nine years old at the time
- (B) at the time when she was eighty-nine
- (C) upon becoming an eighty-nine year old
- (D) when she was eighty-nine
- (E) at the age of eighty-nine years old

SAMPLE ANSWER: Ⓐ Ⓑ Ⓒ ● Ⓔ

Tips For Handling Improving Sentence Questions

1. **If you spot an error in the underlined section, eliminate any answer that repeats it.** If something in the underlined section of a sentence correction question strikes you as an obvious error, you can immediately ignore any answer choices that repeat it. Remember, you still don't have to be able to explain what is wrong. You just need to find a correct equivalent. If the error you found in the underlined section is absent from more than one of the answer choices, look over those choices again to see if they add any new errors.

2. If you don't spot the error in the underlined section, look at the answer choices to see what is changed. Sometimes it's hard to spot what's wrong with the underlined section in a sentence correction question. When that happens, turn to the answer choices. Find the changes in the answers. The changes will tell you what kind of error is being tested. When you substitute the answer choices in the original sentence, ask yourself which of these choices makes the sentence seem clearest to you. That may well be the correct answer choice.

3. Make sure that all parts of the sentence are logically connected. Not all parts of a sentence are created equal. Some parts should be subordinated to the rest, connected with subordinating conjunctions or relative pronouns, not just added on with *and*. Overuse of *and* frequently makes sentences sound babyish. Compare "We had dinner at the Hard Rock Cafe, and we went to a concert" with "After we had dinner at the Hard Rock Cafe, we went to a concert."

4. Make sure that all parts of a sentence given in a series are similar in form. If they are not, the sentence suffers from a lack of parallel structure. The sentence "I'm taking classes in algebra, history, and how to speak French" lacks parallel structure. *Algebra* and *history* are nouns, names of subjects. The third subject should also be a noun: *conversational French*.

5. Pay particular attention to the shorter answer choices. (This tactic also applies to certain paragraph correction questions.) Good prose is economical. Often the correct answer choice will be the shortest, most direct way of making a point. If you spot no grammatical errors or errors in logic in a concise answer choice, it may well be right.

EXAMPLE 1

Being as I had studied for the test with a tutor, I was confident.

(A) Being as I had studied for the test
(B) Being as I studied for the test
(C) Since I studied for the test
(D) Since I had studied for the test
(E) Because I studied for the test

Since you immediately recognize that *Being as* is not acceptable as a conjunction in standard written English, you can eliminate Choices A and B right away. But you also know that both *Since* and *Because* are perfectly acceptable conjunctions, so you have to look more closely at Choices C, D, and E. The only other changes these choices make are in the tense of the verb. Since the studying occurred before the taking of the test, the past perfect tense, *had studied*, is correct, so the answer is Choice D. Even if you hadn't known that, you could have figured it out. Since *Because* and *Since* are both acceptable conjunctions, and since Choices C and E both use the same verb, *studied,* in the simple past tense, those two choices must be wrong. Otherwise, they would both be right, and the PSAT doesn't have questions with two right answers.

EXAMPLE 2

Even the play's most minor characters work together with extraordinary skill, their interplay creates a moving theatrical experience.

(A) their interplay creates a moving theatrical experience
(B) a moving theatrical experience is created by their interplay
(C) and their interplay creates a moving theatrical experience
(D) and a moving theatrical experience being the creation of their interplay
(E) with their interplay they create a moving theatrical experience

Look at the underlined section of the sentence. Nothing seems wrong with it. It could stand on its own as an independent sentence: *Their interplay creates a moving theatrical experience.* Choices B and E are similar to it, for both could stand as independent sentences. Choices C and D, however, are not independent sentences; both begin with the linking word *and.* The error needing correction here is the common comma splice, in which two sentences are carelessly linked with only a comma. Choice C corrects this error in the simplest way possible, adding the word *and* to tie these sentences together.

EXAMPLE 3

The rock star always had enthusiastic fans and they loved him.

(A) and they loved him
(B) and they loving him
(C) what loved him
(D) who loved him
(E) which loved him

The original version of this sentence doesn't have any grammatical errors, but it is a poor sentence because it doesn't connect its two clauses logically. The second clause ("and they loved him") is merely adding information about the fans, so it should be turned into an adjective clause, introduced by a relative pronoun. Choices D and E both seem to fit, but you know that *which* should never be used to refer to people, so Choice D is obviously the correct answer.

EXAMPLE 4

> In this chapter we'll analyze both types of questions, <u>suggest useful techniques for tackling them, providing some sample items for you to try</u>.

(A) suggest useful techniques for tackling them, providing some sample items for you to try

(B) suggest useful techniques for tackling them, providing some sample items which you can try

(C) suggest useful tactics for tackling them, and provide some sample items for you to try

(D) and suggest useful techniques for tackling them by providing some sample items for you to try

(E) having suggested useful techniques for tackling them and provided some sample items for you to try

To answer questions like this correctly, you must pay particular attention to what the sentence means. You must first decide whether *analyzing, suggesting,* and *providing* are logically equal in importance here. Since they are—all are activities that "we" will do—they should be given equal emphasis. Only Choice C provides the proper parallel structure.

EXAMPLE 5

> The turning point in the battle of Waterloo probably was <u>Blucher, who was arriving</u> in time to save the day.

(A) Blucher, who was arriving

(B) Blucher, in that he arrived

(C) Blucher's arrival

(D) when Blucher was arriving

(E) that Blucher had arrived

Which answer choice uses the fewest words? Choice C, *Blucher's arrival.* It also happens to be the right answer.

Choice C is both concise in style and correct in grammar. Look back at the original sentence. Strip it of its modifiers, and what is left? "The turning point . . . was Blucher." A turning point is not a person; it is a *thing.* The turning point in the battle was not Blucher, but Blucher's *action,* the thing he did. The correct answer is Choice C, *Blucher's arrival.* Pay particular attention to such concise answer choices. If a concise choice sounds natural when you substitute it for the original underlined phrase, it's a reasonable guess.

IMPROVING PARAGRAPHS

In the improving paragraph questions, you will confront a flawed student essay followed by six questions. In some cases, you must select the answer choice that best rewrites and combines portions of two separate sentences. In others, you must decide where in the essay a sentence best fits. In still others, you must choose what sort of additional information would most strengthen the writer's argument. Here are the directions.

The passage below is the unedited draft of a student's essay. Some of the essay needs to be rewritten to make the meaning clearer and more precise. Read the essay carefully.

The essay is followed by six questions about changes that might improve all or part of its organization, development, sentence structure, use of language, appropriateness to the audience, or its use of standard written English. Choose the answer that most clearly and effectively expresses the student's intended meaning. Indicate your choice by filling in the corresponding space on the answer sheet.

Tips For Handling Improving Paragraph Questions

1. First read the passage; then read the questions. Whether you choose to skim the student essay quickly or to read it closely, you need to have a reasonable idea of what the student author is trying to say before you set out to correct this rough first draft.
2. First tackle the questions that ask you to improve individual sentences; then tackle the ones that ask you to strengthen the passage as a whole. In the sentence correction questions, you've just been weeding out ineffective sentences and selecting effective ones. Here you're doing more of the same. It generally takes less time to spot an effective sentence than it does to figure out a way to strengthen an argument or link up two paragraphs.
3. Consider whether the addition of signal words or phrases—transitions—would strengthen the passage or particular sentences within it. If the essay is trying to contrast two ideas, it might benefit from the addition of a contrast signal.

     Contrast Signals: *although, despite, however, in contrast, nevertheless, on the contrary, on the other hand.*

If one portion of the essay is trying to support or continue a thought developed elsewhere in the passage, it might benefit from the addition of a support signal.

Support Signals: *additionally, furthermore, in addition, likewise, moreover.*

If the essay is trying to indicate that one thing causes another, it might benefit from the addition of a cause and effect signal.

Cause and Effect Signals: *accordingly, as a result of, because, consequently, hence, therefore, thus.*

Pay particular attention to answer choices that contain such signal words.

4. When you tackle the questions, *go back to the passage* to verify each answer choice. See whether your revised version of a particular sentence sounds right in its context. Ask yourself whether your choice follows naturally from the sentence before.

COMMON GRAMMAR AND USAGE ERRORS

Some errors are more common than others in this section. Here are a dozen that appear frequently on the examination. Watch out for them when you do the practice exercises and when you take the PSAT.

The Run-On Sentence

Mary's party was very exciting, it lasted until 2 A.M.
It is raining today, I need a raincoat.

You may also have heard this error called a comma splice. It can be corrected by making two sentences instead of one:

Mary's party was very exciting. It lasted until 2 A.M.

or by using a semicolon in place of the comma:

Mary's party was very exciting; it lasted until 2 A.M.

or by proper compounding:

Mary's party was very exciting and lasted until 2 A.M.

You can also correct this error with proper subordination. The second example above could be corrected:

Since it is raining today, I need a raincoat.
It is raining today, so I need a raincoat.

The Sentence Fragment

Since John was talking during the entire class, making it
impossible for anyone to concentrate.

This is the opposite of the first error. Instead of too much in one sentence, here you have too little. Do not be misled by the length of the fragment. It must have a main clause before it can be a complete sentence. All you have in this example is the cause. You still need a result. For example, the sentence could be corrected:

Since John was talking during the entire class, making it
impossible for anyone to concentrate, the teacher made him
stay after school.

Error in the Case of a Noun or Pronoun

Between you and I, this test is not really very difficult.

Case problems usually involve personal pronouns, which are in the nominative case (*I, he, she, we, they, who*) when they are used as subjects or predicate nominatives, and in the objective case (*me, him, her, us, them, whom*) when they are used as direct objects, indirect objects, and objects of prepositions. In this example, if you realize that *between* is a preposition, you know that *I* should be changed to the objective *me* because it is the object of a preposition.

Error in Subject-Verb Agreement

Harvard College, along with several other Ivy League schools,
are sending students to the conference.

Phrases starting with *along with* or *as well as* or *in addition to* that are placed in between the subject and the verb do not affect the verb. The subject of this sentence is *Harvard College,* so the verb should be *is sending.*

There is three bears living in that house.

Sentences that begin with *there* have the subject after the verb. The subject of this sentence is *bears,* so the verb should be *are.*

Error in Pronoun-Number Agreement

Every one of the girls on the team is trying to do their best.

Every pronoun must have a specific noun or noun substitute for an antecedent, and it must agree with that antecedent in number (singular or plural). In this example, *their* refers to *one* and must be singular:

Every one of the girls on the team is trying to do her best.

Error in the Tense or Form of a Verb

> *After the sun set behind the mountain, a cool breeze*
> *sprang up and brought relief from the heat.*

Make sure the verbs in a sentence appear in the proper sequence of tenses, so that it is clear what happened when. Since, according to the sentence, the breeze did not appear until after the sun had finished setting, the setting belongs in the past perfect tense:

> *After the sun had set behind the mountain, a cool breeze*
> *sprang up and brought relief from the heat.*

Error in Logical Comparison

> *I can go to California or Florida. I wonder which is best.*

When you are comparing only two things, you should use the comparative form of the adjective, not the superlative:

> *I wonder which is better.*

Comparisons must also be complete and logical.

> *The rooms on the second floor are larger than the first floor.*

It would be a strange building that had rooms larger than an entire floor. Logically, this sentence should be corrected to:

> *The rooms on the second floor are larger than those on the first floor.*

Adjective and Adverb Confusion

> *She did good on the test.*

> *They felt badly about leaving their friends.*

These are the two most common ways that adjectives and adverbs are misused. In the first example, when you are talking about how someone did, you want the adverb *well*, not the adjective *good:*

> *She did well on the test.*

In the second example, after a linking verb like *feel* you want a predicate adjective to describe the subject:

> *They felt bad about leaving their friends.*

Error in Modification and Word Order

Reaching for the book, the ladder slipped out from under him.

A participial phrase at the beginning of the sentence should describe the subject of the sentence. Since it doesn't make sense to think of a ladder reaching for a book, this participle is left dangling with nothing to modify. The sentence needs some rewriting:

When he reached for the book, the ladder slipped out from under him.

Error in Parallelism

In his book on winter sports, the author discusses ice-skating, skiing, hockey, and how to fish in an ice-covered lake.

Logically, equal and similar ideas belong in similar form. This shows that they are equal. In this sentence, the author discusses four sports, and all four should be presented the same way:

In his book on winter sports, the author discusses ice-skating, skiing, hockey, and fishing in an ice-covered lake.

Error in Diction or Idiom

The affects of the storm could be seen everywhere.

Your ear for the language will help you handle these errors, especially if you are accustomed to reading standard English. These questions test you on words that are frequently misused, on levels of usage (informal versus formal), and on standard English idioms. In this example, the verb *affect,* meaning "to influence," has been confused with the noun *effect,* meaning "result."

The effects of the storm could be seen everywhere.

The exercises that follow will give you practice in answering the three types of questions you'll find on the Identifying Sentence Errors questions, Improving Sentence questions, and Improving Paragraph questions. When you have completed each exercise, check your answers against the answer key. Then, read the answer explanations for any questions you either answered incorrectly or omitted.

Practice Exercise   **Answers given on pages 174–178.**

The sentences in this section may contain errors in grammar, usage, choice of words, or idioms. There is either just one error per sentence or the sentence is correct. Some words or phrases are underlined and lettered; everything else in the sentence is correct.

If an underlined word or phrase is incorrect, choose that letter; if the sentence is correct, select <u>No error</u>. Then blacken the appropriate space on your Answer Sheet.

EXAMPLE: SAMPLE ANSWER:

Ⓐ Ⓑ ● Ⓓ Ⓔ

The fields have soil <u>so rich that</u> corn
                     A

<u>growing here</u> commonly <u>had stood</u> more
   B   C

than six feet <u>tall</u>. <u>No error</u>
              D   E

---

1. We were <u>already</u> <u>to leave for</u> the amusement park when John's car <u>broke down</u>;
            A   B   C

   we <u>were forced</u> to pospone our outing. <u>No error</u>
      D   E

2. <u>By order of</u> the Student Council, the <u>wearing</u> of slacks by <u>we</u> girls in school
   A   B   C

   <u>has been permitted</u>. <u>No error</u>
   D   E

3. <u>Each</u> one of the dogs in the show <u>require</u> a <u>special</u> <u>kind</u> of diet. <u>No error</u>
   A   B   C   D   E

4. The major difficulty <u>confronting</u> the authorities <u>was</u> the reluctance of the people
                        A   B

   to talk; they had been warned not to <u>say nothing</u> to the police. <u>No error</u>
   C   D   E

5. If I <u>were</u> you, I would never permit <u>him</u> to <u>take part</u> in such an
        A   B   C

   <u>exhausting and painful</u> activity. <u>No error</u>
   D   E

6. Stanford White, who is one of America's most notable architects,
A   B

have designed many famous buildings, among them the original Madison
C   D

Square Garden. No error
     E

7. The notion of allowing the institution of slavery to continue to exist in a
     A   B   C

democratic society had no appeal to either the violent followers of John Brown

nor the peaceful disciples of Sojourner Truth. No error
D   E

8. Some students prefer watching filmstrips to textbooks because they feel
     A   B

uncomfortable with the presentation of information in a non-oral form. No error
   C   D   E

9. There was so much conversation in back of me that I couldn't hear the actors
  A   B   C D

on the stage. No error
     E

10. This book is too elementary; it can help neither you nor I. No error
     A   B   C D E

11. In a way we may say that we have reached the end of the Industrial Revolution.
    A   B C   D

No error
E

12. Although the books are altogether on the shelf, they are not arranged in
  A   B   C

any kind of order. No error
D   E

13. The reason for my prolonged absence from class was because I was ill for
   A   B   C D

three weeks. No error
    E

14. According to researchers, the weapons and work implements used by
    A   B

Cro-Magnon hunters appear being actually quite "modern." No error
                      C   D   E

15. Since we were caught completely unawares, the affect of Ms. Rivera's remarks
                              A   B

was startling; some were shocked, but others were angry. No error
   C   D   E

16. The committee had intended both you and I to speak at the assembly; however,
                A   B   C

only one of us will be able to talk. No error
 D   E

17. The existence of rundown "welfare hotels" in which homeless families reside
                                  A   B

at enormous cost to the taxpayer provides a shameful commentary of
               C   D

America's commitment to house the poor. No error
                             E

18. We have heard that the prinicpal has decided whom the prize winners will be
                            A   B   C

and will announce the names in the assembly today. No error
 D   E

19. As soon as the sun had rose over the mountains, the valley became
     A   B   C

unbearably hot and stifling. No error
   D   E

20. They are both excellent books, but this one is best. No error
  A   B   C D   E

21. Although the news had come as a surprise to all in the room, both Jane and
              A   B

Oprah tried to do her work as though nothing had happened. No error
          C   D   E

22. Even well-known fashion designers have difficulty staying on top
    ‾‾‾
     A
    from one season to another because of changeable moods and needs in
    ‾‾‾‾‾‾‾‾‾‾‾‾‾‾‾‾‾‾‾‾‾‾‾‾ ‾‾‾‾‾‾‾‾‾ ‾‾‾‾‾‾‾‾‾‾‾‾‾‾‾‾‾
              B   C   D
    the marketplace. No error
                     ‾‾‾‾‾‾‾‾
                        E

23. Arms control has been under discussion for decades with the former Soviet
                        ‾‾‾‾‾‾‾‾‾‾‾‾‾‾‾‾
                              A
    Union, but solutions are still alluding the major powers. No error
          ‾‾‾ ‾‾‾‾‾‾‾‾‾‾‾‾‾ ‾‾‾‾‾‾‾‾   ‾‾‾‾‾‾‾‾
           B   C   D   E

24. Perhaps sports enthusiasts are realizing that jogging is not easy on joints and
                                              ‾‾‾‾   ‾‾‾‾‾‾‾‾‾‾
                                               A   B
    tendons, for the latest fad is being walking. No error
                   ‾‾‾‾‾‾ ‾‾‾‾‾‾‾‾‾‾‾‾‾‾‾‾‾ ‾‾‾‾‾‾‾‾
                      C   D   E

25. Technological advances can cause factual data to become obsolete within
                          ‾‾‾‾‾‾‾‾
                             A
    a short time; yet, students should concentrate on reasoning skills, not facts.
    ‾‾‾‾‾‾‾‾‾‾‾ ‾‾‾   ‾‾‾‾‾‾‾‾‾‾‾‾‾‾‾
         B   C   D
    No error
    ‾‾‾‾‾‾‾‾
       E

26. If anyone cares to join me in this campaign, either now or in the near future,
       ‾‾‾‾‾‾   ‾‾‾‾   ‾‾‾‾‾‾
         A   B   C
    they will be welcomed gratefully. No error
    ‾‾‾‾   ‾‾‾‾‾‾‾‾
     D   E

27. The poems with which he occasionally desired to regale the fashionable world
             ‾‾‾‾‾‾‾‾‾‾‾   ‾‾‾‾‾‾‾‾‾‾‾‾‾‾‾‾
                  A   B
    were invariably bad—stereotyped, bombastic, and even ludicrous. No error
    ‾‾‾‾‾‾‾‾‾‾‾‾‾‾‾‾   ‾‾‾‾‾‾‾‾‾‾‾‾ ‾‾‾‾‾‾‾‾
           C   D   E

28. Ever since the quality of teacher education came under public scrutiny,
        ‾‾‾‾‾ ‾‾‾‾‾‾‾‾
          A   B
    suggestions for upgrading the profession are abounding. No error
                   ‾‾‾‾‾‾‾‾‾   ‾‾‾‾‾‾‾‾‾‾‾‾ ‾‾‾‾‾‾‾‾
                       C   D   E

29. Because the door was locked and bolted, the police were forced to break into
    ‾‾‾‾‾‾‾   ‾‾‾‾   ‾‾‾‾‾
       A   B   C
    the apartment through the bedroom window. No error
                   ‾‾‾‾‾‾‾   ‾‾‾‾‾‾‾‾
                      D   E

30. I will always remember you standing by me offering me encouragement.
    A   B   C   D

No error
 E

31. With special training, capuchin monkeys can enable quadriplegics as well as
                                             A   B

other handicapped individuals to become increasingly independent. No error
                          C   D   E

32. Contrary to what had previously been reported, the conditions governing the
    A   B

truce between Libya and Chad arranged by the United Nations has not yet
                               C   D

been revealed. No error
            E

33. Avid readers generally either admire or dislike Ernest Hemingway's journalistic
                                      A

style of writing; few have no opinion of him. No error
  B   C   D   E

34. In 1986, the nuclear disaster at Chernobyl has aroused intense speculation
                                        A

about the long-term effects of radiation that continued for the better part of
 B   C   D

a year. No error
      E

35. Howard Hughes, who became the subject of bizarre rumors as a result of his
               A   B   C

extreme reclusiveness, was well-known as an aviator, industrialist, and

in producing motion pictures. No error
              D   E

Some or all parts of the following sentences are underlined. The first answer choice, (A), simply repeats the underlined part of the sentence. The other four choices present four alternate ways to phrase the underlined part. Select the answer that produces the most effective sentence, one that is clear and exact, and blacken the appropriate space on your answer sheet. In selecting your choice, be sure that it is standard written English, and that it expresses the meaning of the original sentence.

EXAMPLE:

The first biography of author Eudora Welty came out in 1998 and she was eighty-nine years old at the time.

(A) and she was eighty-nine years old at the time
(B) at the time when she was eighty-nine
(C) upon becoming an eighty-nine year old
(D) when she was eighty-nine
(E) at the age of eighty-nine years old

SAMPLE ANSWER:

36. The child is neither encouraged to be critical or to examine all the evidence before forming an opinion.

   (A) neither encouraged to be critical or to examine
   (B) neither encouraged to be critical nor to examine
   (C) either encouraged to be critical or to examine
   (D) encouraged either to be critical nor to examine
   (E) not encouraged either to be critical or to examine

37. The process by which the community influence the actions of its members is known as social control.

   (A) influence the actions of its members
   (B) influences the actions of its members
   (C) had influenced the actions of its members
   (D) influences the actions of their members
   (E) will influence the actions of its members

38. Play being recognized as an important factor improving mental and physical health and thereby reducing human misery and poverty.

(A) Play being recognized as
(B) By recognizing play as
(C) Their recognizing play as
(D) Recognition of it being
(E) Play is recognized as

39. To be sure, there would be scarcely any time left over for other things if school children would have been expected to have considered all sides of every matter, on which they hold opinions.

(A) would have been expected to have considered
(B) should have been expected to have considered
(C) were expected to consider
(D) will be expected to have considered
(E) were expected to be considered

40. Using it wisely, leisure promotes health, efficiency and happiness.

(A) Using it wisely
(B) If it is used wisely
(C) Having used it wisely
(D) Because of its wise use
(E) Because of usefulness

41. In giving expression to the play instincts of the human race, new vigor and effectiveness are afforded by recreation to the body and to the mind.

(A) new vigor and effectiveness are afforded by recreation to the body and to the mind
(B) recreation affords new vigor and effectiveness to the body and to the mind
(C) there are afforded new vigor and effectiveness to the body and to the mind
(D) by recreation the body and the mind are afforded new vigor and effectiveness
(E) to the body and to the mind afford new vigor and effectiveness to themselves by recreation

42. Depending on skillful suggestion, argument is seldom used in advertising.

(A) Depending on skillful suggestion, argument is seldom used in advertising.
(B) Argument is seldom used in advertising, which depends instead on skillful suggestion.
(C) Skillful suggestion is depended on by advertisers instead of argument.
(D) Suggestion, which is more skillful, is used in place of argument by advertisers.
(E) Instead of suggestion, depending on argument is used by skillful advertisers.

43. When this war is over, no nation will either be isolated in war or peace.

(A) either be isolated in war or peace
(B) be either isolated in war or peace
(C) be isolated in neither war nor peace
(D) be isolated either in war or in peace
(E) be isolated neither in war or peace

44. Thanks to the prevailing westerly winds, dust blowing east from the drought-stricken plains travels halfway across the continent to fall on the cities of the East Coast.

(A) blowing east from the drought-stricken plains
(B) that, blowing east from the drought-stricken plains,
(C) from the drought-stricken plains and blows east
(D) that is from the drought-stricken plains blowing east
(E) blowing east that is from the plains that are drought-stricken

45. Americans are learning that their concept of a research worker toiling alone in a laboratory and who discovers miraculous cures has been highly idealized and glamorized.

(A) toiling alone in a laboratory and who discovers miraculous cures
(B) toiling alone in a laboratory and discovers miraculous cures
(C) toiling alone in a laboratory to discover miraculous cures
(D) who toil alone in the laboratory and discover miraculous cures
(E) has toiled alone hoping to discover miraculous cures

46. However many mistakes have been made in our past, the tradition of America, not only the champion of freedom but also fair play, still lives among millions who can see light and hope scarcely anywhere else.

(A) not only the champion of freedom but also fair play
(B) the champion of not only freedom but also of fair play
(C) the champion not only of freedom but also of fair play
(D) not only the champion but also freedom and fair play
(E) not the champion of freedom only, but also fair play

47. <u>Examining the principal movements sweeping through the world, it can be seen</u> that they are being accelerated by the war.

(A) Examining the principal movements sweeping through the world, it can be seen

(B) Having examined the principal movements sweeping through the world, it can be seen

(C) Examining the principal movements sweeping through the world can be seen

(D) Examining the principal movements sweeping through the world, we can see

(E) It can be seen examining the principal movements sweeping through the world

48. <u>The FCC is broadening its view on what constitutes indecent programming,</u> radio stations are taking a closer look at their broadcasters' materials.

(A) The FCC is broadening its view on what constitutes indecent programming

(B) The FCC, broadening its view on what constitutes indecent programming, has caused

(C) The FCC is broadening its view on what constitutes indecent programming, as a result

(D) Since the FCC is broadening its view on what constitutes indecent programming

(E) The FCC, having broadened its view on what constitutes indecent programming

49. As district attorney, Elizabeth Holtzman not only had the responsibility of supervising a staff of dedicated young lawyers <u>but she had the task of maintaining good relations with the police also.</u>

(A) but she had the task of maintaining good relations with the police also

(B) but she also had the task of maintaining good relations with the police

(C) but also had the task of maintaining good relations with the police

(D) but she had the task to maintain good relations with the police also

(E) but also she had the task to maintain good relations with the police

50. Many politicians are now trying to take uncontroversial positions on <u>issues; the purpose being to allow them to appeal</u> to as wide a segment of the voting population as possible.

(A) issues; the purpose being to allow them to appeal

(B) issues in order to appeal

(C) issues, the purpose is to allow them to appeal

(D) issues and the purpose is to allow them to appeal

(E) issues; that was allowing them to appeal

The passage below is the unedited draft of a student's essay. Some of the essay needs to be rewritten to make the meaning clearer and more precise. Read the essay carefully.

The essay is followed by six questions about changes that might improve all or part of its organization, development, sentence structure, use of language, appropriateness to the audience, or its use of standard written English. Choose the answer that most clearly and effectively expresses the student's intended meaning. Indicate your choice by filling in the corresponding space on the answer sheet.

[1] Throughout history, people have speculated about the future. [2] Will it be a utopia? they wondered. [3] Will injustice and poverty be eliminated? [4] Will people accept ethnic diversity, learning to live in peace? [5] Will the world be clean and unpolluted? [6] Or will technology aid us in creating a trap for ourselves we cannot escape, for example such as the world in 1984? [7] With the turn of the millennium just around the corner these questions are in the back of our minds.

[8] Science fiction often portrays the future as a technological Garden of Eden. [9] With interactive computers, TVs and robots at our command, we barely need to lift a finger to go to school, to work, to go shopping, and education is also easy and convenient. [10] Yet, the problems of the real twentieth century seem to point in another direction. [11] The environment, far from improving, keeps deteriorating. [12] Wars and other civil conflicts breakout regularly. [13] The world's population is growing out of control. [14] The majority of people on earth live in poverty. [15] Many of them are starving. [16] Illiteracy is a problem in most poor countries. [17] Diseases and malnourishment is very common. [18] Rich countries like the U.S.A. don't have the resources to help the "have-not" countries.

[19] Instead, think instead of all the silly inventions such as tablets you put in your toilet tank to make the water blue, or electric toothbrushes. [20] More money is spent on space and defense than on education and health care. [21] Advancements in agriculture can produce enough food to feed the whole country, yet people in the U.S. are starving.

[22] Although the USSR is gone, the nuclear threat continues from small countries like Iraq. [23] Until the world puts its priorities straight, we can't look for a bright future in the twenty-first century, despite the rosy picture painted for us by the science fiction writers.

51. Considering the context of paragraph 1, which of the following is the best revision of sentence 6?

(A) Or will technology create a trap for ourselves from which we cannot escape, for example the world in *1984*?

(B) Or will technology aid people in creating a trap for themselves that they cannot escape; for example, the world in *1984*?

(C) Or will technology create a trap from which there is no escape, as it did in the world in *1984*?

(D) Or will technology trap us in an inescapable world, for example, it did so in the world of *1984*?

(E) Perhaps technology will aid people in creating a trap for themselves from which they cannot escape, just as they did it in the world of *1984*.

52. With regard to the essay as a whole, which of the following best describes the writer's intention in paragraph 1?

(A) To announce the purpose of the essay

(B) To compare two ideas discussed later in the essay

(C) To take a position on the essay's main issue

(D) To reveal the organization of the essay

(E) To raise questions that will be answered in the essay

53. Which of the following is the best revision of the underlined segment of sentence 9 below?

[9] *With interactive computers, TVs and robots at our command, we barely need to lift a finger to go to school, to work,* <u>*to go shopping, and education is also easy and convenient*</u>.

(A) and to go shopping, while education is also easy and convenient

(B) to go shopping, and getting an education is also easy and convenient

(C) to go shopping as well as educating ourselves are all easy and convenient

(D) to shop, and an easy and convenient education

(E) to shop, and to get an easy and convenient education

54. Which of the following is the most effective way to combine sentences 14, 15, 16, and 17?

(A) The majority of people on earth are living in poverty and are starving, with illiteracy, and disease and being malnourished are also a common problems.

(B) Common problems for the majority of people on earth are poverty, illiteracy, diseases, malnourishment, and many are illiterate.

(C) The majority of people on earth are poor, starving, sick, malnourished and illiterate.

(D) Common among the poor majority on earth is poverty, starvation, disease, malnourishment, and illiteracy.

(E) The majority of the earth's people living in poverty with starvation, disease, malnourishment and illiteracy a constant threat.

55. Considering the sentences that precede and follow sentence 19, which of the following is the most effective revision of sentence 19?

(A) Instead they are devoting resources on silly inventions such as tablets to make toilet tank water blue or electric toothbrushes.

(B) Instead, they waste their resources on producing silly inventions like electric toothbrushes and tablets for bluing toilet tank water.

(C) Think of all the silly inventions: tablets you put in your toilet tank to make the water blue and electric toothbrushes.

(D) Instead, tablets you put in your toilet tank to make the water blue or electric toothbrushes are examples of useless products on the market today.

(E) Instead of spending on useful things, think of all the silly inventions such as tablets you put in your toilet tank to make the water blue or electric toothbrushes.

56. Which of the following revisions would most improve the overall coherence of the essay?

(A) Move sentence 7 to paragraph 2

(B) Move sentence 10 to paragraph 1

(C) Move sentence 22 to paragraph 2

(D) Delete sentence 8

(E) Delete sentence 23

Answer Key

1. **A**	20. **D**	39. **C**
2. **C**	21. **C**	40. **B**
3. **B**	22. **E**	41. **B**
4. **D**	23. **D**	42. **B**
5. **E**	24. **D**	43. **D**
6. **C**	25. **C**	44. **A**
7. **D**	26. **D**	45. **C**
8. **B**	27. **E**	46. **C**
9. **B**	28. **D**	47. **D**
10. **D**	29. **E**	48. **D**
11. **E**	30. **C**	49. **C**
12. **B**	31. **E**	50. **B**
13. **D**	32. **D**	51. **C**
14. **C**	33. **D**	52. **E**
15. **B**	34. **A**	53. **E**
16. **B**	35. **D**	54. **C**
17. **D**	36. **E**	55. **B**
18. **B**	37. **B**	56. **C**
19. **B**	38. **E**	

Answer Explanations

1. **(A)** Error in diction. Should be *all ready*. *All ready* means the group is ready; *already* means prior to a given time, previously.

2. **(C)** Error in pronoun case. Should be *us*. The expression *us girls* is the object of the preposition *by*.

3. **(B)** Error in subject-verb agreement. Should be *requires*. Verb should agree with the subject (*each one*).

4. **(D)** Should be *to say anything*. *Not to say nothing* is a double negative.

5. **(E)** Sentence is correct.

6. **(C)** Error in subject-verb agreement. Since the subject is Stanford White (singular), change *have designed* to *has designed*.

7. **(D)** Error in use of correlatives. Change *nor* to *or*. The correct form of the correlative pairs *either* with *or*.

8. **(B)** Error in parallel structure. Change *textbooks* to *reading textbooks*. To have parallel structure, the linked sentence elements must share the same grammatical form.

9. **(B)** Error in diction. Change *in back of* to *behind*.

10. **(D)** Error in pronoun case. Should be *me*. Pronoun is the object of the verb *can help*.

11. **(E)** Sentence is correct.

12. **(B)** Error in diction. Should be *all together. All together* means in a group; *altogether* means entirely.

13. **(D)** Improper use of *because.* Change to *that* (*The reason . . . was that . . . .*).

14. **(C)** Incorrect verbal. Change the participle *being* to the infinitive *to be.*

15. **(B)** Error in diction. Change *affect* (a verb meaning to influence or pretend) to *effect* (a noun meaning result).

16. **(B)** Error in pronoun case. Should be *me.* Subjects of infinitives are in the objective case.

17. **(D)** Error in idiom. Change *commentary of* to *commentary on.*

18. **(B)** Error in pronoun case. Should be *who.* The pronoun is the predicate complement of *will be* and is in the nominative case.

19. **(B)** Should be *had risen.* The past participle of the verb *to rise* is *risen.*

20. **(D)** Error in comparison of modifiers. Should be *better.* Do not use the superlative when comparing two things.

21. **(C)** Error in pronoun-number agreement. Should be *their* instead of *her.* The antecedent of the pronoun is *Jane and Oprah* (plural).

22. **(E)** Sentence is correct.

23. **(D)** Error in diction. Change *alluding* (meaning to refer indirectly) to *eluding* (meaning to evade).

24. **(D)** Confusion of verb and gerund (verbal noun). Change *is being walking* to *is walking.*

25. **(C)** Error in coordination and subordination. Change *yet* to *therefore* or another similar connector to clarify the connection between the clauses.

26. **(D)** Error in pronoun-number agreement. Should be *he* or *she.* The antecedent of the pronoun is *anyone* (singular).

27. **(E)** Sentence is correct.

28. **(D)** Error in sequence of tenses. Change *are abounding* to *have abounded.* The present perfect tense talks about an action that occurs at one time, but is seen in relation to another time.

29. **(E)** Sentence is correct.

30. **(C)** Error in pronoun case. Should be *your.* The pronoun modifying a gerund (verbal noun) should be in the possessive case.

31. **(E)** Sentence is correct.

32. **(D)** Error in subject-verb agreement. Since the subject is *conditions* (plural), change *has* to *have.*

33. **(D)** Error in pronoun. Since the sentence speaks about Hemingway's style rather than about Hemingway, the phrase should read *of it,* not *of him.*

34. **(A)** Error in sequence of tenses. Change *has aroused* to *aroused.* The present perfect tense (*has aroused*) is used for indefinite time. In this sentence, the time is defined as *the better part of a year.*

35. **(D)** Lack of parallel structure. Change *in producing motion pictures* to *motion picture producer.*

36. **(E)** This question involves two aspects of correct English. *Neither* should be followed by *nor; either* by *or.* Choices A and D are, therefore, incorrect. The words *neither . . . nor* and *either . . . or* should be placed before the two items being discussed—*to be critical* and *to examine.* Choice E meets both requirements.

37. **(B)** This question tests agreement. Errors in subject-verb agreement and pronoun-number agreement are both involved. *Community* (singular) needs a singular verb, *influences.* Also, the pronoun that refers to *community* should be singular *(its).*

38. **(E)** Error in following conventions. This is an incomplete sentence or fragment. The sentence needs a verb to establish a principal clause. Choice E provides the verb (*is recognized*) and presents the only complete sentence in the group.

39. **(C)** *Would have been expected* is incorrect as a verb in a clause introduced by the conjunction *if. Had been expected* or *were expected* is preferable. *To have considered* does not follow correct sequence of tense and should be changed to *to consider.*

40. **(B)** Error in modification and word order. One way of correcting a dangling participle is to change the participial phrase to a clause. Choices B and D substitute clauses for the phrase. However, Choice D changes the meaning of the sentence. Choice B is correct.

41. **(B)** Error in modification and word order. As it stands, the sentence contains a dangling modifier. This is corrected by making *recreation* the subject of the sentence, in the process switching from the passive to the active voice. Choice E also provides a subject for the sentence; however, the meaning of the sentence is changed in Choice E.

42. **(B)** Error in modification and word order. As presented, the sentence contains a dangling participle, *depending.* Choice B corrects this error. The other choices change the emphasis presented by the author.

43. **(D)** Error in word order. *Either . . . or* should precede the two choices offered (*in war* and *in peace*).

44. **(A)** Sentence is correct.

45. **(C)** Error in parallelism. In the underlined phrase, you will find two modifiers of *worker-toiling* and *who discovers.* The first is a participial phrase and the second a clause. This results in an error in parallel structure. Choice B also has an error in parallel structure. Choice C corrects this by eliminating one of the modifiers of *worker.* Choice D corrects the error in parallel structure but introduces an error in agreement between subject and verb—*who* (singular) and *toil* (plural). Choice E changes the tense and also the meaning of the original sentence.

46. **(C)** Error in parallelism. Parallel structure requires that *not only* and *but also* immediately precede the words they limit.

47. (D) Error in modification and word order. Choices A, B, and E are incorrect because of the dangling participle. Choice C is incoherent. Choice D correctly eliminates the dangling participle by introducing the subject *we*.

48. (D) Error in comma splice. The punctuation in Choices A and C creates a run-on sentence. Choices B and E are both ungrammatical. Choice D corrects the run-on sentence by changing the beginning clause into the adverb clause that starts with the subordinating conjunction *since*.

49. (C) Error in parallelism. Since the words *not only* immediately precede the verb in the first half of the sentence, the words *but also* should immediately precede the verb in the second half. This error in parallel structure is corrected in Choice C.

50. (B) Error in coordination and subordination. The punctuation in Choices A, C, D, and E creates an incomplete sentence or fragment. Choice B corrects the error by linking the elements with *in order to*.

51. (C) Choice A is awkward and shifts the pronoun usage in the paragraph from third to first person. Choice B is awkward and contains a semicolon error. A semicolon is used to separate two independent clauses. The material after the semicolon is a sentence fragment. Choice C is succinctly and accurately expressed. It is the best answer. Choice D contains a comma splice between *world* and *for*. A comma may not be used to join two independent clauses. Choice E is awkwardly expressed and contains the pronoun *it*, which lacks a clear referent.

52. (E) Choice A indirectly describes the purpose of paragraph 1 but does not identify the writer's main intention. Choices B, C, and D fail to describe the writer's main intention. Choice E accurately describes the writer's main intention. It is the best answer.

53. (E) Choice A is grammatically correct but cumbersome. Choice B contains an error in parallel construction. The clause that begins *and getting* is not grammatically parallel to the previous items on the list. Choice C contains a mixed construction. The first and last parts of the sentence are grammatically unrelated. Choice D contains faulty parallel structure. Choice E is correct and accurately expressed. It is the best answer.

54. (C) Choice A is wordy and awkwardly expressed. Choice B contains an error in parallel structure. The clause *and many are illiterate* is not grammatically parallel to the previous items on the list of problems. Choice C is concise and accurately expressed. It is the best answer. Choice D is concise, but it contains an error in subject-verb agreement. The subject is *poverty, starvation . . . etc.*, which requires a plural verb; the verb *is* is singular. Choice E is a sentence fragment; it has no main verb.

55. (B) Choice A contains an error in idiom. The standard phrase is *devoting to*, not *devoting on*. Choice B ties sentence 19 to the previous sentence and is accurately expressed. It is the best answer. Choice C fails to improve the coherence of the paragraph. Choice D is unrelated to the context of the paragraph. Choice E is insufficiently related to the context of the paragraph.

56. (C) Choice A should stay put because it provides a transition between the questions in paragraph 1 and the beginning of paragraph 2. Choice B is a pivotal sentence in paragraph 2 and should not be moved. Choice C fits the topics of paragraph 2, therefore, sentence 22 should be moved to paragraph 2. Choice C is the best answer. Choice D is needed as an introductory sentence in paragraph 2. It should not be deleted. Choice E provides the essay with a meaningful conclusion and should not be deleted.

9 Two Model Tests

Many students, after taking the PSAT/NMSQT, report that they found the experience very exhausting. More than two hours on difficult test material may prove to be very grueling.

To alleviate this situation, the authors wish to offer two suggestions:

1. Become acquainted with the time situation before taking the actual test. Taking the model tests in this chapter under timed conditions will make you familiar with the situation before you take the actual test. This familiarity should enable you to find the actual test less rigorous.

2. If you recognize that the two-hour test may be physically tiring, you should recognize that you need to be physically fit. The best advice we can offer is that you stop preparation for the test several days before the scheduled date. Rest and relaxation will enable you to avoid the fatigue of a long examination and will prove to be more profitable than last-minute cramming.

ANSWER SHEET—MODEL TEST 1

Section 1

1 Ⓐ Ⓑ Ⓒ Ⓓ Ⓔ
2 Ⓐ Ⓑ Ⓒ Ⓓ Ⓔ
3 Ⓐ Ⓑ Ⓒ Ⓓ Ⓔ
4 Ⓐ Ⓑ Ⓒ Ⓓ Ⓔ
5 Ⓐ Ⓑ Ⓒ Ⓓ Ⓔ
6 Ⓐ Ⓑ Ⓒ Ⓓ Ⓔ
7 Ⓐ Ⓑ Ⓒ Ⓓ Ⓔ
8 Ⓐ Ⓑ Ⓒ Ⓓ Ⓔ
9 Ⓐ Ⓑ Ⓒ Ⓓ Ⓔ
10 Ⓐ Ⓑ Ⓒ Ⓓ Ⓔ
11 Ⓐ Ⓑ Ⓒ Ⓓ Ⓔ
12 Ⓐ Ⓑ Ⓒ Ⓓ Ⓔ
13 Ⓐ Ⓑ Ⓒ Ⓓ Ⓔ
14 Ⓐ Ⓑ Ⓒ Ⓓ Ⓔ
15 Ⓐ Ⓑ Ⓒ Ⓓ Ⓔ
16 Ⓐ Ⓑ Ⓒ Ⓓ Ⓔ
17 Ⓐ Ⓑ Ⓒ Ⓓ Ⓔ
18 Ⓐ Ⓑ Ⓒ Ⓓ Ⓔ
19 Ⓐ Ⓑ Ⓒ Ⓓ Ⓔ
20 Ⓐ Ⓑ Ⓒ Ⓓ Ⓔ
21 Ⓐ Ⓑ Ⓒ Ⓓ Ⓔ
22 Ⓐ Ⓑ Ⓒ Ⓓ Ⓔ
23 Ⓐ Ⓑ Ⓒ Ⓓ Ⓔ
24 Ⓐ Ⓑ Ⓒ Ⓓ Ⓔ
25 Ⓐ Ⓑ Ⓒ Ⓓ Ⓔ

Section 2

1 Ⓐ Ⓑ Ⓒ Ⓓ Ⓔ
2 Ⓐ Ⓑ Ⓒ Ⓓ Ⓔ
3 Ⓐ Ⓑ Ⓒ Ⓓ Ⓔ
4 Ⓐ Ⓑ Ⓒ Ⓓ Ⓔ
5 Ⓐ Ⓑ Ⓒ Ⓓ Ⓔ
6 Ⓐ Ⓑ Ⓒ Ⓓ Ⓔ
7 Ⓐ Ⓑ Ⓒ Ⓓ Ⓔ
8 Ⓐ Ⓑ Ⓒ Ⓓ Ⓔ
9 Ⓐ Ⓑ Ⓒ Ⓓ Ⓔ
10 Ⓐ Ⓑ Ⓒ Ⓓ Ⓔ
11 Ⓐ Ⓑ Ⓒ Ⓓ Ⓔ
12 Ⓐ Ⓑ Ⓒ Ⓓ Ⓔ
13 Ⓐ Ⓑ Ⓒ Ⓓ Ⓔ
14 Ⓐ Ⓑ Ⓒ Ⓓ Ⓔ
15 Ⓐ Ⓑ Ⓒ Ⓓ Ⓔ
16 Ⓐ Ⓑ Ⓒ Ⓓ Ⓔ
17 Ⓐ Ⓑ Ⓒ Ⓓ Ⓔ
18 Ⓐ Ⓑ Ⓒ Ⓓ Ⓔ
19 Ⓐ Ⓑ Ⓒ Ⓓ Ⓔ
20 Ⓐ Ⓑ Ⓒ Ⓓ Ⓔ

Section 3

26 Ⓐ Ⓑ Ⓒ Ⓓ Ⓔ	40 Ⓐ Ⓑ Ⓒ Ⓓ Ⓔ
27 Ⓐ Ⓑ Ⓒ Ⓓ Ⓔ	41 Ⓐ Ⓑ Ⓒ Ⓓ Ⓔ
28 Ⓐ Ⓑ Ⓒ Ⓓ Ⓔ	42 Ⓐ Ⓑ Ⓒ Ⓓ Ⓔ
29 Ⓐ Ⓑ Ⓒ Ⓓ Ⓔ	43 Ⓐ Ⓑ Ⓒ Ⓓ Ⓔ
30 Ⓐ Ⓑ Ⓒ Ⓓ Ⓔ	44 Ⓐ Ⓑ Ⓒ Ⓓ Ⓔ
31 Ⓐ Ⓑ Ⓒ Ⓓ Ⓔ	45 Ⓐ Ⓑ Ⓒ Ⓓ Ⓔ
32 Ⓐ Ⓑ Ⓒ Ⓓ Ⓔ	46 Ⓐ Ⓑ Ⓒ Ⓓ Ⓔ
33 Ⓐ Ⓑ Ⓒ Ⓓ Ⓔ	47 Ⓐ Ⓑ Ⓒ Ⓓ Ⓔ
34 Ⓐ Ⓑ Ⓒ Ⓓ Ⓔ	48 Ⓐ Ⓑ Ⓒ Ⓓ Ⓔ
35 Ⓐ Ⓑ Ⓒ Ⓓ Ⓔ	49 Ⓐ Ⓑ Ⓒ Ⓓ Ⓔ
36 Ⓐ Ⓑ Ⓒ Ⓓ Ⓔ	50 Ⓐ Ⓑ Ⓒ Ⓓ Ⓔ
37 Ⓐ Ⓑ Ⓒ Ⓓ Ⓔ	51 Ⓐ Ⓑ Ⓒ Ⓓ Ⓔ
38 Ⓐ Ⓑ Ⓒ Ⓓ Ⓔ	52 Ⓐ Ⓑ Ⓒ Ⓓ Ⓔ
39 Ⓐ Ⓑ Ⓒ Ⓓ Ⓔ	

Section 4

21 Ⓐ Ⓑ Ⓒ Ⓓ
22 Ⓐ Ⓑ Ⓒ Ⓓ
23 Ⓐ Ⓑ Ⓒ Ⓓ
24 Ⓐ Ⓑ Ⓒ Ⓓ
25 Ⓐ Ⓑ Ⓒ Ⓓ
26 Ⓐ Ⓑ Ⓒ Ⓓ
27 Ⓐ Ⓑ Ⓒ Ⓓ
28 Ⓐ Ⓑ Ⓒ Ⓓ
29 Ⓐ Ⓑ Ⓒ Ⓓ
30 Ⓐ Ⓑ Ⓒ Ⓓ
31 Ⓐ Ⓑ Ⓒ Ⓓ
32 Ⓐ Ⓑ Ⓒ Ⓓ

33

34

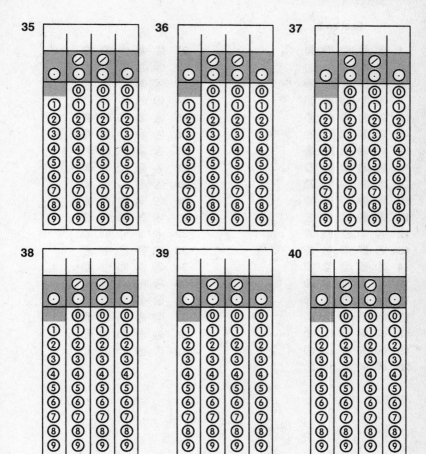

Section 5

1 Ⓐ Ⓑ Ⓒ Ⓓ Ⓔ
2 Ⓐ Ⓑ Ⓒ Ⓓ Ⓔ
3 Ⓐ Ⓑ Ⓒ Ⓓ Ⓔ
4 Ⓐ Ⓑ Ⓒ Ⓓ Ⓔ
5 Ⓐ Ⓑ Ⓒ Ⓓ Ⓔ
6 Ⓐ Ⓑ Ⓒ Ⓓ Ⓔ
7 Ⓐ Ⓑ Ⓒ Ⓓ Ⓔ
8 Ⓐ Ⓑ Ⓒ Ⓓ Ⓔ
9 Ⓐ Ⓑ Ⓒ Ⓓ Ⓔ
10 Ⓐ Ⓑ Ⓒ Ⓓ Ⓔ
11 Ⓐ Ⓑ Ⓒ Ⓓ Ⓔ
12 Ⓐ Ⓑ Ⓒ Ⓓ Ⓔ
13 Ⓐ Ⓑ Ⓒ Ⓓ Ⓔ
14 Ⓐ Ⓑ Ⓒ Ⓓ Ⓔ
15 Ⓐ Ⓑ Ⓒ Ⓓ Ⓔ
16 Ⓐ Ⓑ Ⓒ Ⓓ Ⓔ
17 Ⓐ Ⓑ Ⓒ Ⓓ Ⓔ
18 Ⓐ Ⓑ Ⓒ Ⓓ Ⓔ
19 Ⓐ Ⓑ Ⓒ Ⓓ Ⓔ
20 Ⓐ Ⓑ Ⓒ Ⓓ Ⓔ

21 Ⓐ Ⓑ Ⓒ Ⓓ Ⓔ
22 Ⓐ Ⓑ Ⓒ Ⓓ Ⓔ
23 Ⓐ Ⓑ Ⓒ Ⓓ Ⓔ
24 Ⓐ Ⓑ Ⓒ Ⓓ Ⓔ
25 Ⓐ Ⓑ Ⓒ Ⓓ Ⓔ
26 Ⓐ Ⓑ Ⓒ Ⓓ Ⓔ
27 Ⓐ Ⓑ Ⓒ Ⓓ Ⓔ
28 Ⓐ Ⓑ Ⓒ Ⓓ Ⓔ
29 Ⓐ Ⓑ Ⓒ Ⓓ Ⓔ
30 Ⓐ Ⓑ Ⓒ Ⓓ Ⓔ
31 Ⓐ Ⓑ Ⓒ Ⓓ Ⓔ
32 Ⓐ Ⓑ Ⓒ Ⓓ Ⓔ
33 Ⓐ Ⓑ Ⓒ Ⓓ Ⓔ
34 Ⓐ Ⓑ Ⓒ Ⓓ Ⓔ
35 Ⓐ Ⓑ Ⓒ Ⓓ Ⓔ
36 Ⓐ Ⓑ Ⓒ Ⓓ Ⓔ
37 Ⓐ Ⓑ Ⓒ Ⓓ Ⓔ
38 Ⓐ Ⓑ Ⓒ Ⓓ Ⓔ
39 Ⓐ Ⓑ Ⓒ Ⓓ Ⓔ

MODEL TEST 1

SECTION 1

Time—25 minutes   25 questions (1–25)

Select the best answer to the following questions, then fill in the appropriate space on your answer sheet.

Each of the following sentences contains one or two blanks; these blanks indicate that a word or set of words has been left out. Below the sentence are five words or phrases, lettered A through E. Select the word or set of words that best completes the sentence.

Example:

Fame is ----; today's rising star is all too soon tomorrow's washed-up has-been.

(A) rewarding   (B) gradual   (C) essential
(D) spontaneous   (E) transitory

---

1. Impressed by the extraordinary potential of the new superconductor, scientists predict that its use will ---- the computer industry, creating new products overnight.

   (A) justify   (B) alienate   (C) nullify
   (D) revolutionize   (E) overestimate

2. No matter how ---- the revelations of the coming year may be, they will be hard put to match those of the past decade, which have ---- transformed our view of the emergence of Mayan civilization.

   (A) minor..dramatically
   (B) profound..negligibly
   (C) striking..radically
   (D) bizarre..nominally
   (E) questionable..possibly

3. Few other plants can grow beneath the canopy of the sycamore tree, whose leaves and pods produce a natural herbicide that leaches into the soil, ---- other plants that might compete for water and nutrients.

(A) inhibiting   (B) distinguishing
(C) nourishing   (D) encouraging
(E) refreshing

4. Black women authors such as Zora Neale Hurston, originally ---- by both white and black literary establishments to obscurity as minor novelists, are being rediscovered by black feminist critics today.

(A) inclined   (B) relegated   (C) subjected
(D) diminished   (E) characterized

5. Critics of the movie version of *The Color Purple* ---- its saccharine, over-optimistic mood as out of keeping with the novel's more ---- tone.

(A) applauded..somber
(B) condemned..hopeful
(C) acclaimed..positive
(D) denounced..sanguine
(E) decried..acerbic

Each of the following questions introduces a pair of words or phrases in capital letters, linked by a colon(:); this colon indicates that these words are related in some way. Following the capitalized pair are five pairs of words or phrases lettered A through E. Select the pair whose relationship is most similar to the relationship illustrated by the capitalized pair.

EXAMPLE:

CLOCK:TIME::   (A) watch:wrist
(B) pedometer:speed
(C) thermometer:temperature
(D) hourglass:sand   (E) radio:sound

---

6. DOOR:LATCH::   (A) window:pane
(B) necklace:clasp   (C) lock:key
(D) wall:plaster   (E) house:foundation

7. CAPTION:PHOTOGRAPH::   (A) frame:painting
   (B) subject:portrait   (C) signature:letter
   (D) title:article   (E) stanza:poem

8. TYRANNOSAUR:DINOSAUR::
   (A) lizard:crocodile   (B) whale:fish
   (C) condor:bird   (D) frog:tadpole
   (E) tiger:leopard

9. PROLIFIC:AUTHOR::   (A) melodious:singer
   (B) veracious:witness   (C) dynamic:actor
   (D) loquacious:speaker   (E) agile:acrobat

10. MENTOR:PROTEGE::   (A) competitor:rival
    (B) writer:plagiarist   (C) doctor:surgeon
    (D) sponsor:candidate   (E) truant:dawdler

11. TRAVELER:ITINERARY::   (A) lecturer:outline
    (B) tourist:vacation   (C) pedestrian:routine
    (D) explorer:safari   (E) soldier:furlough

Read each of the passages below, then answer the questions that follow each
passage. The correct response may be <u>stated</u> <u>outright</u> or merely <u>suggested</u> in the
passage and in any introductory or footnoted material included.

Questions 12–17 are based on the following passage.

In the following passage from Jane Austen's novel Pride and Prejudice, *the heroine
Elizabeth Bennet faces an unexpected encounter with her father's cousin (and
prospective heir), the clergyman Mr. Collins.*

It was absolutely necessary to interrupt him now.

"You are too hasty, Sir," she cried. "You forget that I have made no
answer. Let me do it without further loss of time. Accept my thanks for
Line the compliment you are paying me. I am very sensible of the honour of
(5) your proposals, but it is impossible for me to do otherwise than decline
them."

"I am not now to learn," replied Mr. Collins with a formal wave of the
hand, "that it is usual with young ladies to reject the addresses of the
man whom they secretly mean to accept, when he first applies for their
(10) favour; and that sometimes the refusal is repeated a second or even a

third time. I am therefore by no means discouraged by what you have just said, and shall hope to lead you to the altar ere long."

"Upon my word, Sir," cried Elizabeth, "your hope is rather an extraordinary one after my declaration. I do assure you that I am not one of
(15) those young ladies (if such young ladies there are) who are so daring as to risk their happiness on the chance of being asked a second time. I am perfectly serious in my refusal. You could not make *me* happy, and I am convinced that I am the last woman in the world who would make *you* so. Nay, were your friend Lady Catherine to know me, I am persuaded
(20) she would find me in every respect ill qualified for the situation."

"Were it certain that Lady Catherine would think so," said Mr. Collins very gravely—"but I cannot imagine that her ladyship would at all disapprove of you. And you may be certain that when I have the honour of seeing her again I shall speak in the highest terms of your modesty,
(25) economy, and other amiable qualifications."

"Indeed, Mr. Collins, all praise of me will be unnecessary. You must give me leave to judge for myself, and pay me the compliment of believing what I say. I wish you very happy and very rich, and by refusing your hand, do all in my power to prevent your being otherwise. In making me
(30) the offer, you must have satisfied the delicacy of your feelings with regard to my family, and may take possession of Longbourn estate whenever it falls, without any self-reproach. This matter may be considered, therefore, as finally settled." And rising as she thus spoke, she would have quitted the room, had not Mr. Collins thus addressed her.
(35)   "When I do myself the honour of speaking to you next on this subject I shall hope to receive a more favourable answer than you have now given me; though I am far from accusing you of cruelty at present, because I know it to be the established custom of your sex to reject a man on the first application, and perhaps you have even now said as
(40) much to encourage my suit as would be consistent with the true delicacy of the female character."

"Really, Mr. Collins," cried Elizabeth with some warmth, "you puzzle me exceedingly. If what I have hitherto said can appear to you in the form of encouragement, I know not how to express my refusal in such a
(45) way as may convince you of its being one."

12. It can be inferred that in the paragraphs immediately preceding this passage

    (A) Elizabeth and Mr. Collins quarreled

    (B) Elizabeth met Mr. Collins for the first time

    (C) Mr. Collins asked Elizabeth to marry him

    (D) Mr. Collins gravely insulted Elizabeth

    (E) Elizabeth discovered that Mr. Collins was a fraud

13. The word "sensible" in line 4 means

(A) logical   (B) perceptible
(C) sound in judgment   (D) keenly aware
(E) appreciable

14. Instead of having the intended effect, Elizabeth's initial refusal of Mr. Collins (lines 4–6)

(A) causes her to rethink rejecting him
(B) makes him less inclined to wed
(C) gives her the opportunity to consider other options
(D) persuades him she dislikes him intensely
(E) fails to put an end to his suit

15. It can be inferred from lines 21–23 that Mr. Collins

(A) will take Elizabeth's words seriously
(B) admires Elizabeth's independence
(C) is very disappointed by her decision
(D) would accept Lady Catherine's opinion
(E) means his remarks as a joke

16. The reason Elizabeth insists all praise of her "will be unnecessary" (line 26) is because she

(A) feels sure Lady Catherine will learn to admire her in time
(B) is too shy to accept compliments readily
(C) has no intention of marrying Mr. Collins
(D) believes a clergyman should be less effusive
(E) values her own worth excessively

17. On the basis of his behavior in this passage,
Mr. Collins may best be described as

(A) malicious in intent
(B) both obtuse and obstinate
(C) unsure of his acceptance
(D) kindly and understanding
(E) sensitive to Elizabeth's wishes

Questions 18–25 are based on the following passage.

African elephants now are an endangered species. The following passage, taken from a newspaper article written in 1989, discusses the potential ecological disaster that might occur if the elephant were to become extinct.

The African elephant—mythic symbol of a continent, keystone of its ecology and the largest land animal remaining on earth—has become the object of one of the biggest, broadest international efforts yet

Line mounted to turn a threatened species off the road to extinction. But it is
(5)   not only the elephant's survival that is at stake, conservationists say.
Unlike the endangered tiger, unlike even the great whales, the African
elephant is in great measure the architect of its environment. As a
voracious eater of vegetation, it largely shapes the forest-and-savanna
surroundings in which it lives, thereby setting the terms of existence for
(10)   millions of other storied animals—from zebras to gazelles to giraffes and
wildebeests—that share its habitat. And as the elephant disappears, scientists and conservationists say, many other species will also disappear
from vast stretches of forest and savanna, drastically altering and impov-
erishing whole ecosystems.
(15)   Just as the American buffalo was hunted almost to extinction a century ago, so the African elephant is now the victim of an onslaught of
commercial killing, stimulated in this case by soaring global demand for
ivory. Most of the killing is illegal, and conservationists say that although
the pressure of human population and development contributes to the
(20)   elephants' decline, poaching is by far the greatest threat. The elephant
may or may not be on the way to becoming a mere zoological curiosity
like the buffalo, but the trend is clear.
In an atmosphere of mounting alarm among conservationists, a new
international coordinating group backed by 21 ivory-producing and
(25)   ivory-consuming countries has met and adopted an ambitious plan of
action. Against admittedly long odds, the multinational rescue effort is
aimed both at stopping the slaughter of the elephants in the short term
and at nurturing them as a vital "keystone species" in the long run.
It is the elephant's metabolism and appetite that make it a disturber
(30)   of the environment and therefore an important creator of habitat. In a
constant search for the 300 pounds of vegetation it must have every day,
it kills small trees and underbrush and pulls branches off big trees as
high as its trunk will reach. This creates innumerable open spaces in both
deep tropical forests and in the woodlands that cover part of the African
(35)   savannas. The resulting patchwork, a mosaic of vegetation in various
stages of regeneration, in turn creates a greater variety of forage that
attracts a greater variety of other vegetation-eaters than would otherwise
be the case.
In studies over the last 20 years in southern Kenya near Mount
(40)   Kilimanjaro, Dr. David Western has found that when elephants are
allowed to roam the savannas naturally and normally, they spread out at
"intermediate densities." Their foraging creates a mixture of savanna
woodlands (what the Africans call bush) and grassland. The result is a
highly diverse array of other plant-eating species: those like the zebra,
(45)   wildebeest and gazelle, that graze; those like the giraffe, bushbuck and

lesser kudu, that browse on tender shoots, buds, twigs and leaves; and plant-eating primates like the baboon and vervet monkey. These herbivores attract carnivores like the lion and cheetah.

When the elephant population thins out, Dr. Western said, the wood-
(50) lands become denser and the grazers are squeezed out. When pressure from poachers forces elephants to crowd more densely onto reservations, the woodlands there are knocked out and the browsers and primates disappear.

Something similar appears to happen in dense tropical rain forests.
(55) In their natural state, because the overhead forest canopy shuts out sunlight and prevents growth on the forest floor, rain forests provide slim pickings for large, hoofed plant-eaters. By pulling down trees and eating new growth, elephants enlarge natural openings in the canopy, allowing plants to regenerate on the forest floor and bringing down vegetation
(60) from the canopy so that smaller species can get at it.

In such situations, the rain forest becomes hospitable to large plant-eating mammals such as bongos, bush pigs, duikers, forest hogs, swamp antelopes, forest buffaloes, okapis, sometimes gorillas and always a host of smaller animals that thrive on secondary growth. When
(65) elephants disappear and the forest reverts, the larger animals give way to smaller, nimbler animals like monkeys, squirrels and rodents.

18. The passage is primarily concerned with

(A) explaining why elephants are facing the threat of extinction

(B) explaining difficulties in providing sufficient forage for plant-eaters

(C) explaining how the elephant's impact on its surroundings affects other species

(D) distinguishing between savannas and rain forests as habitats for elephants

(E) contrasting elephants with members of other endangered species

19. The word "mounted" in line 4 means

(A) ascended   (B) increased   (C) launched
(D) attached   (E) exhibited

20. In the opening paragraph, the author mentions tigers and whales in order to emphasize which point about the elephant?

(A) Like them, it faces the threat of extinction

(B) It is herbivorous rather than carnivorous

(C) It moves more ponderously than either the tiger or the whale

(D) Unlike them, it physically alters its environment

(E) It is the largest extant land mammal

21. A necessary component of the elephant's ability to transform the landscape is its

(A) massive intelligence (B) fear of predators
(C) ravenous hunger (D) lack of grace (E) ability to regenerate

22. It can be inferred from the passage that

(A) the lion and the cheetah commonly prey upon elephants
(B) the elephant is dependent upon the existence of smaller plant-eating mammals for its survival
(C) elephants have an indirect effect on the hunting patterns of certain carnivores
(D) the floor of the tropical rain forest is too overgrown to accommodate larger plant-eating species
(E) the natural tendency of elephants is to crowd together in packs

23. The passage contains information that would answer which of the following questions?

  I. How does the elephant's foraging affect its surroundings?
 II. How do the feeding patterns of gazelles and giraffes differ?
III. What occurs in the rain forest when the elephant population dwindles?

(A) I only (B) II only (C) I and II only
(D) II and III only (E) I, II, and III

24. The word "host" in line 64 means

(A) food source for parasites
(B) very large number
(C) provider of hospitality
(D) military force
(E) angelic company

25. Which of the following statements best expresses the author's attitude toward the damage to vegetation caused by foraging elephants?

(A) It is a regrettable by-product of the feeding process.
(B) It is a necessary but undesirable aspect of elephant population growth.
(C) It fortuitously results in creating environments suited to diverse species.
(D) It has the unexpected advantage that it allows scientists access to the rain forest.
(E) It reinforces the impression that elephants are a disruptive force.

IF YOU FINISH IN LESS THAN 25 MINUTES,
YOU MAY CHECK YOUR WORK ON THIS
SECTION ONLY. DO NOT TURN TO ANY   **S T O P**
OTHER SECTION IN THE TEST.

SECTION 2

Time—25 minutes   **20 questions (1–20)**

For each problem in this section, determine which of the five choices is correct and blacken that choice on your answer sheet. You may use any blank space on the page for your work.

Notes:

- You may use a calculator whenever you believe it will be helpful.
- Use the diagrams provided to help you solve the problems. Unless you see the phrase "<u>Note</u>: Figure not drawn to scale" under a diagram, it has been drawn as accurately as possible. Unless it is stated that a figure is three-dimensional, you may assume that it lies in a plane.

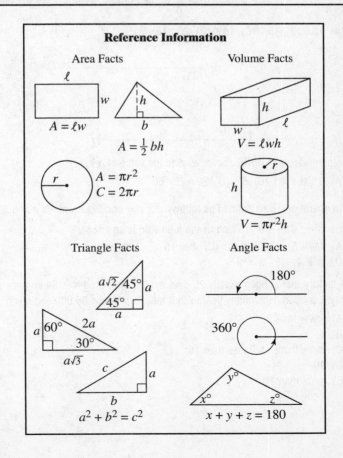

Reference Information

Area Facts

$A = \ell w$

$A = \frac{1}{2} bh$

$A = \pi r^2$
$C = 2\pi r$

Volume Facts

$V = \ell w h$

$V = \pi r^2 h$

Triangle Facts

$a\sqrt{2}$, $45°$, a, $45°$, a

a, $60°$, $2a$, $30°$, $a\sqrt{3}$

c, a, b

$a^2 + b^2 = c^2$

Angle Facts

$180°$

$360°$

$x°$, $y°$, $z°$

$x + y + z = 180$

1. If Mr. Beck earns $16 per hour, how many hours will he have to work in order to earn $88?

(A) 5   (B) 5.5   (C) 6.5   (D) 23.5   (E) 1408

2. Sarah saves $8 every day. If 11 days ago she had $324, how many dollars will she have 11 days from now?

(A) 148   (B) 236   (C) 412   (D) 500   (E) 566

3. Which of the following is an expression for "the product of 7 and the average (arithmetic mean) of a and b?"

(A) $\dfrac{7a+b}{2}$ (B) $\dfrac{7a+7b}{2}$ (C) $\dfrac{7+a+b}{3}$

(D) $7+\dfrac{a+b}{2}$ (E) $\dfrac{7+7a+7b}{3}$

4. If $\dfrac{3}{4}$ of a number is 7 more than $\dfrac{1}{6}$ of the number, what is $\dfrac{5}{3}$ of the number?

(A) 12   (B) 15   (C) 18   (D) 20   (E) 24

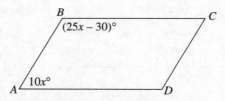

5. In parallelogram *ABCD* above, what is the value of x?

(A) 2   (B) 4   (C) 6   (D) 20   (E) 60

6. An operation, $*$, is defined as follows: for any positive numbers a and b,

$a * b = \sqrt{a+\sqrt{b}}$. Which of the following is an integer?

(A) $11 * 5$ (B) $4 * 9$ (C) $4 * 16$
(D) $7 * 4$ (E) $9 * 9$

7. A factory that is open exactly 25 days each month produces 64 engines each day it is open. How many years will it take to produce 96,000 engines?

(A) fewer than 5
(B) 5
(C) more than 5 but less than 10
(D) 10
(E) more than 10

8. In the figure on the right, what is the value of x?

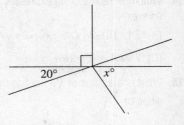

(A) 20
(B) 70
(C) 60
(D) 110
(E) It cannot be determined from the information given.

9. If $x - y = 5$, and $x^2 - y^2 = 75$, what is the value of y?

(A) -10 (B) -5 (C) 5   (D) 10
(E) It cannot be determined from the information given.

10. Julie inherited 40% of her father's estate. After paying a tax equal to 30% of her inheritance, what percent of her father's estate did she own?

(A) 10%   (B) 12%   (C) 18%
(D) 28%   (E) 30%

11. For any positive integer $n > 1$: $n!$ represents the product of the first n positive integers. For example, $3! = 1 \times 2 \times 3 = 6$. Which of the following is (are) equal to $(3!)(4!)$?

I. 7!
II. 12!
III. $4! + 5!$

(A) I only   (B) II only   (C) III only   (D) I and III   (E) I, II, and III

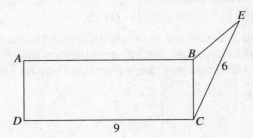

12. In the figure above, $BC = BE$. If R represents the perimeter of rectangle $ABCD$, and T represents the perimeter of triangle CBE, what is the value of $R - T$?

(A) 3   (B) 12   (C) 30   (D) $18 - 6\sqrt{2}$
(E) It cannot be determined from the information given.

13. There are 12 men on a basketball team, and in a game 5 of them play at any one time. If the game is one hour long, and if each man plays exactly the same amount of time, how many minutes does each man play?

(A) 10   (B) 12   (C) 24   (D) 25   (E) 30

14. Which of the following expresses the circumference of a circle in terms of A, its area?

(A) $2A$ (B) $2A\sqrt{\pi}$ (C) $2\pi\sqrt{A}$

(D) $2\sqrt{\pi A}$ (E) $2\pi A$

15. What is the value of k if the line that passes through $(3, -3)$ and $(k, 5)$ has a slope of $\dfrac{2}{3}$?

(A) 0   (B) 6   (C) $8\dfrac{1}{3}$ (D) 15

(E) It cannot be determined from the information given.

16. If x is an odd number, what is the difference between the smallest odd number greater than $5x + 4$ and the largest odd number less than $3x + 7$?

(A) $2x$ (B) $2x - 3$ (C) $8x + 7$ (D) $8x + 8$

(E) It cannot be determined from the information given.

17. The measures of the angles of a triangle are in the ratio of 1:2:3. What is the ratio of the length of the smallest side to the length of the longest side?

(A) $1:\sqrt{2}$ (B) $1:\sqrt{3}$ (C) 1:2   (D) 1:3

(E) It cannot be determined from the information given.

18. A car going 50 miles per hour set out on a 200-mile trip at 12:00 P.M. Exactly 20 minutes later, a second car left from the same place and followed the same route. How fast, in miles per hour, was the second car going if it caught up with the first car at 2:00 P.M.?

(A) 55   (B) 60   (C) 65   (D) 70   (E) 75

19. A store sells f fountain pens and b ballpoint pens. If a fountain pen costs twice as much as a ballpoint pen, and if the store takes in a total of d dollars from the sales of these pens, how many dollars does a ballpoint pen cost?

(A) $\dfrac{d}{b+2f}$ (B) $\dfrac{b+2f}{d}$ (C) $\dfrac{2b+f}{d}$

(D) $\dfrac{d}{2b+f}$ (E) $d(b + 2f)$

20. If in 1965 Yann was four times as old as Isabel, and in 1970 he was three times as old as she was, how old was Yann when Isabel was born?

(A) 25   (B) 30   (C) 35

(D) 40   (E) 45

IF YOU FINISH IN LESS THAN 25 MINUTES, YOU MAY CHECK YOUR WORK ON THIS SECTION ONLY. DO NOT TURN TO ANY OTHER SECTION IN THE TEST.   **STOP**

SECTION 3

Time—25 minutes   27 questions (26–52)

Each of the following sentences contains one or two blanks; these blanks indicate that a word or set of words has been left out. Below the sentence are five words or phrases, lettered A through E. Select the word or set of words that best completes the sentence.

EXAMPLE:

Fame is ----; today's rising star is all too soon tomorrow's washed-up has-been.

(A) rewarding   (B) gradual   (C) essential
(D) spontaneous   (E) transitory

---

26. In order that they may be able to discriminate wisely among the many conflicting arguments put before them, legislators must be trained to ---- the truth.

(A) confuse   (B) condemn   (C) ignore
(D) condone   (E) discern

27. In their new collections of lighthearted, provocative dresses, French fashion designers are gambling that even ---- professional women are ready for a bit of ---- in style.

(A) strict..reticence
(B) serious..frivolity
(C) elegant..tradition
(D) modern..harmony
(E) unsentimental..propriety

28. Irony can, after a fashion, become a mode of escape: to laugh at the terrors of life is in some sense to ---- them.

(A) exaggerate   (B) revitalize   (C) corroborate
(D) evade   (E) justify

29. People who find themselves unusually ---- and ready to drowse off at unexpected moments may be suffering from a hormonal imbalance.

(A) lethargic   (B) distracted   (C) obdurate
(D) benign   (E) perfunctory

30. The expression "he passed away" is ---- for "he died."

(A) a reminder   (B) a commiseration
(C) a simile   (D) a euphemism
(E) an exaggeration

31. Despite the enormous popularity and influence of his book, *Thunder Out of China,* White's career ----.

(A) soared   (B) endured   (C) accelerated
(D) revived   (E) foundered

32. Written just after King's assassination, Lomax's book has all the virtues of historical ----, but lacks the greater virtue of historical ----, which comes from long and mature reflection upon events.

(A) precision..accuracy
(B) criticism..distance
(C) immediacy..perspective
(D) outlook..realism
(E) currency..testimony

33. Relishing his triumph, Costner especially ---- the chagrin of the critics who had predicted his ----.

(A) regretted..success
(B) acknowledged..comeback
(C) understated..bankruptcy
(D) distorted..mortification
(E) savored..failure

Each of the following questions introduces a pair of words or phrases in capital letters, linked by a colon(:); this colon indicates that these words are related in some way. Following the capitalized pair are five pairs of words or phrases lettered A through E. Select the pair whose relationship is most similar to the relationship illustrated by the capitalized pair.

EXAMPLE:

CLOCK:TIME::   (A) watch:wrist
(B) pedometer:speed
(C) thermometer:temperature
(D) hourglass:sand   (E) radio:sound

34. PEBBLE:SLINGSHOT::   (A) arrow:quiver
(B) ball:cannon   (C) missile:target
(D) hilt:dagger   (E) barrel:rifle

35. DRIZZLE:POUR::   (A) rumple:fold
(B) moisten:waterproof   (C) tingle:chill
(D) dam:flood   (E) smolder:blaze

36. ERADICATE:ERROR::   (A) acknowledge:fault
(B) arbitrate:dispute   (C) penalize:foul
(D) uproot:weed   (E) erase:blackboard

37. GANDER:GOOSE::   (A) fawn:deer
(B) porpoise:whale   (C) mare:horse
(D) panda:bear   (E) ram:sheep

38. LOCOMOTION:FEET::   (A) perspiration:sweat
(B) amnesia:brain   (C) sensation:hands
(D) digestion:stomach   (E) sound:ears

39. GARBLED:COMPREHEND::
(A) controversial:dispute
(B) negligible:disregard
(C) mangled:believe
(D) methodical:organize
(E) camouflaged:discern

40. PURIST:CORRECTNESS::

(A) miser:generosity
(B) saint:elevation
(C) nomad:refuge
(D) judge:accuracy
(E) martinet:discipline

The questions that follow the two passages in this section relate to the content of both, and to their relationship. The correct response may be <u>stated outright</u> or merely <u>suggested</u> in the passages and in any introductory or footnoted material included.

Questions 41–52 are based on the following passages.

The following passages are excerpted from two recent essays that relate writing to sports. The author of Passage 1 deals with having had a novel rejected by his publisher. The author of Passage 2 explores how his involvement in sports affected his writing career.

Passage 1

In consigning this manuscript to a desk drawer, I am comforted by the behavior of baseball players. There are *no* pitchers who do not give up home runs, there are *no* batters who do not strike out. There are *no*
Line major league pitchers or batters who have not somehow learned to
(5) survive giving up home runs and striking out. That much is obvious.

What seems to me less obvious is how these "failures" must be digested, or put to use, in the overall experience of the player. A jogger once explained to me that the nerves of the ankle are so sensitive and complex that each time a runner sets his foot down, hundreds of
(10) messages are conveyed to the runner's brain about the nature of the terrain and the requirements for weight distribution, balance, and muscle-strength. I'm certain that the ninth-inning home run that Dave Henderson hit off Donny Moore registered complexly and permanently in Moore's mind and body and that the next time Moore faced Henderson, his
(15) pitching was informed by his awful experience of October 1986. Moore's continuing baseball career depended to some extent on his converting that encounter with Henderson into something useful for his pitching. I can also imagine such an experience destroying an athlete, registering in his mind and body in such a negative way as to produce a debilitating
(20) fear.

Of the many ways in which athletes and artists are similar, one is that, unlike accountants or plumbers or insurance salesmen, to succeed

at all they must perform at an extraordinary level of excellence. Another
is that they must be willing to extend themselves irrationally in order to
(25) achieve that level of performance. A writer doesn't have to write all-out
all the time, but he or she must be ready to write all-out any time the
story requires it. Hold back and you produce what just about any literate
citizen can produce, a "pretty good" piece of work. Like the cautious
pitcher, the timid writer can spend a lifetime in the minor leagues.
(30)   And what more than failure—the strike out, the crucial home run
given up, the manuscript criticized and rejected—is more likely to produce caution or timidity? An instinctive response to painful experience is
to avoid the behavior that produced the pain. To function at the level of
excellence required for survival, writers like athletes must go against
(35) instinct, must absorb their failures and become stronger, must endlessly
repeat the behavior that produced the pain.

Passage 2
           The athletic advantages of this concentration, particularly for an ath-
lete who was making up for the absence of great natural skill, were
considerable. Concentration gave you an edge over many of your
(40) opponents, even your betters, who could not isolate themselves to that
degree. For example, in football if they were ahead (or behind) by several
touchdowns, if the game itself seemed to have been settled, they tended
to slack off, to ease off a little, certainly to relax their own concentration.
It was then that your own unwavering concentration and your own
(45) indifference to the larger point of view paid off. At the very least you
could deal out surprise and discomfort to your opponents.
           But it was more than that. Do you see? The ritual of physical concen-
tration, of acute engagement in a small space while disregarding all the
clamor and demands of the larger world, was the best possible lesson in
(50) precisely the kind of selfish intensity needed to create and to finish a
poem, a story, or a novel. This alone mattered while all the world going
on, with and without you, did not.
           I was learning first in muscle, blood, and bone, not from literature
and not from teachers of literature or the arts or the natural sciences,
(55) but from coaches, in particular this one coach who paid me enough
attention to influence me to teach some things to myself. I was learning
about art and life through the abstraction of athletics in much the same
way that a soldier is, to an extent, prepared for war by endless parade
ground drill. His body must learn to be a soldier before heart, mind, and
(60) spirit can.
           Ironically, I tend to dismiss most comparisons of athletics to art and
to "the creative process." But only because, I think, so much that is

claimed for both is untrue. But I have come to believe—indeed I have to
believe it insofar as I believe in the validity and efficacy of art—that what
(65) comes to us first and foremost through the body, as a sensuous affec-
tive experience, is taken and transformed by mind and self into a thing of
the spirit. Which is only to say that what the body learns and is taught is
of enormous significance—at least until the last light of the body fails.

41. Why does the author of Passage 1 consign his manuscript to a desk drawer?

(A) To protect it from the inquisitive eyes of his family
(B) To prevent its getting lost or disordered
(C) Because his publisher wishes to take another look at it
(D) Because he chooses to watch a televised baseball game
(E) To set it aside as unmarketable in its current state

42. Why is the author of Passage 1 "comforted by the behavior of baseball
players" (lines 1–2)?

(A) He treasures the timeless rituals of America's national pastime.
(B) He sees he is not alone in having to confront failure and move on.
(C) He enjoys watching the frustration of the batters who strike out.
(D) He looks at baseball from the viewpoint of a behavioral psychologist.
(E) He welcomes any distraction from the task of revising his novel.

43. What function in the passage is served by the discussion of the nerves in the
ankle in lines 7–12?

(A) It provides a momentary digression from the overall narrative flow.
(B) It emphasizes how strong a mental impact Henderson's home run must
have had on Moore.
(C) It provides scientific confirmation of the neuromuscular abilities of athletes.
(D) It illustrates that the author's interest in sports is not limited to baseball
alone.
(E) It conveys a sense of how confusing it is for the mind to deal with so
many simultaneous messages.

44. The word "registered" in line 13 means

(A) enrolled formally
(B) expressed without words
(C) corresponded exactly
(D) made an impression
(E) qualified officially

45. The attitude of the author of Passage 1 to accountants, plumbers, and insurance salesmen (lines 22–23) can best be described as

(A) respectful   (B) cautious   (C) superior
(D) cynical   (E) hypocritical

46. In the concluding paragraphs of Passage 1, the author appears to

   (A) romanticize the writer as someone heroic in his or her accomplishments
   (B) deprecate athletes for their inability to react to experience instinctively
   (C) minimize the travail that artists and athletes endure to do their work
   (D) advocate the importance of literacy to the common citizen
   (E) suggest a cautious approach would reduce the likelihood of future failure

47. The author of Passage 2 prizes

   (A) his innate athletic talent
   (B) the respect of his peers
   (C) his ability to focus
   (D) the gift of relaxation
   (E) winning at any cost

48. The word "settled" in line 42 means

   (A) judged   (B) decided   (C) reconciled   (D) pacified   (E) inhabited

49. What does the author mean by "indifference to the larger point of view" (line 45)?

   (A) Inability to see the greater implications of the activity in which you were involved
   (B) Hostility to opponents coming from larger, better trained teams
   (C) Reluctance to look beyond your own immediate concerns
   (D) Refusing to care how greatly you might be hurt by your opponents
   (E) Being more concerned with the task at hand than with whether you win or lose

50. What is the function of the phrase "to an extent" in line 58?

   (A) It denies a situation
   (B) It conveys a paradox
   (C) It qualifies a statement
   (D) It represents a metaphor
   (E) It minimizes a liability

51. The author finds it ironic that he tends to "dismiss most comparisons of athletics to art" (line 61) because

   (A) athletics is the basis for great art
   (B) he finds comparisons generally unhelpful
   (C) he is making such a comparison
   (D) he typically is less cynical
   (E) he rejects the so-called "creative process"

52. The authors of both passages would agree that

(A) the lot of the professional writer is more trying than that of the professional athlete

(B) athletics has little to do with the actual workings of the creative process

(C) both artists and athletes learn hard lessons in the course of mastering their art

(D) it is important to concentrate on the things that hurt us in life

(E) participating in sports provides a distraction from the isolation of a writer's life

IF YOU FINISH IN LESS THAN 25 MINUTES, YOU MAY CHECK YOUR WORK ON THIS SECTION ONLY. DO NOT TURN TO ANY OTHER SECTION IN THE TEST.

STOP

SECTION 4

Time—25 minutes   **20 questions (21–40)**

This section has two types of questions. The directions for each type are given right before those questions. You may use any blank space on the page for your work.

Notes:

- You may use a calculator whenever you believe it will be helpful.
- Use the diagrams provided to help you solve the problems. Unless you see the phrase "<u>Note</u>: Figure not drawn to scale" under a diagram, it has been drawn as accurately as possible. Unless it is stated that a figure is three-dimensional, you may assume that it lies in a plane.

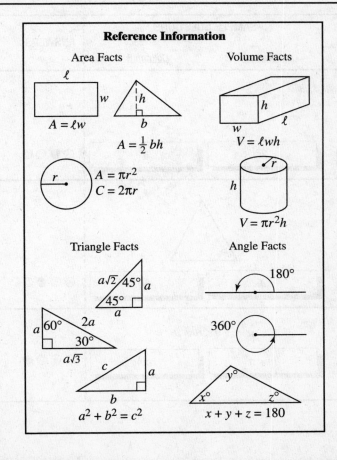

Reference Information

Area Facts

$A = \ell w$

$A = \frac{1}{2} bh$

$A = \pi r^2$
$C = 2\pi r$

Volume Facts

$V = \ell wh$

$V = \pi r^2 h$

Triangle Facts

$a\sqrt{2}$, $45°$, $45°$, a, a

a, $60°$, $2a$, $30°$, $a\sqrt{3}$

c, a, b, $a^2 + b^2 = c^2$

Angle Facts

$180°$

$360°$

$x°$, $y°$, $z°$, $x + y + z = 180$

Directions for the Quantitative Comparison Questions

In each of questions 21–32, two quantities appear in boxes: one in Column A and one in Column B. You must compare them. The correct answer to a question is

A if the quantity in Column A is greater;
B if the quantity in Column B is greater;
C if the two quantities are equal;
D if it is impossible to determine which quantity is greater.

<u>Notes:</u>
- Sometimes information about one or both of the quantities is centered above the two boxes.
- If the same symbol appears in both columns, it represents the same thing each time.
- All variables represent real numbers.

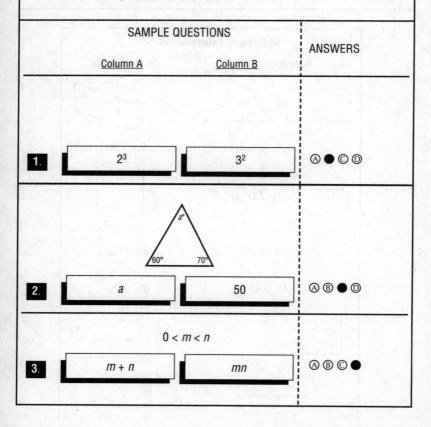

SAMPLE QUESTIONS

ANSWERS

Column A | Column B

1. | 2^3 | 3^2 | Ⓐ ● Ⓒ Ⓓ

2. | a | 50 | Ⓐ Ⓑ ● Ⓓ

$a°$
$60°$ $70°$

3. $0 < m < n$ | $m + n$ | mn | Ⓐ Ⓑ Ⓒ ●

SUMMARY DIRECTIONS FOR QUANTITATIVE
COMPARISON QUESTIONS

<u>Answer:</u> A if the quantity in Column A is greater;
B if the quantity in Column B is greater;
C if the two quantities are equal;
D if the relationship cannot be determined from the information given.

<u>Column A</u>	<u>Column B</u>

$$a = -1$$

21. $(a^2 + a)^2$ | 0

---

a and *b* are primes.
$$a + b = 8$$

22. b | 6

---

a and *b* are positive.
$$a + b = 1$$

23. ab | 1

---

24. $(-1)^{1998}$ | $(-1)^{1999}$

---

n is an odd positive integer.

25. The number of prime factors of n | The number of prime factors of $2n$

$$a > b > 0$$

26. a^3b^2 | a^2b^3

$$0 < a < b < 1$$

27. $\sqrt{a+b}$ | $\sqrt{a} + \sqrt{b}$

SUMMARY DIRECTIONS FOR QUANTITATIVE
COMPARISON QUESTIONS

<u>Answer:</u> A if the quantity in Column A is greater;
B if the quantity in Column B is greater;
C if the two quantities are equal;
D if the relationship cannot be determined from the information given.

<u>Column A</u>   <u>Column B</u>

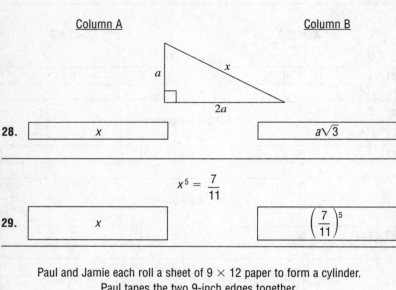

28. | x | | $a\sqrt{3}$ |

$$x^5 = \frac{7}{11}$$

29. | x | | $\left(\dfrac{7}{11}\right)^5$ |

Paul and Jamie each roll a sheet of 9×12 paper to form a cylinder.
Paul tapes the two 9-inch edges together.
Jamie tapes the two 12-inch edges together.

30. | The volume of
Paul's cylinder | | The volume of
Jamie's cylinder |

The circumference of a circle is $a\pi$ inches
The area of the same circle is $b\pi$ square inches

31. | a | | b |

Column A   Column B

The figure below consists of 4 circles with the same center.
The radii of the 4 circles are 1, 2, 3, and 4.

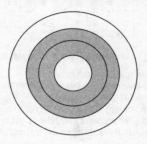

32. | The area of the shaded region | | The area of the white region |

Directions for Student-Produced Response Questions (Grid-ins)

In questions 33–40, first solve the problem, and then enter your answer on the grid provided on the answer sheet. The instructions for entering your answers follow.

- First, write your answer in the boxes at the top of the grid.
- Second, grid your answer in the columns below the boxes.
- Use the fraction bar in the first row or the decimal point in the second row to enter fractions and decimals.

Answer: $\frac{8}{15}$ Answer: 1.75

Write your answer in the boxes

Grid in your answer

Answer: 100

Either position is acceptable

- Grid only one space in each column.
- Entering the answer in the boxes is recommended as an aid in gridding, but is not required.
- The machine scoring your exam can read only what you grid, so you **must grid in your answers correctly to get credit.**
- If a question has more than one correct answer, grid in only one of them.
- The grid does not have a minus sign, so no answer can be negative.
- A mixed number *must* be converted to an improper fraction or a decimal before it is gridded. Enter $1\frac{1}{4}$ as 5/4 or 1.25; the machine will interpret 1 1/4 as $\frac{11}{4}$ and mark it wrong.

- **All decimals must be entered as accurately as possible.** Here are the three acceptable ways of gridding

$$\frac{3}{11} = 0.272727...$$

| 3/11 | .272 | .273 |

- Note that rounding to .273 is acceptable, because you are using the full grid, but you would receive **no credit** for .3 or .27, because they are less accurate.

33. If $a * b = (a + b)^2 - (a - b)^2$, what is the value of $7 * 11$?

34. If $3x - 11 = 11 - 3x$, what is the value of x?

35. What is the average (arithmetic mean) of 1, 2.3, and 4.56?

36. Jim, Kim, Ben, and Len divided $1000 as follows: Kim got twice as much as Jim, Ben got 3 times as much as Jim, and Len got $100. How much, in dollars, did Jim get?

37. If x, y, and z are different positive integers less than 10, what is the greatest possible value of $\dfrac{x^2 - y}{z}$?

38. In a jar containing only red and blue marbles, 40% of the marbles are red. If the average weight of a red marble is 40 grams and the average weight of a blue marble is 60 grams, what is the average weight, in grams, of all the marbles in the jar?

39. How many sides does a polygon have if the measure of each interior angle is twice the measure of each exterior angle?

40. A jar contained 3 times as many red marbles as blue marbles. After Lior removed n % of the red marbles and increased the number of blue marbles by n %, there were the same number of marbles of each color. What is the value of n?

IF YOU FINISH IN LESS THAN 25 MINUTES,
YOU MAY CHECK YOUR WORK ON THIS
SECTION ONLY. DO NOT TURN TO ANY   **S T O P**
OTHER SECTION IN THE TEST.

SECTION 5

Time—30 minutes　39 questions (1–39)

The sentences in this section may contain errors in grammar, usage, choice of words, or idioms. There is either just one error per sentence or the sentence is correct. Some words or phrases are underlined and lettered; everything else in the sentence is correct.

If an underlined word or phrase is incorrect, choose that letter; if the sentence is correct, select <u>No error</u>. Then blacken the appropriate space on your Answer Sheet.

EXAMPLE:

The region has a climate <u>so severe that</u> plants
　　　　　　　　　　　　　A

<u>growing there</u> rarely <u>had been</u> more than
　　　　B　　　　　　　　C

twelve inches <u>high</u>. <u>No error</u>　　　　Ⓐ Ⓑ ● Ⓓ Ⓔ
　　　　　　　　D　　　E

---

1. Notice the <u>immediate</u> <u>affect</u> <u>this</u> drug has on the <u>behavior of</u> the rats in the
　　　　　　　　A　　　　B　　C　　　　　　　　　D

   cage. <u>No error</u>
　　　　　E

2. I believe the <u>commissioner and she to be honest</u>: <u>nevertheless</u>, corruption
　　　　　　　　　A　　　　　　　　　　　　　　　　B

   by public officals and their staffs <u>appears to be</u> a <u>continual</u> political problem.
　　　　　　　　　　　　　　　　　　C　　　　　　　D

   <u>No error</u>
　　E

3. <u>In spite</u> of official denials, news sources reported <u>that</u> the bombs that hit
　　A　　　　　　　　　　　　　　　　　　　　　　B

   Tripoli in 1986 were <u>really</u> <u>intended to kill</u> Muammar al-Qaddafi. <u>No error</u>
　　　　　　　　　　　C　　　　D　　　　　　　　　　　　　　　E

4. <u>Are you going</u> to <u>lie</u> there <u>all day</u> and refuse <u>to see</u> your friends? <u>No error</u>
　　A　　　　　　B　　　　C　　　　　　D　　　　　　　E

5. Neither the teacher nor her pupils were enthused about going on the field
   <u>A</u>   <u>B</u>   <u>C</u>   <u>D</u>
   trip. <u>No error</u>
          E

6. While Egyptian President Anwar El-Sadat was reviewing a military parade in
   <u>A</u>
   1981, <u>a band of</u> commandos <u>had shot</u> him and others <u>in the vicinity</u>. <u>No error</u>
          B   C   D   E

7. Please do not be <u>aggravated</u> by his <u>bad manners</u> <u>since</u> he is <u>merely</u> trying
                      A   B   C   D
   to attract attention. <u>No error</u>
                          E

8. Neither the opera singers <u>or</u> the general public <u>had seen</u> <u>as much glitter</u>
                              A   B   C
   in years as they did during *Turandot,* the <u>finale of</u> the opera season. <u>No error</u>
                                                 D   E

9. His story about the <u>strange beings</u> in a space ship was <u>so</u> <u>incredulous</u> <u>that</u>
                        A   B   C   D
   no one believed him. <u>No error</u>
                         E

10. The hot air balloon had burst as they <u>were preparing</u> <u>for launch</u>, and the
                                           A   B
    platform <u>had broke</u> <u>as a result</u>. <u>No error</u>
              C   D   E

11. I fail <u>to understand</u> <u>why</u> you are seeking my <u>council</u> after the way you <u>ignored</u>
            A   B   C   D
    my advice last week. <u>No error</u>
                          E

12. Ann Landers, <u>whose</u> name is a household word <u>to millions of</u> readers, <u>are</u>
                  A   B   C
    <u>well-known</u> for family advice. <u>No error</u>
     D   E

13. Between <u>you and I</u>, the highway department must review bridge construction
A

<u>across the country</u> <u>in order to</u> avoid major catastrophes <u>resulting from</u> metal
B   C   D

fatigue. <u>No error</u>
E

14. Child custody in surrogate mother cases is just <u>one of the many</u> controversial
A

issues <u>that</u> <u>are</u> currently being <u>decided upon</u> in the courts. <u>No error</u>
B   C   D   E

15. John usually eats a quick lunch, <u>ignoring</u> the question of <u>whether</u> <u>what</u> he eats
A   B   C

is <u>healthy</u> or not. <u>No error</u>
D   E

16. <u>If</u> you continue to drive <u>so recklessly</u>, you <u>are likely</u> to have a serious accident
A   B   C

in the <u>very</u> near future. <u>No error</u>
D   E

17. The general, <u>along with</u> the members of his <u>general staff</u>, <u>seem</u> to favor
A   B   C

<u>immediate retaliation</u>. <u>No error</u>
D   E

18. We resented <u>him</u> <u>criticizing</u> our efforts because he <u>had ignored</u> our requests
A   B   C

for assistance <u>up to that time</u>. <u>No error</u>
D   E

19. Casey Jones, <u>who was</u> killed in the <u>line of duty</u>, <u>became</u> a hero to fellow
A   B   C

railroad workers and <u>was to be immortalized</u> by a ballad. <u>No error</u>
D   E

Some or all parts of the following sentences are underlined. The first answer choice, (A), simply repeats the underlined part of the sentence. The other four choices present four alternate ways to phrase the underlined part. Select the answer that produces the most effective sentence, one that is clear and exact, and blacken the appropriate space on your answer sheet. In selecting your choice, be sure that it is standard written English, and that it expresses the meaning of the original sentence.

EXAMPLE:

The first biography of author Eudora Welty came out in 1998
and she was eighty-nine years old at the time.

(A) and she was eighty-nine years old at the time.
(B) at the time when she was eighty-nine.
(C) upon becoming an eighty-nine year old.
(D) when she was eighty-nine.
(E) at the age of eighty-nine years old.

20. The police officer refused to permit us to enter the apartment, saying that he had orders to stop him going into the building.

(A) stop him going   (B) prevent him going
(C) stop his going   (D) stop us going
(E) stop our going

21. After conducting the orchestra for six concerts, Beethoven's *Ninth Symphony* was scheduled.

(A) After conducting
(B) After he conducted
(C) While conducting
(D) Although he conducted
(E) After he had conducted

22. Jackie Robinson became the first black player in major league baseball, he paved the way for black athletes to be accepted on the field.

(A) Jackie Robinson became the first black player in major league baseball, he

(B) Jackie Robinson, in becoming the first black player in major league baseball, he

(C) Jackie Robinson became the first black player in major league baseball; he

(D) Jackie Robinson, the first black player in major league baseball; he

(E) Jackie Robinson had become the first black player in major league baseball and he

23. Sitting in the Coliseum, the music couldn't hardly be heard because of the cheering and yelling of the spectators.

(A) the music couldn't hardly be heard because of

(B) the music couldn't hardly be heard due to

(C) the music could hardly be heard due to

(D) we could hardly be heard because of

(E) we could hardly hear the music because of

24. The contents of the examination came as a shock to the student, everything on it having no resemblance to what she had studied.

(A) as a shock to the student, everything on it having

(B) to the student as a shock, being that everything on it had

(C) to the student as a shock, with everything on it having

(D) as a shock to the student, everything on it has

(E) as a shock to the student; everything on it had

25. Across the nation, curricular changes sweeping the universities as schools reassess the knowledge that educated people should have.

(A) curricular changes sweeping the universities as schools

(B) curricular changes are sweeping the universities as schools

(C) changes are sweeping the curricular since schools

(D) curricular changes sweeping the universities causing schools to

(E) curricular changes sweep the universities, but schools

26. If you have enjoyed these kind of programs, write to your local public television station and ask for more.

(A) these kind of programs

(B) those kind of programs

(C) these kinds of programs

(D) these kind of a program

(E) those kind of a program

27. In her critique of the newly opened restaurant, the reviewer discussed the elaborate menu, the impressive wine list, and how the waiters functioned.

    (A) list, and how the waiters functioned
    (B) list and how the waiters functioned
    (C) list, and the excellent service
    (D) list, and even the excellent service
    (E) list, and how the waiters usually function

28. Contemporary poets are not abandoning rhyme, but some avoiding it.

    (A) but some avoiding it
    (B) but it is avoided by some of them
    (C) but it is being avoided
    (D) but some are avoiding it
    (E) but it has been being avoided by some

29. Your complaint is no different from the last customer who expected a refund.

    (A) Your complaint is no different from the last customer
    (B) Your complaint is no different from that of the last customer
    (C) Your complaint is similar to the last customer
    (D) Your complaint is no different then that of the last customer
    (E) Your complaint is the same as the last customer

30. According to the review board, many laboratory tests were ordered by the staff of the hospital that had no medical justification.

    (A) many laboratory tests were ordered by the staff of the hospital that
    (B) many laboratory tests were ordered by the staff of the hospital who
    (C) the staff of the hospital ordered many laboratory tests that
    (D) the staff of the hospital, who ordered many laboratory tests that
    (E) the ordering of many laboratory tests by the staff of the hospital which

31. Confident about the outcome, President Clinton, along with his staff, are traveling to the conference.

    (A) Confident about the outcome, President Clinton along with his staff are traveling
    (B) Confident about the outcome, President Clinton's party are traveling
    (C) Confident about the outcome, President Clinton along with his staff is traveling
    (D) With confidence about the outcome, President Clinton along with his staff are traveling
    (E) President Clinton along with his staff is traveling confidently about the outcome

32. Helen Keller was blind and deaf from infancy and she learned to communicate using both sign language and speech.

(A) Helen Keller was blind and deaf from infancy and she

(B) Although blind and deaf from infancy, Helen Keller

(C) Although being blind and deaf from the time she was an infant, Helen Keller

(D) Being blind and deaf from infancy, Helen Keller

(E) Helen Keller, being blind and deaf from infancy, she

33. Standing alone beside her husband's grave, grief overwhelmed the widow and she wept inconsolably.

(A) grief overwhelmed the widow and she wept inconsolably

(B) grief overwhelmed the widow, who wept inconsolably

(C) grief overwhelmed the widow that wept inconsolably

(D) the widow, overwhelmed by grief, wept inconsolably

(E) the widow was overwhelmed by grief, she wept inconsolably

---

The passage below is the unedited draft of a student's essay. Some of the essay needs to be rewritten to make the meaning clearer and more precise. Read the essay carefully.

The essay is followed by six questions about changes that might improve all or part of its organization, development, sentence structure, use of language, appropriateness to the audience, or its use of standard written English. Choose the answer that most clearly and effectively expresses the student's intended meaning. Indicate your choice by filling in the corresponding space on the answer sheet.

---

[1] Members of our community have objected to the inclusion of various pieces of art in the local art exhibit. [2] They say that these pieces offend community values. [3] The exhibit in its entirety should be presented.

[4] The reason for this is that people have varied tastes, and those who like this form of art have a right to see the complete exhibit. [5] An exhibit like this one gives the community a rare chance to see the latest modern art nearby, and many people have looked forward to it with great anticipation. [6] It would be an unfortunate blow to those people for it not to be shown.

[7] The exhibit may contain pieces of art that tend to be slightly erotic, but what is being shown that most people haven't already seen? [8] So, give it an R or an X rating and don't let small children in. [9] But how many small children voluntarily go to see an art exhibit? [10] The exhibit includes examples of a new style of modern

art. [11] The paintings show crowds of nude people. [12] The exhibit is at the library's new art gallery. [13] For centuries artists have been painting and sculpting people in the nude. [14] Why are these works of art different? [15] Perhaps they are more graphic in some respects, but we live in a entirely different society than from the past. [16] It is strange indeed for people in this day and age to be offended by the sight of the human anatomy.

[17] If people don't agree with these pieces, they simply should just not go. [18] But they should not be allowed to prevent others from seeing it.

34. Taking into account the sentences that precede and follow sentence 3, which of the following is the best revision of sentence 3?

(A) On the other hand, the whole exhibit should be presented.

(B) The exhibit, however, should be presented in its entirety.

(C) The exhibit should be entirely presented regardless of what the critics say.

(D) But another point of view is that the exhibit should be presented in its entirety.

(E) Still other members also say the whole exhibit should be presented in its entirety.

35. In the context of paragraph 3, which of the following is the best revision of sentence 8?

(A) So, an R or X rating will warn people with small children to keep them out.

(B) Therefore, giving it an R or an X rating and not letting small children in.

(C) To satisfy everyone objecting to the exhibit, perhaps the exhibit could be given an R or an X rating to advise parents that some of the art on exhibit may not be suitable for young children.

(D) Let an R or an X rating caution the public that some of the art may be offensive and be unsuitable for young children.

(E) In conclusion, small children will be kept out by giving it an R or an X rating.

36. In the context of paragraph 3, which of the following is the best revision of sentences 10, 11, and 12?

(A) Paintings on exhibit at the library showing crowds of nude people and done in a new style of modern art.

(B) The exhibit, on display at the library, includes paintings of crowds of nude people done in a new style of modern art.

(C) The exhibit includes paintings in a new style of modern art, which shows crowds of nude people at the library.

(D) The library is the site of the exhibit which shows a new style of modern art, with paintings showing crowds of nude people.

(E) The new style of modern art includes examples of paintings showing crowds of nude people on exhibit in the library.

37. To improve the clarity and coherence of the whole essay, where is the best place to relocate the ideas contained in sentences 10, 11, and 12?

(A) Before sentence 1

(B) Between sentences 1 and 2

(C) Between sentences 8 and 9

(D) Between sentences 15 and 16

(E) After sentence 18

38. Which of the following is the best revision of the underlined segment of sentence 15 below?

Perhaps they are more graphic in some respects, but we live in a <u>*entirely*</u> <u>*different society than from the past*</u>.

(A) an entirely different society than of the past

(B) a completely different society than the past

(C) a society completely different than from past societies

(D) a society which is entirely different from the way societies have been in the past

(E) an entirely different society from that of the past

39. Which of the following revisions of sentence 17 provides the best transition between paragraphs 3 and 4?

(A) If anyone doesn't approve of these pieces, they simply should not go to the exhibit.

(B) Anyone disagreeing with the pieces in the exhibit shouldn't go to it.

(C) Anyone who disapproves of nudity in art simply shouldn't go to the exhibit.

(D) If anyone dislikes the sight of nudes in art, this show isn't for them.

(E) Don't go if you disapprove of nudity in art.

IF YOU FINISH IN LESS THAN 30 MINUTES, YOU MAY CHECK YOUR WORK ON THIS SECTION ONLY. DO NOT TURN TO ANY OTHER SECTION IN THE TEST.   **S T O P**

Answer Key

Section 1 Verbal Reasoning

1. D	10. D	19. C
2. C	11. A	20. D
3. A	12. C	21. C
4. B	13. D	22. C
5. E	14. E	23. E
6. B	15. D	24. B
7. D	16. C	25. C
8. C	17. B	
9. D	18. C	

Section 2 Mathematical Reasoning

1. B	8. E	15. D
2. D	9. C	16. A
3. B	10. D	17. C
4. D	11. C	18. B
5. C	12. B	19. A
6. D	13. D	20. B
7. B	14. D	

Section 3 Verbal Reasoning

26. E	35. E	44. D
27. B	36. D	45. C
28. D	37. E	46. A
29. A	38. D	47. C
30. D	39. E	48. B
31. E	40. E	49. E
32. C	41. E	50. C
33. E	42. B	51. C
34. B	43. B	52. C

Section 4 Mathematical Reasoning

21. C	25. B	29. A
22. B	26. A	30. A
23. B	27. B	31. D
24. A	28. A	32. C

Grid-in Questions

33. 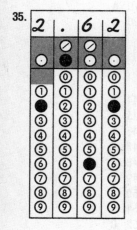   **34.**

35.   **36.**

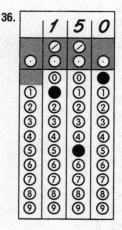

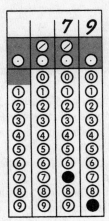

37. 7 9

38. 5 2

39. 6

40. 5 0

Section 5 Writing Skills

1. **B**	14. **D**	27. **C**
2. **A**	15. **E**	28. **D**
3. **E**	16. **E**	29. **B**
4. **E**	17. **C**	30. **C**
5. **C**	18. **A**	31. **C**
6. **C**	19. **D**	32. **B**
7. **A**	20. **E**	33. **D**
8. **A**	21. **E**	34. **D**
9. **C**	22. **C**	35. **D**
10. **C**	23. **E**	36. **B**
11. **C**	24. **E**	37. **A**
12. **C**	25. **B**	38. **E**
13. **A**	26. **C**	39. **C**

Answer Explanations

Section 1 Verbal Reasoning

1. **(D)** Such an extraordinarily useful material would *revolutionize* or make radical changes in an industry.

2. **(C)** A contrast is set up here by the expression "no matter how." It tells us that, although future "revelations" (surprising news) may be *striking*, they will not equal past ones. These past revelations *radically* transformed or thoroughly changed our view.

3. **(A)** Since "few other plants can grow beneath the canopy of the sycamore," it must be *inhibiting* or restraining the other plants.

4. **(B)** Certain authors have been *relegated* or sent off to "obscurity," a state of being hidden or forgotten. There they must be "rediscovered."

5. **(E)** Critics sometimes praise, but more often *decry* or condemn things. Here the critics see the "saccharine" (too sweet) mood of the movie as inconsistent with the *acerbic* (sour, bitter) tone of the book.

6. **(B)** A *latch* is the part of the *door* that closes it; a *clasp* is the part of the *necklace* that closes it.

(Function)

7. **(D)** A *caption* is a title or explanatory heading for a *photograph*; a *title* is the equivalent for an *article*.

(Function)

8. **(C)** A *tyrannosaur* is a kind of *dinosaur*; a *condor* is a kind of *bird*.

(Member and Class)

9. **(D)** An *author* who is *prolific* (highly productive) by definition writes a lot; a *speaker* who is *loquacious* (talkative) by definition talks a lot.

(Defining Characteristic)

10. **(D)** A *mentor*, by definition, aims to assist a *protégé*; a *sponsor*, by definition, aims to assist a *candidate*.

(Function)

11. **(A)** A *traveler* follows an *itinerary* or plan of his or her journey; a *lecturer* follows an *outline* or plan of his or her lecture.

(Worker and Tool)

12. **(C)** Among other clues, Mr. Collins states that he hopes to lead Elizabeth "to the altar ere long."

13. **(D)** Elizabeth is "sensible of the honour" Mr. Collins is paying her by proposing. She is all too *keenly aware* of his intentions and wants nothing to do with them.

14. **(E)** Eliizabeth expects that by refusing Mr. Collins' proposal she will *put an end to his suit;* that is the result she desires. However, her rejection *fails* to have this intended effect. Instead, Mr. Collins in his stubbornness and conceit continues to pursue her and even takes her refusal as an encouraging sign.

15. **(D)** Mr. Collins breaks off in the middle of a sentence that begins: "Were it certain that Lady Catherine would think so . . . ." He then finishes it awkwardly by saying, "but I cannot imagine that her ladyship would at all disapprove of you." By implication, his unspoken thought was that, if Lady Catherine *didn't* approve of Elizabeth, then Mr. Collins wouldn't want to marry her after all.

16. **(C)** Mr. Collins plans to praise Elizabeth to Lady Catherine in order to ensure Lady Catherine's approval of his bride. Elizabeth insists all such praise will be unnecessary because she *has no intention of marrying* Mr. Collins and thus has no need of Lady Catherine's approval.

17. **(B)** *Obtuse* means thick-headed and *obstinate* means stubborn. Both apply to Mr. Collins, who can't seem to understand that Elizabeth is telling him "no."

18. **(C)** The author's emphasis is on the elephant as an important "creator of habitat" for other creatures.

19. **(C)** To mount an effort to rescue an endangered species is to *launch* or initiate a campaign.

20. **(D)** The elephant is the architect of its environment in that it *physically alters its environment,* transforming the landscape around it.

21. **(C)** The author states that it is the elephant's metabolism and appetite—in other words, its voracity or *ravenous hunger*—that leads to its creating open spaces in the woodland and transforming the landscape.

22. **(C)** Since the foraging of elephants creates a varied landscape that attracts a diverse group of plant-eating animals and since the presence of these plant-eaters in turn attracts carnivores, it follows that elephants *have an indirect effect on the hunting patterns of carnivores.*

23. **(E)** You can arrive at the correct answer choice through the process of elimination.

    Question I is answerable on the basis of the passage. The elephant's foraging opens up its surroundings by knocking down trees and stripping off branches. Therefore, you can eliminate Choices B and D.

    Question II is answerable on the basis of the passage. Gazelles are grazers; giraffes are browsers. Therefore, you can eliminate Choice A.

    Question III is answerable on the basis of the passage. The concluding sentence states that when elephants disappear, the forest reverts. Therefore, you can eliminate Choice C.

    Only Choice E is left. It is the correct answer.

24. **(B)** The author is listing the many species that depend on the elephant as a creator of habitat. Thus, the host of smaller animals is the *very large number* of these creatures that thrive in the elephant's wake.

25. **(C)** The author is in favor of the effect of elephants on the environment; he feels an accidental or *fortuitous result* of their foraging is that it allows a greater variety of creatures to exist in mixed-growth environments.

Section 2 Mathematical Reasoning

In each mathematics section, for some of the problems, an alternative solution, indicated by two asterisks (**), follows the first solution. When this occurs, one of the solutions is the direct mathematical one and the other is based on one of the tactics discussed in Chapter 7.

1. **(B)** $88 ÷ $16 per hour = 5.5 hours. If you prefer, set up a ratio and cross-multiply:

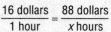

$$\frac{16 \text{ dollars}}{1 \text{ hour}} = \frac{88 \text{ dollars}}{x \text{ hours}} \cdot$$

2. **(D)** In 11 days Sarah saves $88. If 11 days ago she had $324, she now has $324 + $88 = $412, and 11 days from now will have $412 + $88 = $500.

3. **(B)** The average of a and b is $\dfrac{a+b}{2}$, and the product of that with 7 is

$$7\left(\frac{a+b}{2}\right) = \frac{7a+7b}{2}.$$

**It is easier and quicker to do this directly. So substitute for a and b, only if you get stuck or confused. If $a = 2$ and $b = 4$, their average is 3, and the product of 7 and their average is 21. Only Choice B is equal to 21 when $a = 2$ and $b = 4$.

4. **(D)** Let the number be x, and write the equation:

$$\frac{3}{4}x = 7 + \frac{1}{6}x.$$

Multiply both sides by 12: $9x = 84 + 2x$

Subtract $2x$ from each side and divide by 7: $7x = 84 \Rightarrow x = 12$

Be careful: 12 is *not* the answer. You were asked for $\dfrac{5}{3}$ of the number.

$\dfrac{5}{3}(12) = 20.$

5. **(C)** The sum of the measures of two adjacent angles of a parallelogram is 180°. Therefore, $180 = 10x + 25x - 30 = 35x - 30$, which implies that $35x = 210$ and $x = 6$.

6. **(D)** There's nothing to do except check the choices, although it is often faster to start with E and work toward A.

E: $9 * 9 = \sqrt{9+\sqrt{9}} = \sqrt{9+3} = \sqrt{12}$, which is not an integer.

D: $7 * 4 = \sqrt{7+\sqrt{4}} = \sqrt{7+2} = \sqrt{9} = 3$, an integer. The answer is D. Once you find the answer, do not waste any time trying the other choices—they won't work.

7. (B) The factory produces 64 engines per day × 25 days per month × 12 months per year = 19,200 engines per year, and 96,000 ÷ 19,200 = 5.

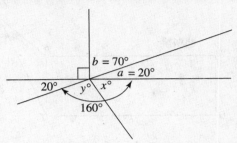

8. (E) Since vertical angles are equal, $a = 20$, and so $x + y = 160$. We can see that $b = 70$, but there are no other vertical angles, and it is impossible to determine x or y from the information given.

9. (C) Since $x^2 - y^2 = (x - y)(x + y)$, then
$$75 = x^2 - y^2 = (x - y)(x + y) = 5(x + y).$$
Therefore, $x + y = 15$. Adding the equations
$$x + y = 15 \text{ and } x - y = 5, \text{ we get}$$
$$2x = 20 \Rightarrow x = 10 \Rightarrow y = 5.$$
**Use TACTIC 10: backsolve. Choice C works.

10. (D) If Julie had to pay 30% of the value of her inheritance in taxes, she still owned 70% of her inheritance: 70% of 40% is 28% ($0.70 \times 0.40 = 0.28$).

**Assume the estate was worth $100. Julie received 40% or $40. Her tax was 30% of $40, or $12. She still had $28, or 28% of the $100 estate.

11. (C) The given expression $(3!)(4!) = 6(24) = 144$. Now, evaluate the three choices.

I: $7! = 5040$, which is much too big (false).

II: $12!$ is even bigger (false).

III: $4! + 5! = 24 + 120 = 144$ (true).

III only is true.

12. (B) It is given that $BE = BC$; also $BC = AD$, since they are opposite sides of a rectangle. Label each of them w, as shown in the diagram.

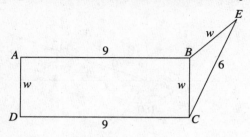

Then $R = 18 + 2w$ and $T = 6 + 2w$.
So $R - T = 18 - 6 = 12$.

13. (D) Since the game takes one hour, or 60 minutes, and there are always 5 men playing, there are a total of $5 \times 60 = 300$ minutes of playing time. If that is evenly divided among the 12 players, each one plays $300 \div 12 = 25$ minutes.

**Try the choices. If 5 men played the first 10 or 12 minutes, and 5 other men played the next 10 or 12 minutes, there wouldn't be 5 men available to play the rest of the game. So 10 and 12 are much too small. Eliminate A and B. If 5 men played for 30 minutes, and 5 other men played the next 30 minutes, the game would be over and 2 men wouldn't have played at all. Eliminate E since 30 is too large. The answer must be 24 or 25.

14. (D) Since $A = \pi r^2$, $r^2 = \dfrac{A}{\pi}$ and $r = \sqrt{\dfrac{A}{\pi}} = \dfrac{\sqrt{A}}{\sqrt{\pi}}$.

The circumference $= 2\pi r = 2\pi \dfrac{\sqrt{A}}{\sqrt{\pi}} = 2\sqrt{\pi}\sqrt{A} = 2\sqrt{\pi A}$.

15. (D) Use the formula: slope $= \dfrac{y_2 - y_1}{x_2 - x_1}$.

Then $\dfrac{2}{3} = \dfrac{5 - (-3)}{k - 3} = \dfrac{8}{k - 3}$. Cross-multiply: $24 = 2k - 6 \Rightarrow 2k = 30 \Rightarrow k = 15$.

**If you don't remember the formula, make a quick sketch:

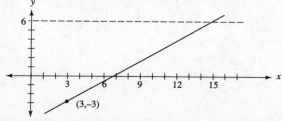

Since the slope is positive, k is greater than 3, and since the slope is less than 1, the line is going up too slowly for k to be 6 or 8. Guess 15

16. (A) If x is odd, so are $5x$ and $5x + 4$. To get the smallest odd number greater than $5x + 4$, add 2: $5x + 6$. On the other hand, $3x + 7$ is even, and the largest odd number smaller than it is 1 less than $3x + 7$, namely $3x + 6$. The required difference is $(5x + 6) - (3x + 6) = 2x$.

Use **TACTIC 11 and let $x = 3$. The smallest odd number greater than 19 is 21 and the largest odd number less than 16 is 15: $21 - 15 = 6$. Which answer equals 6 when $x = 3$? Only A.

17. (C) It's worth remembering that when the three angles of a triangle are in the ratio of 1:2:3, the triangle is a 30-60-90 right triangle. (If you don't know that, solve the equation $x + 2x + 3x = 180$.) In a 30-60-90 right triangle the sides are a, $a\sqrt{3}$, and $2a$, so the desired ratio is a:$2a = 1$:2.

18. (B) At 2:00, the first car had been going 50 miles per hour for 2 hours, and so had gone 100 miles. The second car covered the same 100 miles in 1 hour

and 40 minutes, or $1\dfrac{2}{3} = \dfrac{5}{3}$ hours. Therefore, its rate was $100 \div \dfrac{5}{3} =$

$100 \times \dfrac{3}{5} = 60$ miles per hour.

19. (A) Let $x =$ cost of a ballpoint pen, and $2x =$ cost of a fountain pen. Then f fountain pens and b ballpoint pens cost $f(2x) + bsx = d$ dollars. Now solve for x:

$$2fx + bx = d \Rightarrow x(2f + b) = d \Rightarrow x = \frac{d}{b+2f}$$

Use **TACTIC 11. Suppose a ballpoint pen costs $2 and a fountain pen $4. Then, if 2 ballpoint pens and 3 fountain pens were sold, the store took in $16. Which of the choices equals 2 when $b = 2$, $f = 3$ and $d = 16$?

Only $\dfrac{d}{b+2f}$.

20. (B) Make a table to determine Yann's and Isabel's ages.

Table 1

	1965	1970
Yann	$4x$	$4x + 5$
Isabel	x	$x + 5$

Let x represent Isabel's age in 1965, and fill in Table 1 as shown. In 1970, Yann was 3 times as old as Isabel, so

$$4x + 5 = 3(x + 5) = 3x + 15 \Rightarrow x = 10.$$

So in 1965, Isabel was 10 and Yann was 40. Since he is 30 years older than she is, he was 30 when she was born.

Section 3 Verbal Reasoning

26. (E) To make the correct decisions, the lawmakers must be able to *discern* or recognize the truth.

27. (B) There is a chance that *serious* women may not be attracted by an inappropriate *frivolity* or lightheartedness in style—hence the gamble.

28. (D) If irony is a mode of escape, then the ironic person is *evading* or escaping life's terrors.

29. (A) If you started falling asleep at times you wouldn't normally wish to do so, you clearly would strike yourself as unusually *lethargic* (drowsily slow to respond; sluggish; listless).

30. (D) A *euphemism* is by definition a mild expression used in place of a more unpleasant or distressing one. The blunt expression "he died" is unpleasantly direct for some people, who substitute the vague euphemism "he passed away."

31. (E) *Despite* signals a contrast. If someone writes an enormously popular book, you would expect his career to prosper. Instead, White's career *foundered* or came to grief.

32. (C) Because it was written immediately after the assassination, the book has *immediacy*, but it lacks *perspective;* the author had not had enough time to distance himself from his immediate reactions to the event and think about it.

33. (E) The key word here is "chagrin." Because Costner has triumphed, the critics who predicted his *failure* feel chagrin (great annoyance mixed with disappointment or humiliation). Costner, for his part, greatly enjoys his success and especially enjoys or *savors* their embarrassment and vexation.

34. (B) A *pebble* is shot from a *slingshot;* a *ball* is shot from a *cannon.*

(Function)

35. (E) To *drizzle* or rain lightly is less intense than to *pour;* to *smolder* or barely burn is less intense than to *blaze.*

(Degree of Intensity)

36. (D) To *eradicate* an *error* is to wipe it out or eliminate it; to *uproot* a *weed* is to pull it out or eliminate it.

(Purpose)

37. (E) A *gander* is a male *goose;* a *ram* is a male *sheep.*

(Sex)

38. (D) *Locomotion* is a function of the *feet; digestion* is a function of the *stomach.*

(Function)

39. (E) Something *garbled* or confused is difficult to *comprehend;* something *camouflaged* or hidden is difficult to *discern* or perceive.

(Antonym Variant)

40. (E) A *purist* is concerned with strict *correctness;* a *martinet* is concerned with strict *discipline*.

(Defining Characteristic)

41. (E) The italicized introduction states that the author has had his manuscript rejected by his publisher. He is consigning or committing it to a desk drawer to *set it aside as unmarketable.*

42. (B) The rejected author identifies with these baseball players, who constantly must face "failure." *He sees he is not alone in having to confront failure and move on.*

43. (B) The author uses the jogger's comment to make a point about the *mental impact Henderson's home run must have had on Moore.* He reasons that, if each step a runner takes sends so many complex messages to the brain, then Henderson's ninth-inning home run must have flooded Moore's brain with messages, impressing its image indelibly in Moore's mind.

44. (D) The author is talking of the impact of Henderson's home run on Moore's mind. Registering in Moore's mind, the home run *made an impression* on him.

45. (C) The author looks on himself as someone who "to succeed at all . . . must perform at an extraordinary level of excellence." This level of excellence, he maintains, is not demanded of accountants, plumbers, and insurance salesmen, and he seems to pride himself on belonging to such a demanding profession. Thus, his attitude to members of less demanding professions can best be described as *superior.*

46. (A) The description of the writer defying his pain and extending himself irrationally to create a "masterpiece" despite the rejections of critics and publishers is a highly romantic one that elevates *the writer as someone heroic in his or her accomplishments.*

47. (C) The author of Passage 2 discusses the advantages of his ability to concentrate. Clearly, he prizes *his ability to focus* on the task at hand.

48. (B) When one football team is ahead of another by several touchdowns and there seems to be no way for the second team to catch up, the outcome of the game appears *decided* or settled.

49. (E) The "larger point of view" focuses on what to most people is the big question: the outcome of the game. The author is indifferent to this larger point of view. Concentrating on his own performance, he is *more concerned with the task at hand than with* winning or losing the game.

50. (C) Parade ground drill clearly does not entirely prepare a soldier for the reality of war. It only does so "to an extent." By using this phrase, the author is *qualifying his statement,* making it less absolute.

51. (C) One would expect someone who dismisses or rejects most comparisons of athletics to art to avoid making such comparisons. The author, however, *is* *making such a comparison.* This reversal of what would have been expected is an instance of irony.

52. (C) To learn to overcome failure, to learn to give one's all in performance, to learn to focus on the work of the moment, to learn "the selfish intensity needed to create and to finish a poem, a story, or a novel"—these are hard lessons that *both athletes and artists learn.*

Section 4 Mathematical Reasoning

21. (C) $[(-1)^2 + (-1)]^2 = [1 + (-1)]^2 = [0]^2 = 0$. The columns are equal (C).

22. (B) The only primes whose sum is 8 are 3 and 5, both of which are less than 6. [*Note:* $1 + 7 = 8$, but 1 is *not* a prime.] Column B is greater.

23. (B) Since a and b are positive, $a + b = 1 \Rightarrow a < 1$ and $b < 1 \Rightarrow ab < 1$. Column B is greater.

24. (A) Since 1998 is even, $(-1)^{1998} = 1$, whereas since 1999 is odd, $(-1)^{1999} = -1$. Column A is greater.

25. (B) Every factor of n is a factor of $2n$, but 2 is a prime factor of $2n$, which is not a factor of n (since n is odd). Therefore, $2n$ has more prime factors than n. Column B is greater.

Use **TACTIC 15, and replace n by an odd number. Let $n = 5$; 5 has one prime factor (5), whereas 10 has two prime factors (2 and 5). Eliminate A and C. Try $n = 15$: 15 has two prime factors (3 and 5) whereas 30 has three prime factors (2, 3, and 5). Choose B.

26. (A) Use **TACTIC 17**.

	Column A	Column B
	a^3b^2	a^2b^3

Since a and b are not 0, we can divide each column by a^2b^2: $\dfrac{a^3b^2}{a^2b^2} = a$ $\qquad$ $\dfrac{a^2b^3}{a^2b^2} = b$

Since it is given that $a > b$, Column A is greater.

Use **TACTIC 15 and plug in numbers. If $a = 2$ and $b = 1$, Column A is 8 and Column B is 4 so eliminate B and C. Try some other numbers. A is always greater.

	Column A	Column B
27. (B)	$\sqrt{a+b}$	$\sqrt{a} + \sqrt{b}$

Since the quantities in each column are positive, we can square them.	$a + b$	$a + 2\sqrt{ab} + b$

Subtract $a + b$ from each column	0	$2\sqrt{ab}$

Since a and b are positive, $2\sqrt{ab}$ is positive; Column B is greater.

Use **TACTIC 10-1: plug in easy-to-use numbers that satisfy the conditions and use your calculator. Let $a = 0.1$ and $b = 0.9$. Column A: $\sqrt{0.1+0.9} = \sqrt{1} = 1$.

Column B: $\sqrt{0.1} + \sqrt{0.9} \approx .32 + .95 = 1.27$. Column B is greater. Eliminate A and C. Try other values; each time Column B is larger. Choose B.

28. (A) By the Pythagorean theorem, $a^2 + (2a)^2 = x^2$, so

$$x^2 = a^2 + (2a)^2 = a^2 + 4a^2 = 5a^2.$$

Therefore, $x = a\sqrt{5}$, which is greater than $a\sqrt{3}$. Column A is greater.

29. (A) Column B $= \left(\dfrac{7}{11}\right)^5 = (x^5)^5 = x^{25}$. Since $0 < x < 1$, $x^{25} < x$.

**Use a scientific calculator. $\left(\dfrac{7}{11}\right)^5 \approx 0.1$, whereas $x \approx .95$ (raise $\dfrac{7}{11}$ to

the $\dfrac{1}{5}$ or .2 power).

30. (A) Drawing a picture makes it easier to visualize the problem. The volume of a cylinder is $\pi r^2 h$. In each case, we know the height but have to determine the radius in order to calculate the volume.

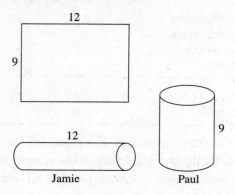

Jamie   Paul

Paul's cylinder has a circumference of 12:

$$2\pi r = 12 \Rightarrow r = \frac{12}{2\pi} = \frac{6}{\pi} \Rightarrow$$

$$V = \pi \left(\frac{6}{\pi}\right)^2 (9) = \pi \left(\frac{36}{\pi^2}\right)(9) = \frac{324}{\pi}.$$

Jamie's cylinder has a circumference of 9:

$$2\pi r = 9 \Rightarrow r = \frac{9}{2\pi} \Rightarrow$$

$$V = \pi \left(\frac{9}{2\pi}\right)^2 (12) = \pi \left(\frac{81}{4\pi^2}\right)(12) = \frac{243}{\pi}.$$

Column A is greater.

31. (D) Let r, C, and A represent the radius, circumference, and area of the circle: $C = 2\pi r = a\pi$ and $a = \frac{2\pi r}{\pi} = 2r$. Similarly, $A = \pi r^2 = b\pi \Rightarrow b = \frac{\pi r^2}{\pi}$ $= r^2$. The value of Column A is $2r$ and the value of Column B is r^2. Which is greater? If $r = 2$, the columns are equal; if $r = 1$, they aren't. Neither column is *always* greater, and the two columns are not *always* equal (D).

Use TACTIC 15. Let $r = 1$. Then, $C = 2\pi$ and $A = \pi$; so $a = 2$ and $b = 1$. Column B is greater: eliminate A and C. Try $r = 2$. Now, $C = 4\pi$ and $A = 4\pi$. So, this time $a = b$ and the columns are equal. Eliminate B. The answer is D.

32. (C) Since the entire region is a circle of radius 4, its area is $\pi(4)^2 = 16\pi$. The shaded region is a circle of radius 3 minus the small white circle of radius 1, so its area is $9\pi - \pi = 8\pi$. So, the shaded region is one-half of the total, and the white region is the other half. The columns are equal (C).

33. (308) Don't do any algebra. Just replace a and b by 7 and 11 in the original expression:

$$(7 + 11)^2 - (7 - 11)^2 =$$
$$18^2 - (-4)^2 = 324 - 16 = 308.$$

34. $\left(\dfrac{22}{6} \text{ or } \dfrac{11}{3} \text{ or } 3.66\right)$ Notice that the left-hand side of the equation is the negative of the righthand side, meaning that each side is equal to 0. Therefore,

$$3x - 11 = 0 \Rightarrow 3x = 11 \Rightarrow x = \frac{11}{3}$$

**Just solve the equation:

$3x - 11 = 11 - 3x \Rightarrow 6x = 22 \Rightarrow x = \dfrac{22}{6}$. Note that it is *not* necessary to reduce $\dfrac{22}{6}$. (It's not even advisable.)

35. (2.62) Just add the three numbers and divide by 3:

$$(1 + 2.3 + 4.56) \div 3 = 7.86 \div 3 = 2.62.$$

36. (150) Since Len got $100, the other three shared the remaining $900. If x represents Jim's share, then Kim got $2x$ and Ben got $3x$. Then $900 = x + 2x + 3x = 6x \Rightarrow x = 150$.

37. (79) For a fraction to be large, the numerator should be as large as possible and the denominator as small as possible. The greatest value that $x^2 - y$ could have is 80, by letting $x = 9$ and $y = 1$. Since x, y, and z are different, the least that z could be is 2, and the value of the fraction would be $\dfrac{80}{2}$ or 40. However, if you interchange x and y, you get 79 for the numerator $(9^2 - 2)$ and 1 for the denominator: $\dfrac{79}{1}$ or 79.

38. (52) This is a weighted average:

$$\frac{40\%(40) + 60\%(60)}{100\%} = \frac{16 + 36}{1} = 52.$$

**If you prefer, assume there are 100 marbles, 40 of which are red and 60 of which are blue: $\dfrac{40(40) + 60(60)}{100} = \dfrac{1600 + 3600}{100} = 52$.

39. (6) Let $x =$ measure of each exterior angle, and $2x =$ measure of each interior angle. Since the sum of the measures of an interior and exterior angle is 180: $180 = x + 2x = 3x \Rightarrow x = 60$. Since the sum of the measures of all the exterior angles is 360°, there are $360 \div 60 = 6$ angles and, of course, 6 sides.

40. (50) Even if you can do this completely algebraically, you should use **TACTIC 21** since it's much easier to plug in numbers. Of course, since you're dealing with percents, the best number to use is 100. Assume the jar contains 100 blue marbles and 300 red ones. Since $n\%$ of 100 is n and $n\%$ of 300 is $3n$, the jar now has $300 - 3n$ red marbles and $100 + n$ blue ones. Therefore,

$$100 + n = 300 - 3n \Rightarrow 100 + 4n = 300 \Rightarrow 4n = 200 \Rightarrow n = 50.$$

Section 5 Writing Skills

1. **(B)** Error in diction. *Affect* is a verb and should not be used in place of *effect*.
2. **(A)** Error in case. The subject of an infinitive *(to be)* should be in the objective case. Therefore, change *commissioner and she* to *commissioner and her.*
3. **(E)** Sentence is correct.
4. **(E)** Sentence is correct.
5. **(C)** Error in diction. There is no such verb as *enthuse*. Change *enthused* to *enthusiastic.*
6. **(C)** Error in tense. Change *had shot* to *shot.*
7. **(A)** Error in diction. Use *irritated* instead of *aggravated.*
8. **(A)** Error in idiom. Change *neither . . . or* to *neither . . . nor.*
9. **(C)** Error in diction. Change *incredulous* to *incredible.*
10. **(C)** Error in tense. Change *had broke* to *had broken.*
11. **(C)** Error in diction. Change *council* to *counsel.*
12. **(C)** Error in subject-verb agreement. The subject, *Ann Landers,* is singular; the verb should be singular—*is.*
13. **(A)** Error in pronoun case. The preposition *between* requires the objective case. Therefore, change *you and I* to *you and me.*
14. **(D)** Error in diction. Issues are *decided* or settled. The actual choice made is what is *decided upon*. Delete *upon.*
15. **(E)** Sentence is correct.
16. **(E)** Sentence is correct.
17. **(C)** Error in subject-verb agreement. The subject, *general,* is singular; the verb should be singular—*seems.*
18. **(A)** Error in pronoun case. The possessive pronoun precedes a gerund. Change *him* to *his.*
19. **(D)** Error in tense. Change *was to be immortalized* to *was immortalized.*
20. **(E)** Error in pronoun case. The noun or pronoun preceding a gerund *(going)* should be in the possessive case.
21. **(E)** Error in modification. The dangling modifier is best corrected in Choice E. Choices B and D introduce an error in tense. Choice C changes the meaning of the sentence.
22. **(C)** Comma splice. Choices A and B are run-on sentences. Choices D and E are ungrammatical.
23. **(E)** Error in modification and double negative. Both are corrected in Choice E.
24. **(E)** Error in coordination and subordination. By changing *having* to *had* and connecting the two main clauses with a semicolon, you tighten the sentence and eliminate wordiness.
25. **(B)** Sentence fragment. Choice B expresses the author's meaning directly and concisely. All other choices are indirect, ungrammatical, or fail to retain the meaning of the original statement.

26. (C) Error in agreement. *Kind* should be modified by *this* or *that; kinds,* by *these* or *those.*

27. (C) Error in parallelism. *Menu, list,* and *service* are all nouns. Thus, parallel structure is retained in Choice C.

28. (D) This corrects the sentence fragment smoothly.

29. (B) Error in logical comparison. Compare *complaints* with *complaints,* not with *customers.* The faulty comparison is corrected in Choice B.

30. (C) Error in modification. Choice C corrects the misplaced modifier and eliminates the unnecessary use of the passive voice.

31. (C) Error in subject-verb agreement. The phrase *along with his staff* is not part of the subject of the sentence. The subject is *President Clinton* (singular); the verb should be *is traveling* (singular).

32. (B) Error in coordination and subordination. The use of the subordinating conjunction *Although* and the deletion of unnecessary words strengthen this sentence.

33. (D) Choices A, B, and C have dangling modifiers; Choice E creates a run-on sentence.

34. (D) Choices A, B, and C abruptly state the contrasting point of view without regard to the context.

Choice D takes the context into account and provides for a smooth progression of thought. It is the best answer.

Choice E is confusing. It is unclear until the end of the sentence whether the *other members* support or oppose the exhibit.

35. (D) Choice A is not consistent in style and mood with the rest of the paragraph.

Choice B is a sentence fragment.

Choice C is excessively wordy.

Choice D fits the context of the paragraph and expresses the idea correctly. It is the best answer.

Choice E inappropriately uses *in conclusion* and contains the pronoun *it,* which lacks a specific referent.

36. (B) Choice A lacks a main verb; therefore, it is a sentence fragment.

Choice B accurately combines the sentences. It is the best answer.

Choice C expresses the idea in a way that the writer could not have intended.

Choice D subordinates important ideas and emphasizes a lesser one.

Choice E restates the idea in a manner that changes the writer's intended meaning.

37. (A) Choice A is the best choice because the sentences contain basic information about the topic. Readers are left in the dark unless the information appears as early as possible in the essay.

38. (E) Choice A contains faulty idiom; the phrase *than of the past* is nonstandard usage.

Choice B contains a faulty comparison; *society* and *the past* cannot be logically compared.

Choice C contains an error in idiom; the phrase *than from* is redundant.

Choice D is correct but excessively wordy.

Choice E is the best answer.

39. (C) Choice A provides a reasonable transition, but it contains an error in pronoun-antecedent agreement. The pronoun *they* is plural; its antecedent *anyone* is singular.

Choice B contains an error in diction. One can *disapprove of* but not *disagree with* a piece of art.

Choice C alludes to the content of the previous paragraph and is clearly and succinctly expressed. It is the best answer.

Choice D contains an error in pronoun-antecedent agreement. The pronoun *them* is plural; the antecedent *anyone* is singular.

Choice E is inconsistent in tone and mood with the rest of the essay.

ANSWER SHEET—MODEL TEST 2

Section 1

1. Ⓐ Ⓑ Ⓒ Ⓓ Ⓔ
2. Ⓐ Ⓑ Ⓒ Ⓓ Ⓔ
3. Ⓐ Ⓑ Ⓒ Ⓓ Ⓔ
4. Ⓐ Ⓑ Ⓒ Ⓓ Ⓔ
5. Ⓐ Ⓑ Ⓒ Ⓓ Ⓔ
6. Ⓐ Ⓑ Ⓒ Ⓓ Ⓔ
7. Ⓐ Ⓑ Ⓒ Ⓓ Ⓔ
8. Ⓐ Ⓑ Ⓒ Ⓓ Ⓔ
9. Ⓐ Ⓑ Ⓒ Ⓓ Ⓔ
10. Ⓐ Ⓑ Ⓒ Ⓓ Ⓔ
11. Ⓐ Ⓑ Ⓒ Ⓓ Ⓔ
12. Ⓐ Ⓑ Ⓒ Ⓓ Ⓔ
13. Ⓐ Ⓑ Ⓒ Ⓓ Ⓔ
14. Ⓐ Ⓑ Ⓒ Ⓓ Ⓔ
15. Ⓐ Ⓑ Ⓒ Ⓓ Ⓔ
16. Ⓐ Ⓑ Ⓒ Ⓓ Ⓔ
17. Ⓐ Ⓑ Ⓒ Ⓓ Ⓔ
18. Ⓐ Ⓑ Ⓒ Ⓓ Ⓔ
19. Ⓐ Ⓑ Ⓒ Ⓓ Ⓔ
20. Ⓐ Ⓑ Ⓒ Ⓓ Ⓔ
21. Ⓐ Ⓑ Ⓒ Ⓓ Ⓔ
22. Ⓐ Ⓑ Ⓒ Ⓓ Ⓔ
23. Ⓐ Ⓑ Ⓒ Ⓓ Ⓔ
24. Ⓐ Ⓑ Ⓒ Ⓓ Ⓔ
25. Ⓐ Ⓑ Ⓒ Ⓓ Ⓔ

Section 2

1. Ⓐ Ⓑ Ⓒ Ⓓ Ⓔ
2. Ⓐ Ⓑ Ⓒ Ⓓ Ⓔ
3. Ⓐ Ⓑ Ⓒ Ⓓ Ⓔ
4. Ⓐ Ⓑ Ⓒ Ⓓ Ⓔ
5. Ⓐ Ⓑ Ⓒ Ⓓ Ⓔ
6. Ⓐ Ⓑ Ⓒ Ⓓ Ⓔ
7. Ⓐ Ⓑ Ⓒ Ⓓ Ⓔ
8. Ⓐ Ⓑ Ⓒ Ⓓ Ⓔ
9. Ⓐ Ⓑ Ⓒ Ⓓ Ⓔ
10. Ⓐ Ⓑ Ⓒ Ⓓ Ⓔ
11. Ⓐ Ⓑ Ⓒ Ⓓ Ⓔ
12. Ⓐ Ⓑ Ⓒ Ⓓ Ⓔ
13. Ⓐ Ⓑ Ⓒ Ⓓ Ⓔ
14. Ⓐ Ⓑ Ⓒ Ⓓ Ⓔ
15. Ⓐ Ⓑ Ⓒ Ⓓ Ⓔ
16. Ⓐ Ⓑ Ⓒ Ⓓ Ⓔ
17. Ⓐ Ⓑ Ⓒ Ⓓ Ⓔ
18. Ⓐ Ⓑ Ⓒ Ⓓ Ⓔ
19. Ⓐ Ⓑ Ⓒ Ⓓ Ⓔ
20. Ⓐ Ⓑ Ⓒ Ⓓ Ⓔ

Section 3

26 Ⓐ Ⓑ Ⓒ Ⓓ Ⓔ   40 Ⓐ Ⓑ Ⓒ Ⓓ Ⓔ
27 Ⓐ Ⓑ Ⓒ Ⓓ Ⓔ   41 Ⓐ Ⓑ Ⓒ Ⓓ Ⓔ
28 Ⓐ Ⓑ Ⓒ Ⓓ Ⓔ   42 Ⓐ Ⓑ Ⓒ Ⓓ Ⓔ
29 Ⓐ Ⓑ Ⓒ Ⓓ Ⓔ   43 Ⓐ Ⓑ Ⓒ Ⓓ Ⓔ
30 Ⓐ Ⓑ Ⓒ Ⓓ Ⓔ   44 Ⓐ Ⓑ Ⓒ Ⓓ Ⓔ
31 Ⓐ Ⓑ Ⓒ Ⓓ Ⓔ   45 Ⓐ Ⓑ Ⓒ Ⓓ Ⓔ
32 Ⓐ Ⓑ Ⓒ Ⓓ Ⓔ   46 Ⓐ Ⓑ Ⓒ Ⓓ Ⓔ
33 Ⓐ Ⓑ Ⓒ Ⓓ Ⓔ   47 Ⓐ Ⓑ Ⓒ Ⓓ Ⓔ
34 Ⓐ Ⓑ Ⓒ Ⓓ Ⓔ   48 Ⓐ Ⓑ Ⓒ Ⓓ Ⓔ
35 Ⓐ Ⓑ Ⓒ Ⓓ Ⓔ   49 Ⓐ Ⓑ Ⓒ Ⓓ Ⓔ
36 Ⓐ Ⓑ Ⓒ Ⓓ Ⓔ   50 Ⓐ Ⓑ Ⓒ Ⓓ Ⓔ
37 Ⓐ Ⓑ Ⓒ Ⓓ Ⓔ   51 Ⓐ Ⓑ Ⓒ Ⓓ Ⓔ
38 Ⓐ Ⓑ Ⓒ Ⓓ Ⓔ   52 Ⓐ Ⓑ Ⓒ Ⓓ Ⓔ
39 Ⓐ Ⓑ Ⓒ Ⓓ Ⓔ

Section 4

21 Ⓐ Ⓑ Ⓒ Ⓓ
22 Ⓐ Ⓑ Ⓒ Ⓓ
23 Ⓐ Ⓑ Ⓒ Ⓓ
24 Ⓐ Ⓑ Ⓒ Ⓓ
25 Ⓐ Ⓑ Ⓒ Ⓓ
26 Ⓐ Ⓑ Ⓒ Ⓓ
27 Ⓐ Ⓑ Ⓒ Ⓓ
28 Ⓐ Ⓑ Ⓒ Ⓓ
29 Ⓐ Ⓑ Ⓒ Ⓓ
30 Ⓐ Ⓑ Ⓒ Ⓓ
31 Ⓐ Ⓑ Ⓒ Ⓓ
32 Ⓐ Ⓑ Ⓒ Ⓓ

33 [grid-in answer box with digits 0–9]

34 [grid-in answer box with digits 0–9]

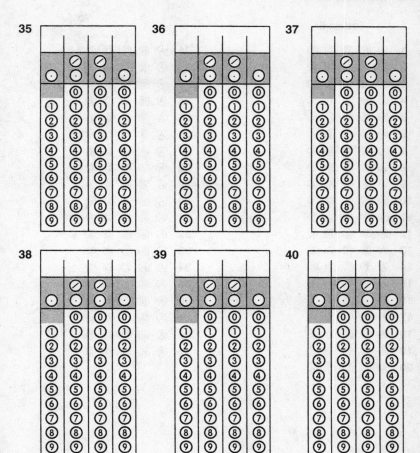

Section 5

1 Ⓐ Ⓑ Ⓒ Ⓓ Ⓔ
2 Ⓐ Ⓑ Ⓒ Ⓓ Ⓔ
3 Ⓐ Ⓑ Ⓒ Ⓓ Ⓔ
4 Ⓐ Ⓑ Ⓒ Ⓓ Ⓔ
5 Ⓐ Ⓑ Ⓒ Ⓓ Ⓔ
6 Ⓐ Ⓑ Ⓒ Ⓓ Ⓔ
7 Ⓐ Ⓑ Ⓒ Ⓓ Ⓔ
8 Ⓐ Ⓑ Ⓒ Ⓓ Ⓔ
9 Ⓐ Ⓑ Ⓒ Ⓓ Ⓔ
10 Ⓐ Ⓑ Ⓒ Ⓓ Ⓔ
11 Ⓐ Ⓑ Ⓒ Ⓓ Ⓔ
12 Ⓐ Ⓑ Ⓒ Ⓓ Ⓔ
13 Ⓐ Ⓑ Ⓒ Ⓓ Ⓔ
14 Ⓐ Ⓑ Ⓒ Ⓓ Ⓔ
15 Ⓐ Ⓑ Ⓒ Ⓓ Ⓔ
16 Ⓐ Ⓑ Ⓒ Ⓓ Ⓔ
17 Ⓐ Ⓑ Ⓒ Ⓓ Ⓔ
18 Ⓐ Ⓑ Ⓒ Ⓓ Ⓔ
19 Ⓐ Ⓑ Ⓒ Ⓓ Ⓔ
20 Ⓐ Ⓑ Ⓒ Ⓓ Ⓔ

21 Ⓐ Ⓑ Ⓒ Ⓓ Ⓔ
22 Ⓐ Ⓑ Ⓒ Ⓓ Ⓔ
23 Ⓐ Ⓑ Ⓒ Ⓓ Ⓔ
24 Ⓐ Ⓑ Ⓒ Ⓓ Ⓔ
25 Ⓐ Ⓑ Ⓒ Ⓓ Ⓔ
26 Ⓐ Ⓑ Ⓒ Ⓓ Ⓔ
27 Ⓐ Ⓑ Ⓒ Ⓓ Ⓔ
28 Ⓐ Ⓑ Ⓒ Ⓓ Ⓔ
29 Ⓐ Ⓑ Ⓒ Ⓓ Ⓔ
30 Ⓐ Ⓑ Ⓒ Ⓓ Ⓔ
31 Ⓐ Ⓑ Ⓒ Ⓓ Ⓔ
32 Ⓐ Ⓑ Ⓒ Ⓓ Ⓔ
33 Ⓐ Ⓑ Ⓒ Ⓓ Ⓔ
34 Ⓐ Ⓑ Ⓒ Ⓓ Ⓔ
35 Ⓐ Ⓑ Ⓒ Ⓓ Ⓔ
36 Ⓐ Ⓑ Ⓒ Ⓓ Ⓔ
37 Ⓐ Ⓑ Ⓒ Ⓓ Ⓔ
38 Ⓐ Ⓑ Ⓒ Ⓓ Ⓔ
39 Ⓐ Ⓑ Ⓒ Ⓓ Ⓔ

MODEL TEST 2

SECTION 1

Time—25 minutes   25 questions (1–25)

Select the best answer to the following questions, then fill in the appropriate space on your answer sheet.

Each of the following sentences contains one or two blanks; these blanks indicate that a word or set of words has been left out. Below the sentence are five words or phrases, lettered A through E. Select the word or set of words that best completes the sentence.

EXAMPLE:

Fame is ----; today's rising star is all too soon tomorrow's washed-up has-been.

(A) rewarding   (B) gradual   (C) essential
(D) spontaneous   (E) transitory

---

1. The traditional French café is slowly becoming ----, a victim to the growing popularity of *le fast food*.

(A) celebrated   (B) indispensable
(C) prevalent   (D) extinct   (E) fashionable

2. Although we expected the women's basketball coach to be ---- over the recent victory of the team, we found her surprisingly ----.

(A) ecstatic..gleeful
(B) ambivalent..devious
(C) triumphant..responsive
(D) elated..naive
(E) jubilant..disheartened

3. The debate coach suggested that he eliminate his---- remarks in his otherwise serious speech because they were ----.

(A) bantering..inappropriate
(B) jesting..accurate
(C) solemn..irrelevant
(D) tacit..digressive
(E) perfunctory..inconsiderate

4. Many young people and adults, uncomfortable with math, feel it is a subject best ---- engineers, scientists, and that small, elite group endowed at birth with a talent for the ---- world of numbers.

   (A) ignored by..abstract
   (B) suited to..accessible
   (C) studied by..interminable
   (D) left to..esoteric
   (E) avoided by..abstruse

5. Her novel published to universal acclaim, her literary gifts acknowledged by the chief figures of the Harlem Renaissance, her reputation as yet ---- by envious slights, Hurston clearly was at the ---- of her career.

   (A) undamaged..ebb
   (B) untarnished..zenith
   (C) untainted..end
   (D) blackened..mercy
   (E) unmarred..whim

Each of the following questions introduces a pair of words or phrases in capital letters, linked by a colon(:); this colon indicates that these words are related in some way. Following the capitalized pair are five pairs of words or phrases lettered A through E. Select the pair whose relationship is most similar to the relationship illustrated by the capitalized pair.

EXAMPLE:

CLOCK:TIME:: (A) watch:wrist
(B) pedometer:speed
(C) thermometer:temperature
(D) hourglass:sand (E) radio:sound

---

6. CONDUCTOR:ORCHESTRA:: (A) ballerina:ballet
   (B) surgeon:hospital (C) director:cast
   (D) lawyer:courtroom (E) tenor:chorus

7. ESSAYIST:WORDS:: (A) sculptor:pedestal
   (B) painter:easel (C) soldier:uniform
   (D) baker:batter (E) butcher:meat

8. INAUGURATE:PRESIDENT:: (A) abdicate:king
   (B) promote:student (C) campaign:candidate
   (D) install:officer (E) succeed:governor

9. OUTFOX:CUNNING::   (A) outline:thought
(B) outstrip:speed   (C) outreach:charity
(D) outrank:bravery   (E) outrage:wrath

10. CACOPHONOUS:HEAR::   (A) intangible:touch
(B) unsavory:taste   (C) olfactory:smell
(D) palpable:feel   (E) credulous:believe

11. IMPERTURBABLE:DISCOMPOSE::
(A) amenable:sway   (B) laconic:interpret
(C) boorish:provoke   (D) incredulous:convince
(E) egregious:intrude

Read each of the passages below, then answer the questions that follow each passage. The correct response may be <u>stated outright</u> or merely <u>suggested</u> in the passage and in any introductory or footnoted material included.

Questions 12–17 are based on the following passage.

The following passage is excerpted from a book on prominent African-Americans during Franklin Delano Roosevelt's presidency.

Like her white friends Eleanor Roosevelt and Aubrey Williams, Mary Bethune believed in the fundamental commitment of the New Deal to assist the black American's struggle and in the need for blacks to
Line assume responsibilities to help win that struggle. Unlike those of her
(5) white liberal associates, however, Bethune's ideas had evolved out of a long experience as a "race leader." Founder of a small black college in Florida, she had become widely known by 1935 as an organizer of black women's groups and as a civil and political rights activist. Deeply religious, certain of her own capabilities, she held a relatively uncluttered
(10) view of what she felt were the New Deal's and her own people's obligations to the cause of racial justice. Unafraid to speak her mind to powerful whites, including the President, or to differing black factions, she combined faith in the ultimate willingness of whites to discard their prejudice and bigotry with a strong sense of racial pride and commitment to
(15) Negro self-help.

More than her liberal white friends, Bethune argued for a strong and direct black voice in initiating and shaping government policy. She pursued this in her conversations with President Roosevelt, in numerous memoranda to Aubrey Williams, and in her administrative work as head
(20) of the National Youth Administration's Office of Negro Affairs. With the assistance of Williams, she was successful in having blacks selected to

NYA posts at the national, state, and local levels. But she also wanted a black presence throughout the federal government. At the beginning of the war she joined other black leaders in demanding appointments to the
(25) Selective Service Board and to the Department of the Army; and she was instrumental in 1941 in securing Earl Dickerson's membership on the Fair Employment Practices Committee. By 1944, she was still making appeals for black representation in "all public programs, federal, state, and local," and "in policy-making posts as well as rank and file jobs."
(30)   Though recognizing the weakness in the Roosevelt administration's response to Negro needs, Mary Bethune remained in essence a black partisan champion of the New Deal during the 1930s and 1940s. Her strong advocacy of administration policies and programs was predicated on a number of factors: her assessment of the low status of black
(35) Americans during the Depression; her faith in the willingness of some liberal whites to work for the inclusion of blacks in the government's reform and recovery measures; her conviction that only massive federal aid could elevate the Negro economically; and her belief that the thirties and forties were producing a more self-aware and self-assured black
(40) population. Like a number of her white friends in government, Bethune assumed that the preservation of democracy and black people's "full integration into the benefits and the responsibilities" of American life were inextricably tied together. She was convinced that, with the help of a friendly government, a militant, aggressive "New Negro" would emerge
(45) out of the devastation of depression and war, a "New Negro" who would "save America from itself," who would lead America toward the full realization of its democratic ideas.

12. The author's primary goal in the passage is to do which of the following?
    (A) Criticize Mary Bethune for adhering too closely to New Deal policies
    (B) Argue that Mary Bethune was too optimistic in her assessment of race relations
    (C) Explore Mary Bethune's convictions and her influence on black progress in the Roosevelt years
    (D) Point out the weaknesses of the white liberal approach to black needs during Roosevelt's presidency
    (E) Summarize the attainments of blacks under the auspices of Roosevelt's New Deal

13. It can be inferred from the passage that Aubrey Williams was which of the following?
    I. A man with influence in the National Youth Administration
    II. A white liberal
    III. A man of strong religious convictions

    (A) I only   (B) II only   (C) I and II only
    (D) II and III only   (E) I, II, and III

14. The author mentions Earl Dickerson (line 26) primarily in order to

(A) cite an instance of Bethune's political impact
(B) contrast his career with that of Bethune
(C) introduce the subject of a subsequent paragraph
(D) provide an example of Bethune's "New Negro"
(E) show that Dickerson was a leader of his fellow blacks

15. The word "instrumental" in line 26 means

(A) subordinate   (B) triumphant   (C) musical
(D) gracious   (E) helpful

16. It can be inferred from the passage that Bethune believed the "New Negro" would "save America from itself " (lines 43–47) by

(A) joining the Army and helping America overthrow its Fascist enemies
(B) helping America accomplish its egalitarian ideals
(C) voting for administration anti-poverty programs
(D) electing other blacks to government office
(E) expressing a belief in racial pride

17. The author uses all the following techniques in the passage EXCEPT

(A) comparison and contrast
(B) development of an extended metaphor
(C) direct quotation
(D) general statement and concrete examples
(E) repetition of central ideas

Questions 18–25 are based on the following passage.

In this excerpt from the novel Hard Times *by Charles Dickens, the reader is introduced to Thomas Gradgrind, headmaster of a so-called model school.*

Thomas Gradgrind, sir. A man of realities. A man of facts and calculations. A man who proceeds upon the principle that two and two are four, and nothing over, and who is not to be talked into allowing for
Line anything over. Thomas Gradgrind, sir—peremptorily Thomas—Thomas
(5) Gradgrind. With a rule and a pair of scales, and the multiplication table always in his pocket, sir, ready to weigh and measure any parcel of human nature, and tell you exactly what it comes to. It is a mere question of figures, a case of simple arithmetic. You might hope to get some other nonsensical belief into the head of George Gradgrind, or Augustus
(10) Gradgrind, or John Gradgrind, or Joseph Gradgrind (all suppositions, non-existent persons), but into the head of Thomas Gradgrind—no, sir!

Mr. Gradgrind walked homeward from the school in a state of considerable satisfaction. It was his school, and he intended it to be a
model. He intended every child in it to be a model—just as the young
(15) Gradgrinds were all models.

There were five young Gradgrinds, and they were models every
one. They had been lectured at from their tenderest years; coursed, like
little hares. Almost as soon as they could run alone, they had been made
to run to the lecture-room. The first object with which they had an
(20) association, or of which they had a remembrance, was a large blackboard with a dry Ogre chalking ghastly white figures on it.

Not that they knew, by name or nature, anything about an Ogre. Fact
forbid! I only use the word to express a monster in a lecturing castle,
with Heaven knows how many heads manipulated into one, taking
(25) childhood captive, and dragging it into gloomy statistical dens by the
hair.

No little Gradgrind had ever seen a face in the moon; it was up in the
moon before it could speak distinctly. No little Gradgrind had ever learnt
the silly jingle, Twinkle, twinkle, little star; how I wonder what you are!
(30) No little Gradgrind had ever known wonder on the subject of the stars,
each little Gradgrind having at five years old dissected the Great Bear like a
Professor Owen, and driven Charles's Wain like a locomotive engine-dri-
ver. No little Gradgrind had ever associated a cow in a field with that
famous cow with the crumpled horn who tossed the dog who worried
(35) the cat who killed the rat who ate the malt, or with that yet more famous
cow who swallowed Tom Thumb: it had never heard of those celebrities,
and had only been introduced to a cow as a graminivorous ruminating
quadruped with several stomachs.

18. The phrase "peremptorily Thomas" in line 4 emphasizes Gradgrind's

(A) absolute insistence upon facts
(B) dislike of the name Augustus
(C) need to remind himself of the simplest details
(D) desire to be on a first name basis with others
(E) inability to introduce himself properly

19. The word "rule" in line 5 means

(A) legal regulation
(B) academic custom
(C) scientific principle
(D) dominion over schoolchildren
(E) straight edge used in measuring

20. Gradgrind's mood as he marches homeward (lines 12–13) can best be characterized as one of

(A) uncertainty   (B) complacency
(C) boredom   (D) relief   (E) cynicism

21. The author's tone in describing Thomas Gradgrind's educational methodology is

(A) openly admiring   (B) acutely concerned
(C) bitterly scornful   (D) broadly satirical   (E) warmly nostalgic

22. The passage suggests that Gradgrind rejects from his curriculum anything that is in the least

(A) analytical   (B) mechanical   (C) fanciful
(D) dogmatic   (E) pragmatic

23. It can be inferred from the passage that the Great Bear and Charles's Wain most likely are

(A) subjects of nursery rhymes   (B) groupings of stars
(C) zoological phenomena   (D) themes of popular songs
(E) popular toys for children

24. Which of the following axioms is closest to Gradgrind's view of education as presented in the passage?

(A) Experience keeps a dear school, but fools will learn in no other.
(B) Let early education be a sort of amusement, that you may be better able to find out the natural bent.
(C) Education is what you have left over after you have forgotten everything you have learned.
(D) A teacher who can arouse a feeling for one single good action accomplishes more than one who fills our memory with rows on rows of natural objects, classified with name and form.
(E) Modern science, as training the mind to an exact and impartial analysis of fact, is an education specially fitted to promote sound citizenship.

25. In line 36, the word "celebrities" refers to

(A) the little Gradgrinds   (B) famous professors   (C) heavenly bodies
(D) locomotive engine-drivers   (E) fictional characters

IF YOU FINISH IN LESS THAN 25 MINUTES, YOU MAY CHECK YOUR WORK ON THIS SECTION ONLY. DO NOT TURN TO ANY OTHER SECTION IN THE TEST.   **S T O P**

SECTION 2

Time—25 minutes   20 questions (1–20)

For each problem in this section, determine which of the five choices is correct and blacken that choice on your answer sheet. You may use any blank space on the page for your work.

Notes:

- You may use a calculator whenever you believe it will be helpful.
- Use the diagrams provided to help you solve the problems. Unless you see the phrase "<u>Note</u>: Figure not drawn to scale" under a diagram, it has been drawn as accurately as possible. Unless it is stated that a figure is three-dimensional, you may assume that it lies in a plane.

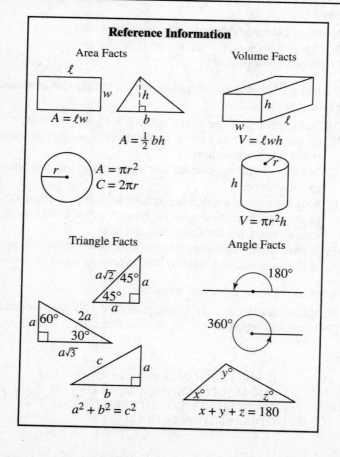

Reference Information

Area Facts

$A = \ell w$

$A = \frac{1}{2} bh$

$A = \pi r^2$
$C = 2\pi r$

Volume Facts

$V = \ell wh$

$V = \pi r^2 h$

Triangle Facts

$a\sqrt{2}$ $45°$ a
$45°$ a

a $60°$ $2a$
$30°$ $a\sqrt{3}$

c a
b
$a^2 + b^2 = c^2$

Angle Facts

$180°$

$360°$

$y°$
$x°$ $z°$
$x + y + z = 180$

1. If the ratio of the number of boys to girls in a club is 2:3, what percent of the club members are girls?

   (A) $33\frac{1}{3}$ %   (B) 40%   (C) 50%

   (D) 60%   (E) $66\frac{2}{3}$ %

2. If $7d + 5 = 5d + 7$, what is the value of d?
   (A) -1 (B) 0   (C) 1   (D) 5   (E) 7

3. The Salem Soccer League is divided into d divisions. Each division has t teams, and each team has p players. How many players are there in the entire league?

   (A) $\dfrac{pt}{d}$ (B) $\dfrac{dt}{p}$ (C) $\dfrac{d}{pt}$ (D) $d + t + p$
   (E) dtp

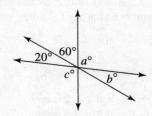

4. In the figure above, what is the value of $a + b + c$?
   (A) 210   (B) 220   (C) 240   (D) 270   (E) 280

5. When a gymnast competes at the Olympics, each of six judges awards a score between 0 and 10. The highest and lowest scores are discarded and the gymnast's final mark is the average (arithmetic mean) of the remaining scores. What would be a gymnast's mark if the judges' scores were 9.6, 9.4, 9.5, 9.7, 9.2, and 9.6?

   (A) 9.5   (B) 9.525   (C) 9.55
   (D) 9.575   (E) 9.6

6. $X = \{3, 4, 5\}$ and $Y = \{4, 5, 6\}$. If x is in X and y is in Y, how many different values are there for the sum of x and y?
   (A) 5   (B) 6   (C) 7   (D) 8   (E) 9

7. Which of the following is *NOT* a solution of $3x^2 + 2y = 5$?

    (A) $x = 1$ and $y = 1$
    (B) $x = -1$ and $y = 1$
    (C) $x = 1$ and $y = -1$
    (D) $x = 3$ and $y = -11$
    (E) $x = -3$ and $y = -11$

8. If $3x + 5y = 23$ and $5x + 3y = 17$, what is the average (arithmetic mean) of x and y?

    (A) 0   (B) 2.5   (C) 5   (D) 8   (E) 20

9. Sally wrote the number 1 on 1 slip of paper, the number 2 on 2 slips of paper, the number 3 on 3 slips of paper, the number 4 on 4 slips of paper, the number 5 on 5 slips of paper, and the number 6 on 6 slips of paper. All the slips of paper were placed in a bag, and Lana drew one slip at random. What is the probability that the number on the slip Lana drew was odd?

    (A) $\dfrac{1}{9}$ (B) $\dfrac{1}{7}$ (C) $\dfrac{3}{7}$ (D) $\dfrac{1}{2}$ (E) $\dfrac{4}{7}$

Questions 10–11 refer to the following definition.

For all integers a and b: $a \div b = a$, if $a + b$ is even;
$$a \div b = b, \text{ if } a + b \text{ is odd.}$$

10. What is the value of $-5 \div 5$?

    (A) 10   (B) 5   (C) 0   (D) -5 (E) -10

11. If $a \ne b$ and $a \div b = 10$, which of the following could be true?

    I. $a + b$ is even
    II. $a + b$ is odd
    III. $b \div a = 10$

    (A) I only   (B) II only   (C) III only
    (D) I and II only   (E) I, II, and III

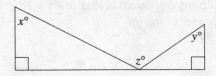

12. In the figure above, which of the following is an expression for *z* in terms of *x* and *y*?

(A) $x + y$ (B) $90 - x - y$ (C) $180 - x - y$
(D) $x + y - 90$ (E) $x + y - 180$

13. Let *P*, *Q*, and *R* be three points in the plane such that $PQ:QR = 2:3$. Which of the following could be the ratio *PQ:PR*?

I. 1:1

II. 2:5

III. 3:5

(A) I only (B) I and II only (C) I and III only
(D) II and III (E) I, II, and III

14. In a calculation, Diana accidentally decreased a number by 60% instead of increasing it by 60%. By what percent must the incorrect number be increased to yield the correct answer?

(A) 60% (B) 120% (C) 300% (D) 400%
(E) It cannot be determined from the information given.

15. For any number $w \neq 3$, $\subset w \supset = \dfrac{w+2}{w-3}$. For what value of *w* is $\subset w \supset = \dfrac{3}{2}$?

(A) 13 (B) 1 (C) 0 (D) −1 (E) −13

16. Paul drove *m* miles in *h* hours; Michelle drove the same distance in $\dfrac{1}{2}$ an hour less. How fast, in miles per hour, did Michelle drive?

(A) $\dfrac{m}{2h}$ (B) $\dfrac{2m+h}{2h}$ (C) $\dfrac{2m-h}{2h}$

(D) $\dfrac{2m}{2h+1}$ (E) $\dfrac{2m}{2h-1}$

17. A bag contains 4 red, 5 white, and 6 blue marbles. Sarah begins removing marbles from the bag at random, one at a time. What is the least number of marbles she must remove to be sure that she has at least one of each color?

(A) 3 (B) 6 (C) 9 (D) 12 (E) 15

18. Which of the following expressions is equal to $2^{3x} + 2^{3x} + 2^{3x} + 2^{3x}$?

(A) 2^{3x+2}　(B) 2^{3x+4}　(C) 2^{6x}

(D) 2^{12x}　(E) 2^{9x^2}

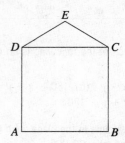

Note: Figure not drawn to scale

19. In the figure above, $ED = EC$, the area of square $ABCD$ is 100, and the area of $\triangle DEC$ is 10. Find the distance from A to E.

(A) 11　(B) 12　(C) $\sqrt{146}$

(D) 13　(E) $\sqrt{244}$

20. The circumference of circle II is 4 feet longer than the circumference of circle I. How many feet longer is the radius of circle II than the radius of circle I?

(A) $\dfrac{1}{4\pi}$　(B) $\dfrac{2}{\pi}$　(C) $\dfrac{1}{\pi}$　(D) 2

(E) It cannot be determined from the information given.

IF YOU FINISH IN LESS THAN 25 MINUTES,
YOU MAY CHECK YOUR WORK ON THIS **STOP**
SECTION ONLY. DO NOT TURN TO ANY
OTHER SECTION IN THE TEST.

SECTION 3
Time—25 minutes   27 questions (26–52)

Each of the following sentences contains one or two blanks; these blanks indicate that a word or set of words has been left out. Below the sentence are five words or phrases, lettered A through E. Select the word or set of words that best completes the sentence.

EXAMPLE:

Fame is ----; today's rising star is all too soon tomorrow's washed-up has-been.

(A) rewarding   (B) gradual   (C) essential
(D) spontaneous   (E) transitory

---

26. Once known only to importers of exotic foreign delicacies, the kiwi fruit has been transplanted successfully to America and is now ---- a much wider market.

(A) accessible to   (B) unknown to
(C) perplexing to   (D) comparable to
(E) uncultivated by

27. Continuously looking for new ways of presenting her material, for fresh methods of capturing her students' attention, she has been ---- in the classroom.

(A) a pedant   (B) a misfit
(C) an innovator   (D) a stoic
(E) a martinet

28. Measurement is, like any other human endeavor, a complex activity, subject to error, not always used ----, and frequently misinterpreted and ----.

(A) mistakenly..derided
(B) erratically..analyzed
(C) systematically..organized
(D) innovatively..refined
(E) properly..misunderstood

29. This coming trip to France should provide me with ---- test of the value of my conversational French class.

(A) an intimate   (B) an uncertain
(C) a pragmatic   (D) a pretentious
(E) an arbitrary

30. In a shocking instance of ---- research, one of the most influential researchers in the field of genetics reported on experiments that were never carried out and published deliberately ---- scientific papers on his nonexistent work.

   (A) comprehensive..abstract
   (B) theoretical..challenging
   (C) erroneous..impartial
   (D) derivative..authoritative
   (E) fraudulent..deceptive

31. Many of the characters portrayed by Clint Eastwood are strong but ---- types, rugged men of few words.

   (A) ruthless   (B) equivocal   (C) laconic
   (D) stingy   (E) vociferous

32. Like sauces, without a certain amount of spice, conversations grow ----.

   (A) eloquent   (B) heated   (C) elaborate
   (D) straightforward   (E) insipid

33. Both ---- and ----, Scrooge seldom smiled and never gave away a halfpenny.

   (A) sanguine..miserly
   (B) acerbic..magnanimous
   (C) morose..munificent
   (D) crabbed..parsimonious
   (E) sullen..philanthropic

Each of the following questions introduces a pair of words or phrases in capital letters, linked by a colon(:); this colon indicates that these words are related in some way. Following the capitalized pair are five pairs of words or phrases lettered A through E. Select the pair whose relationship is most similar to the relationship illustrated by the capitalized pair.

EXAMPLE:

CLOCK:TIME::   (A) watch:wrist
(B) pedometer:speed
(C) thermometer:temperature
(D) hourglass:sand   (E) radio:sound

Ⓐ Ⓑ ● Ⓓ Ⓔ

34. ALPHABET:LETTER::   (A) preface:book
   (B) piano:music   (C) ruler:distance
   (D) deck:card   (E) latch:door

35. SANCTUARY:REFUGE::   (A) oasis:desert
   (B) church:pew   (C) departure:flight
   (D) tree:shade   (E) holiday:resort

36. RUSTLE:CATTLE::   (A) bleat:sheep
   (B) swim:fish   (C) pan:gold
   (D) speculate:stock   (E) hijack:cargo

37. AVARICE:VICE::   (A) charity:virtue
   (B) greed:devil   (C) motive:suspicion
   (D) penury:crime   (E) frugality:economy

38. GLINT:LIGHT::   (A) blare:sound
   (B) whiff:scent   (C) shade:color
   (D) glut:food   (E) wave:tide

39. MERCURIAL:CONSTANCY::
   (A) sturdy:durability
   (B) genial:loyalty
   (C) ephemeral:permanence
   (D) quixotic:idealism
   (E) diffident:fidelity

40. SCOTCH:RUMOR::   (A) divert:traffic
   (B) broach:topic   (C) suppress:riot
   (D) singe:fire   (E) spread:gossip

The questions that follow the two passages in this section relate to the content of both, and to their relationship. The correct response may be stated outright or merely suggested in the passages and in any introductory or footnoted material included.

Questions 41–52 are based on the following passages.

The following passages are excerpted from recent essays about flying.

Passage 1

   Flying alone in an open plane is the purest experience of flight possible. That pure experience is felt at its most intense in acrobatic flying, when you are upside down, or pointed at the sky or at the earth, and

Line   moving in ways that you can only in the unsubstantial medium of the air.
(5)   Acrobatic flying is a useless skill in its particulars—nobody *needs* to do
a loop or a roll, not even a fighter pilot—but this skill extends your control of the plane and yourself and makes extreme actions in the sky comfortable. When you reach the top of a loop, upside down and engine at
full throttle, and tilt your head back to pick up the horizon line behind
(10)   you, you are as far outside instinctive human behavior as you can go—
hanging in space, the sky below you and the earth above, inscribing a
circle on emptiness. And then the nose drops across the horizon; your
speed increases and the plane scoops through into normal flight, and
you are back in the normal world, with the earth put back in its place.
(15)   The going out and coming back are what makes a loop so satisfying.

After a while, that is. At first it was terrifying, like being invited to a
suicide that you didn't want to commit. "This is a loop," my instructor
said casually. He lowered the plane's nose to gain airspeed, and then
pulled sharply up. The earth, and my stomach, fell away from me; and
(20)   we were upside down, and I could feel gravity clawing at me, pulling me
out into the mile of empty space between me and the ground. I grabbed
at the sides of the cockpit and hung on until gravity was on my side
again.

"You seemed a little nervous that time," the instructor said when the
(25)   plane was right side up again. "You've got to have confidence in that
seat belt, or you'll never do a decent loop. So this time, when we get on
top, I want you to put both arms out of the cockpit." And I did it. It was
like stepping off a bridge, but I did it, and the belt held, and the plane
came round. And after that I could fly a loop. It was, as I said, satisfying.

Passage 2

(30)   The black plane dropped spinning, and flattened out spinning the
other way; it began to carve the air into forms that built wildly and musi-
cally on each other and never ended. Reluctantly, I started paying attention. Rahm drew high above the world an inexhaustibly glorious line; it
piled over our heads in loops and arabesques. The plane moved every
(35)   way a line can move, and it controlled three dimensions, so the line
carved massive and subtle slits in the air like sculptures. The plane
looped the loop, seeming to arch its back like a gymnast; it stalled,
dropped, and spun out of it climbing; it spiraled and knifed west on one
side's wings and back east on another; it turned cartwheels, which must
(40)   be physically impossible; it played with its own line like a cat with yarn.
How did the pilot know where in the air he was? If he got lost, the
ground would swat him.

His was pure energy and naked spirit. I have thought about it for
years. Rahm's line unrolled in time. Like music, it split the bulging rim of

(45) the future along its seam. It pried out the present. We watchers waited
for the split-second curve of beauty in the present to reveal itself. The
human pilot, Dave Rahm, worked in the cockpit right at the plane's nose;
his very body tore into the future for us and reeled it down upon us like
a curling peel.

(50) Like any fine artist, he controlled the tension of the audience's longing. You desired, unwittingly, a certain kind of roll or climb, or a return
to a certain portion of the air, and he fulfilled your hope slantingly, like a
poet, or evaded it until you thought you would burst, and then fulfilled it
surprisingly, so you gasped and cried out.

(55) The oddest, most exhilarating and exhausting thing was this: he
never quit. The music had no periods, no rests or endings; the poetry's
beautiful sentence never ended; the line had no finish; the sculptured
forms piled overhead, one into another without surcease. Who could
breathe, in a world where rhythm itself had no periods?

(60) I went home and thought about Rahm's performance that night, and
the next day, and the next.

I had thought I knew my way around beauty a little bit. I knew I had
devoted a good part of my life to it, memorizing poetry and focusing my
attention on complexity of rhythm in particular, on force, movement,

(65) repetition, and surprise, in both poetry and prose. Now I had stood
among dandelions between two asphalt runways in Bellingham,
Washington, and begun learning about beauty. Even the Boston Museum
of Fine Arts was never more inspiring than this small northwestern airport on this time-killing Sunday afternoon in June. Nothing on earth is

(70) more gladdening than knowing we must roll up our sleeves and move
back the boundaries of the humanly possible once more.

41. According to the author of Passage 1, training in acrobatic flying

  (A) has only theoretical value
  (B) expands a pilot's range of capabilities
  (C) is an essential part of general pilot training
  (D) comes naturally to most pilots
  (E) should only be required of fighter pilots

42. The word "medium" in line 4 means

  (A) midpoint   (B) appropriate occupation
  (C) method of communication
  (D) environment   (E) compromise

43. To "pick up the horizon line" (line 9) is to

    (A) lift it higher   (B) spot it visually
    (C) measure its distance   (D) choose it eagerly
    (E) increase its visibility

44. Passage 1 suggests that the author's grabbing at the sides of the cockpit (lines 19–23) was

    (A) instinctive   (B) terrifying   (C) essential
    (D) habit-forming   (E) life-threatening

45. The word "held" (line 28) most nearly means

    (A) carried   (B) detained   (C) accommodated
    (D) remained valid   (E) maintained its grasp

46. By putting both arms out of the cockpit (lines 27–29), the author

    (A) chooses the path of least resistance
    (B) enables himself to steer the plane more freely
    (C) relies totally on his seat belt to keep him safe
    (D) allows himself to give full expression to his nervousness
    (E) is better able to breathe deeply and relax

47. The author's use of the word "satisfying" (line 29) represents

    (A) a simile   (B) an understatement
    (C) a fallacy   (D) a euphemism
    (E) a hypothesis

48. The author of Passage 2 mentions her initial reluctance to watch the stunt flying (lines 32–33) in order to

    (A) demonstrate her hostility to commercial entertainment
    (B) reveal her fear of such dangerous enterprises
    (C) minimize her participation in aerial acrobatics
    (D) indicate how captivating the demonstration was
    (E) emphasize the acuteness of her perceptions

49. By fulfilling "your hope slantingly, like a poet" (lines 52–53), the author means that

    (A) the pilot flew the plane on a diagonal
    (B) Rahm was a writer of popular verse
    (C) the pilot had a bias against executing certain kinds of rolls
    (D) Rahm refused to satisfy your expectations directly
    (E) the pilot's sense of aesthetic judgment was askew

50. At the end of Passage 2, the author is left feeling

    (A) empty in the aftermath of the stunning performance she has seen

    (B) jubilant at the prospect of moving from Boston to Washington

    (C) exhilarated by her awareness of new potentials for humanity

    (D) glad that she has not wasted any more time memorizing poetry

    (E) surprised by her response to an art form she had not previously believed possible

51. Compared to Passage 2, Passage 1 is

    (A) less informative   (B) more tentative

    (C) more argumentative   (D) more speculative

    (E) less lyrical

52. How would the author of Passage 2 most likely react to the assessment of acrobatic flying in lines 5–8?

    (A) She would consider it too utilitarian an assessment of an aesthetic experience.

    (B) She would reject it as an inaccurate description of the pilot's technique.

    (C) She would admire it as a poetic evocation of the pilot's art.

    (D) She would criticize it as a digression from the author's main point.

    (E) She would regard it as too effusive to be appropriate to its subject.

IF YOU FINISH IN LESS THAN 25 MINUTES, YOU MAY CHECK YOUR WORK ON THIS SECTION ONLY. DO NOT TURN TO ANY OTHER SECTION IN THE TEST.

S T O P

SECTION 4

Time—25 minutes   **20 questions (21–40)**

This section has two types of questions. The directions for each type are given right before those questions. You may use any blank space on the page for your work.

Notes:

- You may use a calculator whenever you believe it will be helpful.
- Use the diagrams provided to help you solve the problems. Unless you see the phrase "<u>Note</u>: Figure not drawn to scale" under a diagram, it has been drawn as accurately as possible. Unless it is stated that a figure is three-dimensional, you may assume that it lies in a plane.

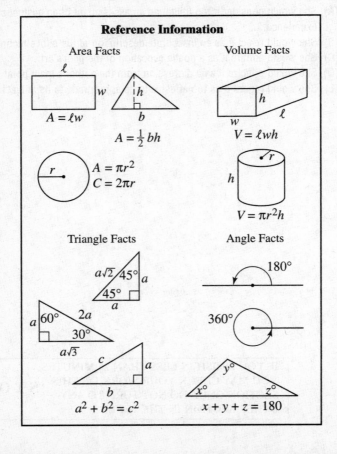

Reference Information

Area Facts

$A = \ell w$

$A = \frac{1}{2} bh$

$A = \pi r^2$
$C = 2\pi r$

Volume Facts

$V = \ell wh$

$V = \pi r^2 h$

Triangle Facts

$a\sqrt{2}$, $45°$, $45°$, a

a, $60°$, $2a$, $30°$, $a\sqrt{3}$

$a^2 + b^2 = c^2$

Angle Facts

$180°$

$360°$

$x + y + z = 180$

Directions for the Quantitative Comparison Questions

In each of questions 21–32, two quantities appear in boxes: one in Column A and one in Column B. You must compare them. The correct answer to a question is

A   if the quantity in Column A is greater;
B   if the quantity in Column B is greater;
C   if the two quantities are equal;
D   if it is impossible to determine which quantity is greater.

Notes:
- *The correct answer is never E.*
- Sometimes information about one or both of the quantities is centered above the two boxes.
- If the same symbol appears in both columns, it represents the same thing each time.
- All variables represent real numbers.

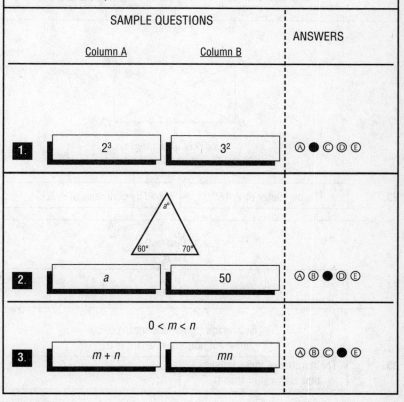

	SAMPLE QUESTIONS		ANSWERS
	Column A	Column B	
1.	2^3	3^2	Ⓐ ● Ⓒ Ⓓ Ⓔ
2.	a	50	Ⓐ Ⓑ ● Ⓓ Ⓔ
3.	$m + n$	mn	Ⓐ Ⓑ Ⓒ ● Ⓔ

For question 2: triangle with $a°$ at top, $60°$ and $70°$ at base.

For question 3: $0 < m < n$

SUMMARY DIRECTIONS FOR QUANTITATIVE
COMPARISON QUESTIONS

<u>Answer:</u> A if the quantity in Column A is greater;
B if the quantity in Column B is greater;
C if the two quantities are equal;
D if it is impossible to determine which quantity is greater.

	<u>Column A</u>	<u>Column B</u>
21.	$\frac{3}{5}$ of 4	$\frac{4}{5}$ of 3

22.	The least multiple of 7 that is greater than 80	The largest multiple of 12 that is less than 90

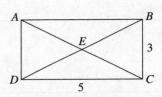

ABCD is a rectangle.
<u>Note:</u> Figure not drawn to scale

23.	The perimeter of △AED	The perimeter of △EDC

$$a > 0, \; b > 0$$
$$a \neq b$$

24.	$\frac{a}{b}$	$\left(\frac{a}{b}\right)^3$

The average (arithmetic mean) of six
different nonzero integers is 0.

25.	The number of these integers that are greater than 0	3

Column A   Column B

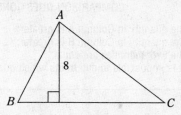

Note: Figure not drawn to scale

| 26. | The area of △ABC | 2 |

$$x > 1$$
$$xy = 12$$
$$zx = 25$$

| 27. | y | z |

$$x < y$$

| 28. | The average (arithmetic mean) of x and y | The average (arithmetic mean) of x, y, and y |

$$x^2 + 6x + 8 = 0$$

| 29. | x | 2 |

x and y are positive integers
$$xy = 20$$

| 30. | x + y | 13 |

**SUMMARY DIRECTIONS FOR QUANTITATIVE
COMPARISON QUESTIONS**

<u>Answer:</u> A if the quantity in Column A is greater;
B if the quantity in Column B is greater;
C if the two quantities are equal;
D if it is impossible to determine which quantity is greater.

<u>Column A</u>   <u>Column B</u>

$$\begin{array}{r} AB \\ + CD \\ \hline AAA \end{array}$$

In the addition problem above, each letter represents a different digit.

31. | $A + C$ | | $B + D$ |

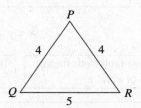

32. | The area of $\triangle PQR$ | | 10 |

Directions for Student-Produced Response Questions (Grid-ins)

In questions 33–40, first solve the problem, and then enter your answer on the grid provided on the answer sheet. The instructions for entering your answers follow:

- First, write your answer in the boxes at the top of the grid.
- Second, grid your answer in the columns below the boxes.
- Use the fraction bar in the first row or the decimal point in the second row to enter fractions and decimal answers.

Answer: $\frac{8}{15}$ Answer: 1.75

Write your answer in the boxes

Grid in your answer

Answer: 100

Either position is acceptable

- Grid only one space in each column.
- Entering the answer in the boxes is recommended as an aid in gridding, but is not required.
- The machine scoring your exam can read only what you grid, so you **must grid in your answers correctly to get credit.**
- If a question has more than one correct answer, grid in only one of them.
- The grid does not have a minus sign, so no answer can be negative.
- A mixed number *must* be converted to an improper fraction or a decimal before it is gridded. Enter $1\frac{1}{4}$ as 5/4 or 1.25; the machine will interpret 1 1/4 as $\frac{11}{4}$ and mark it wrong.

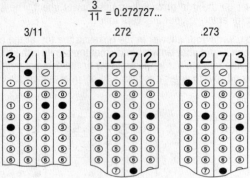

- **All decimals must be entered as accurately as possible.** Here are the three acceptable ways of gridding

$$\frac{3}{11} = 0.272727...$$

- Note that rounding to .273 is acceptable, because you are using the full grid, but you would receive **no credit** for .3 or .27, because they are less accurate.

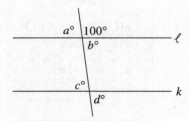

Lines ℓ and k are parallel.

33. In the figure above, what is the value of $a + b + c + d$?

34. What is the area of a right triangle whose hypotenuse is 30 and one of whose legs is 18?

35. If 80% of the freshmen at a particular college eventually graduate, and if 60% of those who graduate attend some graduate school, what percent of the freshmen will *not* attend graduate school?

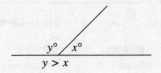

$y > x$

Note: Figure not drawn to scale

36. For the figure above, what is the smallest value of *y* that will fit in the grid?

37. If $\frac{1}{3}$ of a certain number is 4 less than 3 times the number, what is $\frac{3}{5}$ of the number?

38. At Southside High School there are 50 students in the orchestra and 40 students in the chorus. If 10 students are in both the orchestra and chorus, what is the ratio of the number of students who are only in the orchestra to the number who are only in the chorus?

39. A group charters three identical buses and occupies $\frac{4}{5}$ of the seats. After $\frac{1}{4}$ of the passengers leave, the remaining passengers use only two of the buses. What fraction of the seats on the two buses are now occupied?

40. When a group of people were tested for a rare disease, 99.6% of them were found not to have the disease. If 10 people did have the disease, how many people were tested?

IF YOU FINISH IN LESS THAN 25 MINUTES,
YOU MAY CHECK YOUR WORK ON THIS   **S T O P**
SECTION ONLY. DO NOT TURN TO ANY
OTHER SECTION IN THE TEST.

SECTION 5

Time—30 minutes   39 questions (1–39)

The sentences in this section may contain errors in grammar, usage, choice of words, or idioms. There is either just one error per sentence or the sentence is correct. Some words or phrases are underlined and lettered; everything else in the sentence is correct.

If an underlined word or phrase is incorrect, choose that letter; if the sentence is correct, select <u>No error</u>. Then blacken the appropriate space on your Answer Sheet.

EXAMPLE:

The region has a climate <u>so severe that</u> plants
                              A
<u>growing there</u> rarely <u>had been</u> more than
        B   C
twelve inches <u>high</u>. <u>No error</u>   Ⓐ Ⓑ ● Ⓓ Ⓔ
              D   E

---

1. I <u>have been thinking</u> lately about the monsters—or fantasies <u>or whatever</u>—
         A   B
   that frightened <u>myself</u> as a child. <u>No error</u>
   C   D   E

2. We <u>admired</u> his <u>many</u> attempts <u>bravely</u> <u>to enter</u> the burning building. <u>No error</u>
        A   B   C   D   E

3. He worked in the lumber camps <u>during</u> the summer not <u>because of</u> the money
                                    A   B
   <u>but</u> because he wanted to strengthen his muscles by doing <u>hard physical</u>
   C   D
   labor. <u>No error</u>
          E

4. That book is <u>liable</u> to become a best seller because it is <u>well-written</u>,
       A   B
   full of suspense, and <u>very</u> entertaining. <u>No error</u>
   C   D   E

5. $\underset{A}{\underline{\text{According to}}}$ a random poll $\underset{B}{\underline{\text{taken by}}}$ *National Wildlife*, the top three threats

   to the environment $\underset{C}{\underline{\text{is}}}$ water pollution, air pollution, and $\underset{D}{\underline{\text{hazardous}}}$ wastes.

   $\underset{E}{\underline{\text{No error}}}$

6. His three children, Ruth, Frank, and Ellis, are very talented youngsters, $\underset{A}{\underline{\text{but the}}}$

   $\underset{B}{\underline{\text{latter}}}$ $\underset{C}{\underline{\text{shows}}}$ the $\underset{D}{\underline{\text{most}}}$ promise. $\underset{E}{\underline{\text{No error}}}$

7. $\underset{A}{\underline{\text{Passing}}}$ antidrug legislation, calling for more education, and $\underset{B}{\underline{\text{to aid}}}$ Bolivia in

   raids on cocaine dealers are $\underset{C}{\underline{\text{all ways}}}$ that the United States is fighting back

   $\underset{D}{\underline{\text{against}}}$ "crack" use. $\underset{E}{\underline{\text{No error}}}$

8. Cajun cooking, which uses $\underset{A}{\underline{\text{special prepared}}}$ spices, has always been

   well-known in Louisiana, $\underset{B}{\underline{\text{but it is}}}$ $\underset{C}{\underline{\text{only}}}$ now becoming known in other

   $\underset{D}{\underline{\text{parts}}}$ of the country. $\underset{E}{\underline{\text{No error}}}$

9. It seems strange $\underset{A}{\underline{\text{to realize that}}}$ when Harvey Firestone $\underset{B}{\underline{\text{organized}}}$ the Firestone

   Tire and Rubber Company in $\underset{C}{\underline{1900}}$, rubber tires $\underset{D}{\underline{\text{had been}}}$ a novelty. $\underset{E}{\underline{\text{No error}}}$

10. The same laser technology that is $\underset{A}{\underline{\text{being used}}}$ on compact discs $\underset{B}{\underline{\text{is}}}$ also

    $\underset{C}{\underline{\text{under application}}}$ to computers to $\underset{D}{\underline{\text{achieve}}}$ additional memory. $\underset{E}{\underline{\text{No error}}}$

11. The $\underset{A}{\underline{\text{suspenseful}}}$ play *The Mystery of Edwin Drood* permits $\underset{B}{\underline{\text{its}}}$ audience to

    determine the ending; $\underset{C}{\underline{\text{unfortunately}}}$, the play has a $\underset{D}{\underline{\text{new unique}}}$ ending for

    each performance. $\underset{E}{\underline{\text{No error}}}$

12. The Philippine government changed hands when Marcos failed satisfying his
    _____ A _____ B _____ C
    countrymen that he had won the presidential election, and Corazon Aquino

    took over. No error
    _____ D _____ E

13. Was it they who were involved in the recent unruly demonstration? No error
    ___ A B C   D   E

14. We must regard any statement about this controversy, whatever the source,
    _____ A   _____ B
    as gossip until they are confirmed. No error
    C _____ D _____ E

15. She is the only one of the applicants who are fully qualified for the position.
    _____ A _____ B C _____ D
    No error
    E

16. In order to meet publication schedules, publishers often find it necessary to
    _____ A   ____ B _____ C
    trim everyone's schedule and leaving room for unexpected problems.
    _____ D
    No error
    E

17. If the flag is given to him, Juan and him should be at the beginning of the
    A _____ B   _____ C _____ D
    processional. No error
    _____ E

18. People often forget during the winter that lawn maintenance must be started
    _____ A _____ _____ B
    at the onset of spring, in fact they soon remember. No error
    ____ C _____ D _____ E

19. We must come to the realization that it is our obligation to look after the
    _____ A _____ B _____ C
    poorer nations by providing medical care, establishing hospitals and schools,

    and to insure adequate food supplies. No error
    _____ D _____ E

Some or all parts of the following sentences are underlined. The first answer choice, (A), simply repeats the underlined part of the sentence. The other four choices present four alternate ways to phrase the underlined part. Select the answer that produces the most effective sentence, one that is clear and exact, and blacken the appropriate space on your answer sheet. In selecting your choice, be sure that it is standard written English, and that it expresses the meaning of the original sentence.

EXAMPLE:

The first biography of author Eudora Welty came out in 1998
and she was eighty-nine years old at the time.

(A) and she was eighty-nine years old at the time.
(B) at the time when she was eighty-nine.
(C) upon becoming an eighty-nine year old.
(D) when she was eighty-nine.
(E) at the age of eighty-nine years old.

20. Because he spoke out against Hitler's policies was why Dietrich Bonhoeffer, a Lutheran pastor in Nazi Germany, was arrested and eventually hanged by the Gestapo.

(A) Because he spoke out against Hitler's policies was why Dietrich Bonhoeffer, a Lutheran pastor in Nazi Germany, was arrested and eventually hanged by the Gestapo.

(B) Dietrich Bonhoeffer, a Lutheran pastor in Nazi Germany, was arrested and eventually hanged by the Gestapo because he spoke out against Hitler's policies.

(C) Because he spoke out against Hitler's policies, Dietrich Bonhoeffer, a Lutheran pastor in Nazi Germany, was arrested and eventually hung by the Gestapo.

(D) Dietrich Bonhoeffer, a Lutheran pastor in Nazi Germany, being arrested and eventually hung because he spoke out against Hitler's policies.

(E) A Lutheran pastor in Nazi Germany, Dietrich Bonhoeffer, spoke out against Hitler's policies so that he arrested and eventually hung.

21. The difference between Liebniz and Schopenhauer is that the former is optimistic; the latter, pessimistic.

- (A) the former is optimistic; the latter, pessimistic
- (B) the former is optimistic, the latter, pessimistic
- (C) while the former is optimistic; the latter, pessimistic
- (D) the former one is optimistic; the latter one is a pessimistic
- (E) the former is optimistic; the latter being pessimistic

22. Most students like to read these kind of books during their spare time.

- (A) these kind of books
- (B) these kind of book
- (C) this kind of book
- (D) this kinds of books
- (E) those kind of books

23. John was imminently qualified for the position because he had studied computer programming and how to operate an IBM machine.

- (A) imminently qualified for the position because he had studied computer programming and how to operate an IBM machine.
- (B) imminently qualified for the position since studying computer programming and the operation of an IBM machine.
- (C) eminently qualified for the position because he had studied computer programming and how to operate an IBM machine.
- (D) eminently qualified for the position because he had studied computer programming and the operation of an IBM machine.
- (E) eminently qualified for the position because he has studied computer programming and how to operate an IBM machine.

24. The idea of inoculating people with smallpox to protect them from later attacks was introduced into Europe by Mary Wortley Montagu, who learned of it in Asia.

- (A) Mary Wortley Montagu, who learned of it in Asia
- (B) Mary Wortley Montagu, who learned of them in Asia
- (C) Mary Wortley Montagu, who learned it of those in Asia
- (D) Mary Wortley Montagu, learning of it in Asia
- (E) Mary Wortley Montagu, because she learned of it in Asia

25. In general, the fate of Latin American or East Asian countries <u>will affect America more than it does</u> Britain or France.

    (A) will affect America more than it does

    (B) will effect America more than it does

    (C) will affect America more than they do

    (D) will effect America more than they do

    (E) will affect America more than they would

26. While campaigning for President, Dole nearly <u>exhausted his funds and must raise money so that he could pay</u> for last-minute television commercials.

    (A) exhausted his funds and must raise money so that he could pay

    (B) would exhaust his funds to raise money so that he could pay

    (C) exhausted his funds and had to raise money so that he can pay

    (D) exhausted his funds and had to raise money so that he could pay

    (E) exhausted his funds and must raise money so that he can pay

27. Athletic coaches stress <u>not only eating nutritious meals but also to get</u> adequate sleep.

    (A) not only eating nutritious meals but also to get

    (B) to not only eat nutritious meals but also getting,

    (C) not only to eat nutritious meals but also getting,

    (D) not only the eating of nutritious meals but also getting

    (E) not only eating nutritious meals but also getting

28. Oakland, California <u>is where the American novelist Jack London spent his early manhood; it was a busy waterfront town.</u>

    (A) is where the American novelist Jack London spent his early manhood; it was a busy waterfront town

    (B) was the busy waterfront town where the American novelist Jack London spent his early manhood

    (C) is the place where the American novelist Jack London spent his early manhood in a busy waterfront town

    (D) is the site of the busy waterfront which was where the American novelist Jack London was situated in early manhood

    (E) is where the American novelist Jack London spent his early manhood in a busy waterfront town

29. The goal of the remedial program was that it enables the students to master the basic skills they need to succeed in regular coursework.

(A) that it enables
(B) by enabling
(C) to enable
(D) where students are enabled
(E) where it enables

30. Her coach, along with her parents and friends, are confident she will win the tournament.

(A) along with her parents and friends, are confident she
(B) along with her parents and friends, are confident that she
(C) along with her parents and friends, have been confident she
(D) together with her parents and friends, are confident she
(E) along with her parents and friends, is confident she

31. The referee would of stopped the fight if the battered boxer would of risen to his feet.

(A) would of stopped the fight if the battered boxer would of risen
(B) would have stopped the fight if the battered boxer would of risen
(C) would have stopped the fight if the battered boxer had risen
(D) would of stopped the fight if the battered boxer would of rose
(E) would have stopped the fight if the battered boxer had rose

32. When the waitress told me that I could have my choice of vanilla, chocolate, or pistachio ice cream, I selected the former even though I prefer the latter.

(A) the former even though I prefer the latter
(B) the first even though I prefer the latter
(C) the former even though I prefer the last
(D) the former even though it is the latter that I prefer
(E) the first even though I prefer the last

33. In visiting the Tower of London, Mrs. Pomeroy's hat was blown off her head into the river.

(A) In visiting the Tower of London, Mrs. Pomeroy's hat was blown off her head into the river.
(B) Mrs. Pomeroy visited the Tower of London, her hat blew off her head into the river.
(C) Mrs. Pomeroy, who was visiting the Tower of London when her hat blew off her head, saw it fall into the river.
(D) When Mrs. Pomeroy visited the Tower of London, her hat was blown off her head and fell into the river.
(E) Mrs. Pomeroy visited the Tower of London; suddenly her hat was blown off her head which fell into the river.

The passage below is the unedited draft of a student's essay. Some of the essay needs to be rewritten to make the meaning clearer and more precise. Read the essay carefully.

The essay is followed by six questions about changes that might improve all or part of its organization, development, sentence structure, use of language, appropriateness to the audience, or its use of standard written English. Choose the answer that most clearly and effectively expresses the student's intended meaning. Indicate your choice by filling in the corresponding space on the answer sheet.

[1] When you turn on the radio or pop in a tape while the house is quiet or going to work or school in your car, you have several choices of music to listen to. [2] Although, in recent years, CDs have become the medium of choice over records and even tapes. [3] On the radio you have your rap on one station, your classical on another, your New Wave music on another, and then you have your Country. [4] Some young people feel that country is for fat old people, but it isn't. [5] It is music for all ages, fat or thin.

[6] Country music is "fun" music. [7] It has an unmistakable beat and sound that gets you up and ready to move. [8] You can really get into country, even if it is just the clapping of the hands or the stamping of the feet. [9] You can't help feeling cheerful watching the country performers, who all seem so happy to be entertaining their close "friends," although there may be 10,000 of them in the stadium or concert hall. [10] The musicians love it, and the audience flips out with delight. [11] The interpersonal factors in evidence cause a sudden psychological bond to develop into a temporary, but nevertheless tightly knit, family unit. [12] For example, you can imagine June Carter Cash as your favorite aunt and Randy Travis as your long lost cousin.

[13] Some people spurn country music. [14] Why, they ask, would anyone want to listen to singers whine about their broken marriages or their favorite pet that was run over by an 18-wheeler? [15] They claim that Willie Nelson, one of today's country legends, can't even keep his income taxes straight. [16] Another "dynamic" performer is Dolly Parton, whose most famous feature is definitely not her voice. [17] How talented could she be if her body is more famous than her singing?

[18] Loretta Lynn is the greatest. [19] Anyone's negative feelings towards country music would change after hearing Loretta's strong, emotional, and haunting voice. [20] Look, it can't hurt to give a listen. [21] You never know, you might even like it so much that you will go out, pick up a secondhand guitar and learn to strum a few chords.

34. Which is the best revision of the underlined segment of sentence 1 below?

When you turn on the radio or pop in a tape while the house is quiet or going to work or school in your car, you have several choices of music to listen to.

(A) while the house is quiet or in your car going to work or school
(B) driving to work or school while the house is quiet
(C) while the house is quiet or you are driving to work or school
(D) while driving to work or school in your car, and the house is quiet
(E) while there's quiet in the house or you go to work or school in your car

35. To improve the coherence of paragraph 1, which of the following sentences should be deleted?

(A) Sentence 1   (B) Sentence 2
(C) Sentence 3   (D) Sentence 4
(E) Sentence 5

36. Taking into account the sentences that precede and follow sentence 8, which of the following is the best revision of sentence 8?

(A) Clap your hands and stamp your feet is what to do to easily get into country.
(B) You're really into country, even if it is just clapping of the hands or stamping of the feet.
(C) You can easily get into country just by clapping your hands or stamping your feet.
(D) One can get into country music rather easily; one must merely clap one's hands or stamp one's feet.
(E) Getting into country is easy, just clap your hands and stamp your feet.

37. With regard to the writing style and tone of the essay, which is the best revision of sentence 11?

(A) The interpersonal relationship that develops suddenly creates a temporary, but nevertheless a closely knit, family unit.
(B) A family-like relationship develops quickly and rapidly.
(C) A close family-type relation is suddenly very much in evidence between the performer and his or her audience.
(D) All of a sudden you feel like a member of a huge, but tight, family.
(E) A sudden bond develops between the entertainer and the audience that might most suitably be described as a "family," in the best sense of the term.

38. Considering the essay as a whole, which of the following best describes the function of paragraph 3?

    (A) To present some objective data in support of another viewpoint
    (B) To offer a more balanced view of the essay's subject matter
    (C) To ridicule those readers who don't agree with the writer
    (D) To lend further support to the essay's main idea
    (E) To divert the reader's attention from the main idea of the essay

39. Which of the following revisions of sentence 18 provides the smoothest transition between paragraphs 3 and 4?

    (A) Loretta Lynn is one of the great singers of country music.
    (B) Loretta Lynn, however, is the greatest country singer yet.
    (C) But you can bet they've never heard Loretta Lynn.
    (D) The sounds of Loretta Lynn tells a different story, however.
    (E) Loretta Lynn, on the other hand, is superb.

IF YOU FINISH IN LESS THAN 30 MINUTES,
YOU MAY CHECK YOUR WORK ON THIS   **S T O P**
SECTION ONLY. DO NOT TURN TO ANY
OTHER SECTION IN THE TEST.

Answer Key

Section 1 Verbal Reasoning

1. D	10. B	19. E
2. E	11. D	20. B
3. A	12. C	21. D
4. D	13. C	22. C
5. B	14. A	23. B
6. C	15. D	24. E
7. C	16. B	25. E
8. D	17. B	
9. B	18. A	

Section 2 Mathematical Reasoning

1. D	8. B	15. A
2. C	9. C	16. E
3. E	10. D	17. D
4. B	11. D	18. A
5. B	12. A	19. D
6. A	13. E	20. B
7. C	14. C	

Section 3 Verbal Reasoning

26. A	35. D	44. A
27. C	36. E	45. E
28. C	37. A	46. C
29. C	38. B	47. B
30. E	39. C	48. D
31. C	40. C	49. D
32. E	41. B	50. C
33. D	42. D	51. E
34. D	43. B	52. A

Section 4 Mathematical Reasoning

21. C	25. D	29. B
22. C	26. D	30. D
23. B	27. B	31. B
24. D	28. B	32. B

Grid-in Questions

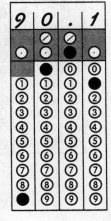

33. 3 2 0

34. 2 1 6

35. 5 2

36. 9 0 . 1

37.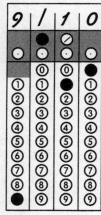

or . **9**

38.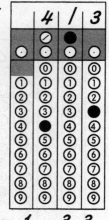

or **1** . **3 3**

39.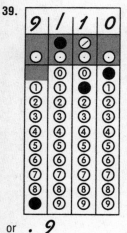

or . **9**

40.

| 2 | 5 | 0 | 0 |

Section 5 Writing Skills

1. **D**	11. **C**	21. **A**	31. **C**
2. **C**	12. **C**	22. **C**	32. **E**
3. **B**	13. **E**	23. **D**	33. **D**
4. **B**	14. **D**	24. **A**	34. **C**
5. **C**	15. **C**	25. **A**	35. **B**
6. **B**	16. **D**	26. **D**	36. **C**
7. **B**	17. **C**	27. **E**	37. **D**
8. **A**	18. **D**	28. **B**	38. **B**
9. **D**	19. **D**	29. **C**	39. **C**
10. **C**	20. **B**	30. **E**	

Answer Explanations

Section 1 Verbal Reasoning

1. **(D)** Fast food restaurants are growing more popular in France. The traditional café is therefore growing less popular (falling "victim to the growing popularity" of McBurgers) and is slowly *becoming extinct* (vanishing; disappearing; dying out).

2. **(E)** *Although* signals a contrast. You would expect the coach to be *jubilant* (extremely joyful) about her team's victory. Instead, she was *disheartened* (discouraged).

3. **(A)** *Bantering* or joking remarks are clearly *inappropriate* in a serious speech.

4. **(D)** People uncomfortable with math would be likely to think the field should be *left to* those gifted in such an *esoteric* (hard to understand; known only to a chosen few) subject.

5. **(B)** A writer whose work was universally acclaimed or applauded and whose reputation was not yet *tarnished* or stained would be at the *zenith* or high point of her career.

6. **(C)** A *conductor* leads or directs an *orchestra*; a *director* guides or directs a *cast*.

    (Function)

7. **(C)** *Words* are the medium an *essayist* employs when creating an essay; *batter* is the material a *baker* uses when preparing a cake.

    (Material and Worker)

8. **(D)** To *inaugurate* a *president* is to introduce him or her into office. To *install* an *officer* is to do the same.

    (Function)

9. **(B)** To *outfox* someone is to surpass that person in *cunning*; to *outstrip* someone is to surpass that person in *speed*.

    (Defining Characteristic)

10. **(B)** Something *cacophonous* (discordant; harsh-sounding) is unpleasant to *hear*; something *unsavory* (unpalatable; disagreeable in taste) is unpleasant to *taste*.

    (Defining Characteristic)

11. **(D)** Someone *imperturbable* (unexcitable; calm) is difficult to *discompose* or agitate; someone *incredulous* (disbelieving) is difficult to *convince*.

    (Antonym Variant)

12. **(C)** The entire passage examines Bethune's beliefs in the ultimate victory of racial justice and in the possibility of winning whites to her cause. In addition, it clearly shows Bethune, in her work to get her people represented in all public programs, having an impact on her people's progress.

13. (C) You can arrive at the correct answer by the process of elimination.

Williams assisted Bethune in influencing the advancement of blacks within the NYA. Therefore, you can eliminate Choices B and D.

The opening sentence of the first paragraph indicates Williams was one of Bethune's white friends; references to him in the second paragraph suggest he was a liberal. Therefore, you can eliminate Choice A.

Nothing in the passage suggests Williams was religious. Therefore, you can eliminate Choice E.

Only Choice C is left. It is the correct answer.

14. (A) Bethune's success in getting Dickerson's appointment is a clear example of her impact.

Choice B is incorrect. The author is stressing how helpful Bethune was to Dickerson, not how different Bethune's career was from Dickerson's. Choice C is incorrect. Dickerson is not the subject of the paragraph that follows. Choice D is incorrect. The author brings up Bethune's belief in the "New Negro" well after he mentions her assistance to Dickerson. He draws no connection between Dickerson and the "New Negro." Choice E is incorrect. The author is making a point about Bethune, not about Dickerson.

15. (D) Bethune was the intermediary who helped arrange for Dickerson's new position. She was instrumental or *helpful* in gaining this end.

16. (B) By leading America to a "full realization of its democratic ideas," the New Negro would be *helping America accomplish its egalitarian goals.*

17. (B) The author compares and contrasts Bethune with her white liberal friends. The author directly quotes the wording of Bethune's 1944 appeals for black representation. The author gives concrete examples of the ways in which Bethune remained a black partisan champion of the New Deal. The author constantly reiterates the idea that Bethune had an ongoing influence on black progress during the Roosevelt years. However, the author uses figurative language only minimally and never develops an extended metaphor.

18. (A) Dickens implies that Gradgrind is so peremptory (absolute; dogmatic) about facts that he would insist upon the fact that his given name was, in fact, Thomas.

19. (E) Gradgrind carries scales and a rule in his pocket to "weigh and measure any parcel of human nature." Though Dickens plays upon several meanings of *rule* here, the word basically refers to a ruler or measuring stick.

20. (B) As he walks home, Gradgrind is in "a state of considerable satisfaction." He is pleased with himself and with the school he has created; his mood is clearly one of *complacency* or smugness.

21. (D) Dickens is poking fun at Gradgrind's teaching methods and is thus *broadly satirical* (full of ridicule).

22. **(C)** Gradgrind never introduces his pupils to nursery rhymes or to fantasy creatures such as ogres. This suggests that he rejects from his curriculum anything that is in the least *fanciful* or imaginative.

23. **(B)** The little Gradgrinds, having studied the Great Bear and Charles's Wain, had never "known wonder on the subject of stars." This suggests that the Great Bear and the Wain are constellations, or *groupings of stars*.

24. **(E)** Gradgrind's main idea is to fill his pupils full of *facts*, particularly facts about *science* (statistics, constellations, graminivorous quadrupeds, etc.).

25. **(E)** The famous cow with the crumpled horn ("The House that Jack Built") and the yet more famous cow who swallowed Tom Thumb in the folk tale are legendary *fictional characters* with whose celebrity the young Gradgrinds are unacquainted.

Section 2 Mathematical Reasoning

In each mathematics section, for some of the problems, an alternative solution, indicated by two asterisks (**), follows the first solution. When this occurs, one of the solutions is the direct mathematical one and the other is based on one of the tactics discussed in Chapter 7.

1. **(D)** Since the ratio of the number of boys to girls is 2:3, the number of boys is $2x$, the number of girls is $3x$, and the total number of members is $2x + 3x = 5x$. So the girls make up $\frac{3x}{5x} = \frac{3}{5} = 60\%$ of the members.

2. **(C)**
$$7d + 5 = 5d + 7 \Rightarrow$$
$$2d + 5 = 7 \Rightarrow 2d = 2 \Rightarrow d = 1.$$
Use **TACTIC 10. Backsolve, starting with C.

3. **(E)** Since d divisions each have t teams, multiply to get dt teams, and since each team has p players, multiply the number of teams (dt) by p to get the total number of players: dtp.
Use **TACTIC 11. Choose easy-to-use numbers for t, d, and p. For example, assume that there are 2 divisions, each with 4 teams So, there are $2 \times 4 = 8$ teams. Then assume that each of the teams has 10 players, for a total of $8 \times 10 = 80$ players. Now check the five choices. Which one is equal to 80 when $d = 2$, $t = 4$, and $p = 10$? Only dtp.

4. **(B)** The unmarked angle opposite the 60° angle also measures 60°, and the sum of the measures of all six angles in the diagram is 360°. Then,
$$360 = a + b + c + 20 + 60 + 60 =$$
$$a + b + c + 140.$$
Subtracting 140 from each side, we get $a + b + c = 220$.

5. (B) Discard the scores of 9.2 and 9.7 and take the average of the other four scores:

$$\frac{9.4+9.5+9.6+9.6}{4} = \frac{38.1}{4} = 9.525.$$

6. (A) The smallest possible value of $x + y$ is 7 (3 + 4), and the largest possible value is 11 (5 + 6). It is easy to check that each of the integers in between (8, 9, and 10) is also possible, so there are 5 different values.

7. (C) Test each set of values to see which one does not work. Only Choice C, $x = 1$ and $y = -1$ does not work: $3(1)^2 + 2(-1) = 3 - 2 = 1$, not 5. The other choices all work.

8. (B) Adding the two equations, we get $8x + 8y = 40$. So $x + y = \frac{40}{8} = 5$, and the average of x and y is $\frac{x+y}{2} = \frac{5}{2} = 2.5$.

9. (C) There is a total of $1 + 2 + 3 + 4 + 5 + 6 = 21$ slips of paper. Since odd numbers are written on $1 + 3 + 5 = 9$ of them, the probability of drawing an odd number is $\frac{9}{21} = \frac{3}{7}$.

10. (D) Since $-5 + 5 = 0$, and 0 is an even integer, $-5 \div 5 = -5$.

11. (D) Since $10 \div 2 = 10$ (10 + 2 is even), I is true; and since $1 \div 10 = 10$ (1 + 10 is odd), II is true.

$$a \div b = b \div a \Rightarrow a = b$$

which by the given information is impossible. III is false. Statements I and II only are true.

12. (A) Since the sum of the measures of the two acute angles of a right triangle is 90°, $a + x = 90$ and $b + y = 90$. Adding these equations, we get: $a + b + x + y = 180$. Since it is also true that $a + b + z = 180$, we get that $z = x + y$.

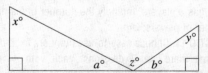

Use TACTIC 11. Substitute numbers for x and y. If $x = 35$ and $y = 25$, then $a = 55$ and $b = 65$. Therefore,

$$z = 180 - (55 + 65) = 180 - 120 = 60.$$

Of the five choices, only $x + y$ equals 60 when $x = 35$ and $y = 25$.

13. **(E)** Assume $PQ = 2$ and $QR = 3$. The most that PR can be is 5, if P is on line QR, so that Q is between P and R; and the least that PR can be is 1, if P is on line QR, between Q and R. In fact, PR can be any length between 5 and 1.

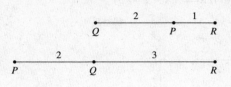 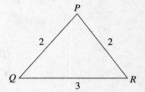

Therefore, the ratio $PQ:PR$ can be any number between 2:5 ($= 0.4$) and 2:1 ($= 2.0$).

All three choices lie in this range. Statements I, II, and III are all true.

14. **(C)** Assume that the number Diana was working with was 100. Decreasing it by 60 she got 40, whereas she should have increased it by 60, getting 160. An increase from 40 to 160 is an actual increase of 120 and a percentage

increase of $\dfrac{\cancel{120}^{\,3}}{\cancel{40}_{\,1}} \times 100\% = 300\%$.

15. **(A)** Cross-multiply to solve the equation $\dfrac{w+2}{w-3} = \dfrac{3}{2}$:

$$2(w + 2) = 3(w - 3) \Rightarrow 2w + 4 = 3w - 9 \Rightarrow w = 13.$$

Use **TACTIC 10 and backsolve. Try the choices. Only 13 works.

16. **(E)** Michelle drove m miles in $h - \dfrac{1}{2}$ hours. Since $r = \dfrac{d}{t}$, to find her rate,

we divide the distance, m, by the time, $\left(h - \dfrac{1}{2}\right)$: $\dfrac{m}{h-\frac{1}{2}} = \dfrac{2m}{2h-1}$

Use **TACTIC 11. If Paul drove 20 miles in 2 hours, Michelle drove 20 miles

in $1\dfrac{1}{2} = \dfrac{3}{2}$ hours. So Michelle drove at $20 \div \dfrac{3}{2} = 20 \times \dfrac{2}{3} = \dfrac{40}{3}$ miles

per hour. Only $\dfrac{2m}{2h-1} = \dfrac{40}{3}$ when $m = 20$ and $h = 2$.

17. **(D)** If Sarah were really unlucky, what could go wrong in her attempt to get one marble of each color? Well, her first 11 picks *might* yield 6 blue marbles and 5 white ones. But then the twelfth marble would be red, and she would have at least one of each color. The answer is 12.

18. **(A)** $2^{3x} + 2^{3x} + 2^{3x} + 2^{3x} = 4(2^{3x}) = 2^2(2^{3x}) = 2^{3x + 2}$.

**Let $x = 1$; then $2^{3x} = 2^3 = 8$, and

$$2^{3x} + 2^{3x} + 2^{3x} + 2^{3x} = 8 + 8 + 8 + 8 = 32.$$

Which of the choices equals 32 when $x = 1$? Only $2^{3x + 2}(2^5 = 32)$.

19. (D) Draw in segment $EXY \perp AB$. Then $XY = 10$ since it is the same length as a side of the square. EX is the height of $\triangle ECD$, whose base is 10 and whose area is 10. So $10 = \frac{1}{2} (10) (EX) \Rightarrow EX = 2 \Rightarrow EY = 12$.

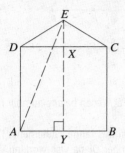

Since $\triangle ECD$ is isosceles, $DX = 5$; so $AY = 5$. Finally, recognize $\triangle AYE$ as a 5-12-13 right triangle, or use the Pythagorean theorem to find the hypotenuse, AE, of the triangle:

$(AE)^2 = 5^2 + 12^2 = 25 + 144 = 169,$

so $AE = 13$.

20. (B) Let r and R be the radii of circle I and circle II, respectively. Since the circumference of circle I is $2\pi r$, the circumference of circle II is $2\pi r + 4 = 2(\pi r + 2)$. But, of course, the circumference of circle II is also $2\pi R$. Therefore,

$$2\pi R = 2(\pi r + 2) \Rightarrow \pi R = \pi r + 2 \Rightarrow$$
$$R = r + \frac{2}{\pi}.$$

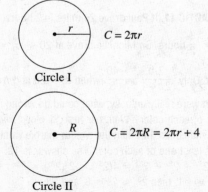

Circle I

Circle II

Section 3 Verbal Reasoning

26. **(A)** Because it can now be grown successfully in America, the once-rare fruit is now *accessible* or readily available to American consumers.

27. **(C)** Someone always searching for new ways to do things is by definition *an innovator* (someone who introduces changes into the existing ways of doing things).

28. **(C)** The sentence lists negative aspects of measurement. One is that it is *not* always used *properly* or correctly. Another is that it is often *misunderstood*. Note that, while the first missing word must be positive, the second must be negative.

29. **(C)** A trip to France, with all the chances for talking in French it would provide, would be a practical or *pragmatic* test of how much you had learned of conversational French.

30. **(E)** Though scientists might be upset by *erroneous* (faulty) or *derivative* (unoriginal) work, the scientific community would be most shocked by *fraudulent* or faked research that was intentionally *deceptive* or deceitful.

31. **(C)** The key phrase "of few words" indicates that Eastwood's characters are *laconic*, untalkative types.

32. **(E)** *Insipid* (flavorless; dull and uninteresting) is a term that applies equally well to food and to conversations.

33. **(D)** Someone *crabbed* (bad-humored; harsh; morose) seldom smiles; someone *parsimonious* (stingy; miserly) never gives away money. Note how parallel structure determines word order: the first missing adjective relates to the first verb ("seldom smiled"); the second missing adjective relates to the second verb ("never gave away").

34. **(D)** An *alphabet* is made up of individual *letters*; a *deck* is made up of individual *cards*.

(Whole to Part)

35. **(D)** A *sanctuary* (place of safety) provides one with shelter or *refuge*; a *tree* provides one with shelter or *shade*.

(Function)

36. **(E)** To *rustle cattle* is to steal them. To *hijack cargo* is to steal it. Note that you are dealing with a secondary meaning of the verb *rustle* here.

(Defining Characteristic)

37. **(A)** *Avarice* or greed is the name of a particular *vice* (evil quality); *charity* or love is the name of a particular *virtue* (good quality).

(Member and Class)

38. **(B)** A *glint* is a small gleam of *light*. A *whiff* is a slight puff of *scent*.

(Degree of Intensity)

39. (C) *Mercurial* (flighty; changeable) by definition means lacking *constancy*, *ephemeral* (temporary; fleeting) by definition means lacking *permanence*.

Beware of eye-catchers. Choice E is incorrect. Someone *diffident* by definition lacks faith in himself; he does not necessarily lack *fidelity* or loyalty to others.

(Antonym Variant)

40. (C) To *scotch* or block a *rumor* is to crush it. To *suppress* or quell a *riot* is to crush it.

(Defining Characteristic)

41. (B) In extending the pilot's control of the plane and making extreme actions (loops, sudden swerves, dives, etc.) comfortable, acrobatic flying *extends a pilot's range of capabilities*.

42. (D) The medium of the air is the *environment* in which flying creatures function.

43. (B) In the course of doing a loop, you lose sight of the horizon and must tilt your head backward to catch sight of the horizon line again. Thus, to pick up the horizon line is to *spot it visually*.

44. (A) Earlier in the passage, the author describes the experience of doing a loop as being "as far outside instinctive human behavior as you can go." In grabbing at the sides of the cockpit during the loop, the author is reverting to *instinctive*, involuntary behavior.

Choice B is incorrect. The experience of doing a loop was terrifying; grabbing the sides of the cockpit was not. Choice C is incorrect. It was not essential for the author to grab the sides of the cockpit; his seat belt was strong enough to keep him from falling out of the plane. Choice D is incorrect. The author did not wind up making a habit of grabbing the sides of the cockpit; he did it only that once. Choice E is incorrect. The experience of doing a loop may have seemed life-threatening; grabbing the sides of the cockpit was not.

45. (E) In saying the belt held, the author means that it did not slip or come unfastened; instead it *maintained its grasp*, keeping him safe.

46. (C) The instructor tells the author to put his arms out of the cockpit so that he can learn to have confidence in his seat belt's ability to hold him in the plane. He does so, *relying totally on his seat belt to keep him safe*.

47. (B) By stressing the terror that went into learning how to fly a loop, the author makes you feel that *satisfying* is an extremely mild word to describe the exhilaration of overcoming such an extreme fear and mastering such an unnatural skill. It is clearly an *understatement*.

48. (D) The author was not a fan of stunt-flying; she was reluctant to pay attention to the aerial display. Therefore, this particular aerial display must have been unusually *captivating* to capture her attention.

49. (D) The author describes the audience's longing for a particular effect in the stunt-flying demonstration ("a certain kind of roll or climb, or a return to a certain portion of the air"). This is akin to a reader's longing for a particular effect in a poem—for example, a certain kind of image or rhyme, or the return of an earlier refrain. Poets, however, play with their readers' expectations, sometimes varying exact end-rhymes with an occasional assonance or consonance (*slant* rhymes), as when Emily Dickinson unexpectedly rhymes *came* with *home*. Thus, in saying that Rahm "fulfilled your hope slantingly, like a poet," the author means that he *refused to satisfy your expectations directly* but gave you something unexpected instead.

50. (C) By "moving back the boundaries of the humanly possible" the author is talking about becoming aware *of new potentials for humanity*. This new knowledge leaves her gladdened and *exhilarated*.

51. (E) Passage 1 is both descriptive and informative. In recounting the story of the flying lesson, it is anecdotal. However, in comparison with Passage 2, it is not particularly poetic or *lyrical*.

52. (A) The author of Passage 1 talks about how useful acrobatic flying is in improving the skills of pilots. The author of Passage 2, however, looks on acrobatic flying as *an aesthetic experience*: she responds to Rahm's aerial demonstration as a new form of beauty, a performance that engages her aesthetically. Therefore, she would most likely consider the assessment of aerial flying in Passage 1 *too utilitarian* (concerned with practical usefulness) to be appropriate for an aesthetic experience.

Section 4 Mathematical Reasoning

21. (C) Multiply: each column is $\frac{12}{5}$. The columns are equal (C).

22. (C) Column A: the multiples of 7 are 7, 14, 21, . . . , 77, 84 . . . . The smallest one greater than 80 is 84. Column B: the multiples of 12 are 12, 24, . . . , 72, 84, 96 . . . . The largest one that is less than 90 is 84. The columns are equal (C).

23. (B) Since the diagonals of a rectangle are equal in length and bisect each other, $AE = ED = EC = BE$. Call this length x. Then the perimeter of $\triangle AED = 2x + 3$, and the perimeter of $\triangle EDC = 2x + 5$. Column B is greater. (Note: you should not waste your time using the Pythagorean theorem to find x.)

24. (D) Use **TACTIC 15** and replace the variables with numbers. If $a = 1$ and $b = 2$, then Column A is $\frac{1}{2}$ and Column B is $\left(\frac{1}{2}\right)^3 = \frac{1}{8}$. This time A is greater; eliminate Choices B and C. If $a = 2$ and $b = 1$, Column A is 2 and Column B is $2^3 = 8$. This time B is greater. Eliminate Choice A. The answer is Choice D.

25. (D) If the average of six numbers is 0, their sum is 0. If the six numbers were −3, −2, −1, 1, 2, 3, Column A would be 3; but if the six numbers were −5, −4, −3, −2, −1, 15, Column A would be only 1. Neither column is *always* greater, and the columns are not *always* equal (D).

26. (D) Use **TACTIC 18**. Could the area of $\triangle ABC = 2$? Since the height is 8, the area would be 2 only if the base were $\frac{1}{2}$:

$$\text{area of } \triangle ABC = 2 = \frac{1}{2}b(8) \Rightarrow 8b = 4 \Rightarrow b = \frac{1}{2}.$$

Could $BC = \frac{1}{2}$? Sure. Does BC have to be $\frac{1}{2}$? No, it could be anything at all. Neither column is *always* greater, and the columns are not *always* equal (D).

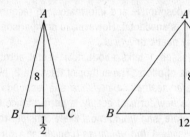

Note: Figures not drawn to scale

27. (B) Column A: $y = \frac{12}{x}$. Column B: $z = \frac{25}{x}$. If two fractions have the same *positive* denominator, the one with the larger numerator—here, B—is greater.
Use **TACTIC 15. Let $x = 2$. Then, $y = 6$ and $z = 12.5$. In this case, Column B is greater, so eliminate Choices A and C. Try another value. Column B is again greater. Guess Choice B.

28. (B) The average of x and y is less than y, so having another y raises the average. Column B is greater.
Use **TACTIC 15. Substitute numbers for the variables. Column A: the average of 2 and 4 is 3. Column B: the average of 2, 4, and 4 is $\frac{2+4+4}{3} = \frac{10}{3}$, which is greater than 3. The answer is Choice B.

29. (B) $x^2 + 6x + 8 = 0 \Rightarrow (x + 2)(x + 4) = 0 \Rightarrow x = -2$ or $x = -4$. In either case, $x < 2$. Column B is greater.

30. (D) If $x = 4$ and $y = 5$, then $x + y = 9$, and Column B is greater. Eliminate Choices A and C. If $x = 1$ and $y = 20$, then $x + y = 21$. This time, Column A is greater. Eliminate Choice B. Neither column is *always* greater, and the columns are not *always* equal (D).

31. (B) Since the sum of two two-digit numbers must be less than 200, A has to be 1, and the sum is 111. Therefore, $B + D$, the quantity in Column B, is 11, whereas $A + C$, the quantity in Column A, is 10 (which when added to the 1 that was carried from the units digit gives 11). Column B is greater.

32. (B) In $\triangle PQR$, draw in height h. Since h is less than PQ and $PQ = 4$, then the area of $\triangle PQR$ is less than $\frac{1}{2}(5)(4) = \frac{1}{2}(20) = 10$.

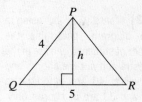

Column B is greater.

33. (320) Since $a + 100 = 180$, $a = 80$. But since ℓ and k are parallel, the four acute angles are all equal: $80 = a = b = c = d$, so their sum is $4 \times 80 = 320$.

34. (216) Draw and label the triangle. By the Pythagorean theorem: $18^2 + b^2 = 30^2 \Rightarrow 324 + b^2 = 900 \Rightarrow b^2 = 576 \Rightarrow b = 24$. The area of the triangle is $\frac{1}{2}(18)(24) = 216$.

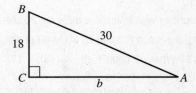

[You can save some work if you recognize this as a 3-4-5 triangle in which each side has been multiplied by 6 (18-24-30).]

35. (52) If there are x freshmen in the college, then $.80x$ of them will graduate and $.60(.80x) = .48x$ will attend graduate school. Therefore, $x - .48x = .52x$ or 52% of the freshmen will not attend graduate school.

**The above solution is straightforward, but there is no reason to use x. Assume there are 100 freshmen. Then 80 of them will graduate and 60% of 80, or 48 of them, will attend graduate school. So 52 will not go to graduate school; 52 is 52% of 100.

36. (90.1) Since $y > x$, y must be greater than 90 and x less than 90. The smallest number greater than 90 that can fit in the grid is 90.1.

37. $\left(\dfrac{9}{10} \text{ or } .9\right)$ Let x be the number. Then,

$$\frac{1}{3}x = 3x - 4 \Rightarrow x = 9x - 12 \Rightarrow 8x = 12 \Rightarrow x = \frac{12}{8} = \frac{3}{2}.$$

Finally, $\dfrac{3}{5}x = \dfrac{3}{5}\left(\dfrac{3}{2}\right) = \dfrac{9}{10}$.

38. $\left(\dfrac{4}{3} \text{ or } 1.33\right)$ Mentally, or by using a Venn diagram, determine the number of students who are in the orchestra and not the chorus and vice versa: 40 are in orchestra only, and 30 are in chorus only. The ratio is 40:30.

Grid in $\dfrac{4}{3}$ or 1.33.

Orchestra   Chorus

40   10   30

39. $\left(\dfrac{9}{10} \text{ or } .9\right)$ If there are x seats on each bus, then the group is using $\dfrac{4}{5}(3x) =$

$\dfrac{12}{5}x$ seats. After $\dfrac{1}{4}$ of them get off, $\dfrac{3}{4}$ of them, or $\dfrac{3}{\cancel{4}_1}\left(\dfrac{\cancel{12}^3}{5}x\right) = \dfrac{9}{5}x$

remain. The fraction of the $2x$ seats now being used on the two buses is

$\dfrac{\frac{9}{5}x}{2x} = \dfrac{\frac{9}{5}}{2} = \dfrac{9}{10}$.

**To avoid working with x, assume there are 20 seats on each bus. At the beginning, the group is using 48 of the 60 seats on the three buses $\left[\dfrac{4}{5}(60) = 48\right]$. When 12 people left $\left[\dfrac{1}{4}(48) = 12\right]$, the 36 remaining

people used $\dfrac{36}{40} = \dfrac{9}{10}$ of the 40 seats on two buses.

40. **(2500)** If 99.6% of the people tested did not have the disease, then 0.4% of them did have the disease. If x = the number of people tested, then 10 $= 0.004x \Rightarrow x = 10 \div .004 = 2500$.

Section 5 Writing Skills

1. **(D)** The reflexive pronoun *myself* cannot be used as the object of the verb *frightened*. Change *myself* to *me*.

2. **(C)** Adjective and adverb confusion. Change *his many attempts bravely to enter* to *his many brave attempts to enter*.

3. **(B)** Error in parallelism. Change *not because of the money* to *not because he needed the money* (a clause) to parallel the clause that follows *but*.

4. **(B)** Error in diction. Change *liable* to *likely*.

5. **(C)** Error in subject-verb agreement. Change *is* to *are*.
6. **(B)** Error in diction. *Latter* should not be used to refer to more than two items. Change *latter* to *last*.
7. **(B)** Error in parallelism. Change *to aid* to *aiding*.
8. **(A)** Adjective and adverb confusion. Change *special prepared* to *specially prepared*.
9. **(D)** Error in tense. Change *had been* to *were*.
10. **(C)** Error in parallelism. Change *under application* to *being applied*.
11. **(C)** Error in coordination and subordination. Change the conjunctive adverb *unfortunately* to *therefore* to clarify the relationship between the clauses.
12. **(C)** Faulty verbal. Change *satisfying* to the infinitive *to satisfy*.
13. **(E)** Sentence is correct.
14. **(D)** Error in subject-verb agreement. Change *they are* to *it is*.
15. **(C)** Error in subject-verb agreement. The antecedent of *who* is *one*. Therefore, *who is* is correct.
16. **(D)** Error in parallelism. Change *leaving room for* to *to leave room for*.
17. **(C)** Error in pronoun case. Change *him* to *he*.
18. **(D)** Error in coordination and subordination. Change *in fact* to *but* in order to clarify the relationship between the clauses.
19. **(D)** Error in parallelism. Change *to insure* to *insuring*.
20. **(B)** Choice B eliminates the excessive wordiness of the original sentence without introducing any errors in diction.
21. **(A)** The use of the semicolon to separate the pair of clauses is correct.
22. **(C)** Error in agreement. *Kind* is singular and requires a singular modifier (*this*).
23. **(D)** Choice D corrects the error in diction and the error in parallel structure.
24. **(A)** The original answer provides the most effective and concise sentence.
25. **(A)** The original sentence is correct. The singular pronoun *it* refers to the subject of the main clause, *fate* (singular).
26. **(D)** Choices A, B, C, and E suffer from errors in the sequence of tenses.
27. **(E)** Error in parallelism. A lack of parallel structure is found in the other four choices.
28. **(B)** Wordiness. Choice B is the clearest, most graceful, and most concise way of expressing the ideas being described.
29. **(C)** Errors in being precise and clear. Choice A provides us with the result of the program rather than the goal. Choice B results in a sentence fragment. Choices D and E use the *was where* construction, which is unclear and should be avoided.
30. **(E)** Choices A, B, C, and D suffer from an error in agreement between the subject and the verb. Remember that the prepositional phrase *along with her parents and friends* is not part of the subject. The subject is the singular word *coach;* it should be followed by the singular verb *is*.
31. **(C)** Error in diction. The use of *of* instead of *have* in Choices A and D is incorrect. The *if* clause requires the subjective mood *had risen* instead of *would have risen* in Choice B. Choices D and E are incorrect, because the past participle of *rise* is *risen*.

32. (E) Error in comparison. *Former* and *latter* should be used only when two items are under consideration. When three or more items are discussed, as in this sentence, use *first* and *last.*

33. (D) Choice A is unacceptable because of the dangling modifier. Choice B is a run-on sentence. Choice C changes the meaning of the sentence. Choice E suffers from a misplaced modifier. Did her head fall into the river? So Choice E would imply.

34. (C) Choice A says that the house is *in your car*, an unlikely place for it to be.

Choice B contains an idea that the writer could not have intended.

Choice C accurately states the intended idea. It is the best answer.

Choice D, like B, contains an idea that is quite absurd.

Choice E is wordy and awkwardly expressed.

35. (B) All sentences except sentence 2 contribute to the development of the essay's topic. Therefore, Choice B is the best answer.

36. (C) Choice A is awkwardly expressed.

Choice B is awkward and contains the pronoun *it*, which has no specific referent.

Choice C is accurately expressed and is consistent with the sentences that precede and follow sentence 8. It is the best answer.

Choice D is written in a style that is different from that of the rest of the essay.

Choice E would be a good choice, but it contains a comma splice. A comma may not be used to join two independent clauses.

37. (D) Choice A is quite formal and is not in keeping with the style and tone of the essay.

Choice B is close to the style and tone of the essay, but it contains the redundance, *quickly and rapidly.*

Choice C has a formal tone inconsistent with the rest of the essay.

Choice D uses the second person pronoun and is consistent with the folksy, conversational style of the essay. It is the best answer.

Choice E uses an objective tone far different from the writing in the rest of the essay.

38. (B) Choice A is only partly true. While the paragraph gives another viewpoint, the data it contains are hardly objective.

Choice B accurately states the writer's intention. It is the best answer.

Choices C, D, and E in no way describe the function of paragraph 3.

39. (C) Choice A provides no particular link to the previous paragraph.

Choice B provides a rather weak transition between paragraphs.

Choice C creates a strong bond between paragraphs by alluding to material in paragraph 3 and introducing the topic of paragraph 4. It is the best answer.

Choice D could be a good transition were it not for the error in subject-verb agreement. The subject *sounds* is plural; the verb *tells* is singular.

Choice E provides a weak transition and its writing style is not consistent with the rest of the essay.